SEASONS of CHANGE

Rural Life in Victorian and Edwardian England

SADIE WARD
with
JONATHAN BROWN
JOHN CREASEY
PATRICIA DAVISON
DAVID EVELEIGH

BOOK CLUB ASSOCIATES
LONDON

**George Allen & Unwin (Publishers) Ltd,
40 Museum Street, London WC1A 1LU, UK**

George Allen & Unwin (Publishers) Ltd,
Park Lane, Hemel Hempstead, Herts HP2 4TE, UK

Allen & Unwin Inc.,
9 Winchester Terrace, Winchester, Mass 01890, USA

George Allen & Unwin Australia Pty Ltd,
8 Napier Street, North Sydney, NSW 2060, Australia

First published in 1982

This edition published 1982 by Book Club Associates
by arrangement with Allen & Unwin

British Library Cataloguing in Publication Data

Seasons of change.
   1. Country life—England—History—19th century
   2. England—Social life and customs—19th century—Sources
I. Ward, Sadie
942'.009'734   DA110

ISBN 0–04–630009–0

Produced by Cameron Books Ltd,
2a Roman Way, London N7 8XG

Designed by Ian Cameron
Managing editor: Jill Hollis
Copy editor: Anthea Zeman

Printed and bound in Great Britain by
R.J. Acford, Terminus Road Industrial Estate, Chichester, Sussex.

Endpapers: pages from *Kelly's Directories* from the last two decades of the nineteenth century.

Frontispiece: women were rarely employed in full-time agricultural work by the 1870s, but they might still help with the harvest and other farm tasks. At such times, they might be compelled to keep children home from school or to take them into the fields.

All illustrations except those listed below are from the collection of the Museum of English Rural Life, University of Reading. The following list includes both copyright holders and owners of original prints or documents.

Beamish Hall, Durham 27b
Bedfordshire Record Office 57a
Brades, Nash, Tyzack 76b
Jonathan Brown 25b, 26a, 26c, 28b
Carlisle Museum and Art Gallery 103a
Curtis Museum, Alton, Hants 165
Mr and Mrs Dines 79b
Essex County Record Office 31a
Dr R.J. Esslemont 181
C.J.O. Evans 85a
Farnham Museum 58b, 58c, 122a
R.G. Grace 81
Guildford Museum 120b
Miles Hadfield 111e
Hampshire County Museum Service 22b, 30b, 50d, 105, 109d,
   112d, 113
Hereford City Library 170a, 176b
Mrs D.N. James 91b
Kodak Museum 115
Mrs Ina Lamb 178b
S. Maclure 73b
Maidstone Museum 109a, 170b
J.K. Major 69a
Museum of Lincolnshire Life 51b
National Union of Agricultural Workers 24a
Norfolk County Library 108b
Oxford City Library 87, 104a, 111a, 166c
J. Patchett 166a
Mrs C.H. Pope 50a
Priest's House Museum, Wimborne Minster, Dorset 111b
The Science Museum 137a
Suffolk Record Office 50e, 111c
John Topham Picture Library 40a, 58a, 85c, 119a, 122b, 125, 130b,
   131a, 132a, 132b, 134a, 135, 137b, 139, 156, 180
Sadie Ward 157
Waterways Museum, Stoke Bruerne 101
Waverley District Council, Godalming Museum 107b, 140a
Wellington Journal and Shrewsbury News 86a
Mrs E.G. Wrightson 172c

Contents

Preface   8

Introduction   9

THE LANDED INTEREST   13
Landlords by Sadie Ward

TENANT FARMS, TIED COTTAGES   25
*Domestic Life by Jonathan Brown, Patricia Davison
and David Eveleigh*

SEED TIME TO HARVEST   37
Agriculture by Sadie Ward

INDUSTRIES OF THE COUNTRYSIDE   66
Manufacturing and Crafts by John Creasey

WATER, ROAD AND RAIL   99
Travel and Transport by Jonathan Brown

IN THE MARKET PLACE   114
Marketing and Shops by Sadie Ward

FOR THE PUBLIC GOOD   141
Welfare, Education and the Police by Sadie Ward

THE LABOURER'S LEISURE   160
Recreation and Sport by Sadie Ward

Bibliography & Acknowledgements   183

Index   186

Preface

This book aims to provide a historical introduction to rural life during six decades of momentous change. The authors have avoided placing undue emphasis on the survival of traditional features. Instead, attention has chiefly been directed to new developments, the speed of their advance and the way in which they affected the occupations and activities of the rural population. The dominant theme is the impact of industrialisation, which had reshaped virtually every aspect of rural life by the Great War.

Industrialisation, through both the industrial and agricultural revolutions, brought about a sharp decline in regional consciousness and self-sufficiency, and the emergence of a national economy. While the leadership of the country was based on land and capital, it had increasingly to take account of the will of the masses, which was being more effectively expressed through wider suffrage and a better educated electorate. Industrial society brought with it the new problems of the growth of poverty, crime and urban squalor that were the concomitants of increasing national wealth. These problems could only be solved through the replacement of the old amateur, aristocratic form of government by the centralised state, with its professional bureaucracy and interventionist intent. The resulting changes were felt first in the towns, and rather more gradually in the countryside.

This book sets out to examine certain aspects of the countryside's adaptation to the conditions of the new industrial state. A number of topics that are not central to this treatment have been dealt with cursorily or omitted. Thus, for instance, there is no detailed account of the conditions of the rural worker, or of the improvements in his material circumstances that were effected either by migration or by the growth of agricultural trade unionism. Other topics, such as developments in rural transport, are seen in a general context, and, for example, detailed lists of carts, carriages and personal conveyances have been avoided. Similarly, the huge subject of rural crime and punishment has been treated only summarily within the framework of increasing public order in the second half of the nineteenth century; improvements resulted from a combination of better policing methods, the creation of other effective channels of social protest and the evolution of a more law-abiding mentality.

Some chapters are concerned mainly to analyse the broad forces of social and economic change, while others look at the introduction of new methods and materials into country areas. The reason for this apparent divergence of emphasis is that each new implement, technique or item of domestic equipment not only reflected a technological advance but would also often involve an adjustment in the previous pattern of life in the countryside.

Although a book of this sort cannot primarily be the product of original research, material from other sources has been supplemented with new work by the authors, particularly in the chapters on rural industries and domestic life. However, the principal aim of the book has been to summarise the existing state of knowledge and to present the results of recent academic studies to a wider readership. The main reference works used in each chapter have been noted in a separate bibliography and acknowledgement section at the end of the book. Any errors arising from oversimplification or misinterpretation of sources are, of course, the responsibility of the authors.

For the many illustrations, the authors are fortunate to have been able fully to exploit the resources of the Institute of Agricultural History and Museum of English Rural Life at the University of Reading, the national centre for information on rural history.

Lastly, we would like to record our gratitude to the Director of the Institute, Dr E.J.T. Collins, for his help with this project, and also to our colleagues, who assisted with the material and much useful criticism. We owe a further debt to Jill Hollis and Ian Cameron of Cameron Books for their constant encouragement and hard work, without which this book could not have been completed. There is a special indebtedness, too, to Phyllis Basten, who expertly typed so much of the original manuscript.

Introduction

The period between 1850 and 1914 witnessed changes that touched every aspect of rural life. In many ways, change was more rapid and fundamental at this time than in the course of the preceding hundred years. The root cause was industrialisation. In the early nineteenth century, the industrial economy was concentrated around a relatively narrow band of industry and technology—coal, iron, heavy engineering and textiles—which offered only limited possibilities for employment and was located only in certain regions. By the mid-century, however, the economy was diversifying at an enormous pace, and the signs of progress were evident in the growth of towns, in improved communications and the appearance of complex consumer industries. The decline in the importance of agriculture was dramatic, and can be judged from the fact that, while in 1811 it was the single most important industry with more than a third share in the national income; this share had been almost halved by 1861, and by 1901 it had slumped to a meagre 6%—a fall which continued after the Great War. One purpose of this book is to give an impression of what these statistics meant in terms of the transformation of country life during these decades.

The full implications of industrialisation in rural areas were not apparent in 1860. Lord Derby's *Return on the Owners of Land* (1872-73), popularly known as the New Domesday survey, established that four-fifths of the land in the United Kingdom was owned by fewer than 7,000 people, and that one-fifth was owned by a mere 525, most of whom were peers of the realm. The ownership of land still conferred great political and social privileges. The composition of the Houses of Lords and Commons continued to be dominated by landed families, and until the third quarter of the century the ownership of land provided the accepted means of entry into Parliament for even the commercial and industrial classes. In the counties, the alliance of landed aristocrat, squire and parson still represented authority and the natural order of things—an order which was at best paternalistic and at worst encouraged habits of deference and

apathy among the labouring classes. Moreover, agriculture itself remained prosperous. The repeal of the Corn Laws in 1846 and the opening up of British markets to foreign competition did not have the dire consequences predicted. For a generation after repeal, the efficiency of home production, limited imports and a swelling urban demand for food combined to keep the industry buoyant. The countryside was well populated, well farmed and provided a spread of employment opportunities—in agriculture and the traditional village industries. In some areas, the small producer-retailer had already been hit by the techniques of mass production—for instance, hand loom weavers were much reduced in numbers— but the shoemaker, carpenter, local ironfounder and woodland worker were not yet seriously affected. Improvements in transport were putting an end to regional self-sufficiency, although the retailing revolution was only just under way. Shops, those Trojan horses of the industrial economy, were proliferating in towns, but were comparitively rare in the smaller villages. While the numbers of workers employed in agriculture remained high, rural wages remained low. Demand for manufactured items was limited, and the old pre-industrial methods of trading—fairs, markets and itinerant retailing, by pedlars, cheapjacks and tinkers, still played an important part in the distribution of commodities. For the poor, life was mainly a matter of constant labour, although the very nature of agricultural work, with its dependence on weather and the seasons, gave some respite from toil. In the countryside, traditional customs, games and pastimes maintained a precarious existence, but their survival was guaranteed only for as long as they embodied, in some measure, the beliefs and values of the majority of the rural population.

By 1914, the picture was very different. Political power had passed decisively to the industrial and commercial middle classes, and the working classes, better educated from the 1870s, were also demanding an effective voice in national government. Wealth and pure ability were sufficient in themselves to ensure entry into Parliament or public life. Farming had left behind its 'golden age' and passed through the 'great depression', from which it emerged only slowly after 1900, with a different structure and a new deployment of productive forces. The former state of near self-sufficiency in home food supplies had been translated into one whereby over half the country's total food requirements were imported, and the more astute observers of international affairs were questioning the country's ability to feed itself during a protracted European War. The air of confidence and bustle, so characteristic of the industry in the 1850s and 1860s, had disappeared and was replaced by a general feeling of insecurity and uncertainty about the future. Many villages were depopulated, and most village industries were in sad decline. Even the traditional popular culture of rural England was all but extinguished. The older forms of folk-song and dance were rare enough to attract the attention of folklorists, and the fact that they had become the object of periodic 'revivals' was a sure sign they no longer represented a living tradition. By 1914, the existence of 'a land problem' was almost universally acknowledged, and the need for land reform—for sweeping measures to try to regenerate rural life—became one of the great political cries of the time. Indeed, it is deeply ironic that had a general election taken place in the urban England of 1915, it would have been fought chiefly on this issue. That this should have been so indicates the truly dramatic nature of the change in the fortunes of the countryside in this period.

Some key factors of change—population trends, urbanisation, rural migration, free trade, the standard of living and transport—are readily identifiable.

A peak of population was reached in most rural areas by about the mid century. After this, there was a general decline in the rate of natural increase, accompanied by heavy losses due to emigration and migration to urban areas. The number of people employed in agriculture, forestry and fishing fell from two million in 1861 to one-and-a-half million by 1901—a loss of no less than a quarter. There appears to have been a limited recovery in population in the first decade or so of the new century, due partly to improved prospects for agriculture and partly to suburban development in rural districts, but after the Great War the long-term trend of depopulation reasserted itself.

In contrast, towns grew at a phenomenal rate. Greater London, for instance, doubled its numbers between 1851 and 1891, and by 1911 it encompassed some seven-and-a-half million, or over a fifth of the total population. Lord Rosebery, speaking as the Chairman of the newly formed London County Council in 1891, discovered:

'No thought of pride associated in my mind with the idea of London. I am always haunted by the awfulness of London... Sixty years ago a great Englishman, Cobbett, called it a wen. If it was a wen then, what is it now? A tumour, an elephantiasis sucking into its gorged system half the life and the blood and the bone of the rural districts.'

Yet many other large towns grew even faster than the metropolis. As Peter Mathias has noted,

'Whereas in 1801 there had been no other city of above 100,000 inhabitants in England and Wales, and only fifteen above 20,000, by 1891 twenty-three centres were in the largest category (possessing together five million inhabitants) and there were 185 others (possessing 15.5 million inhabitants) of over 20,000 inhabitants each.'

The extent to which the nation had been urbanised, however, is perhaps best illustrated by the fact that while in 1851 only half the population lived in towns, by 1901 three quarters of the population did so. The swiftness of this change is largely explained by the high rate of natural increase in cities, but migration was a significant contributory factor. Migrants travelled long distances from all over rural England to the capital, and from Central, West and South West England to the coalfields of South Wales.

The causes of rural migration were complex. Poverty was one. Wages in the countryside, especially in the labour-abundant districts of southern England, were little above subsistence level until the mid century. The conditions of employment were harsh and the atmosphere of village life was often claustrophobic. But by the 1860s, most farm workers were experiencing some limited improvement in wages and their standard of living. By this time, migration out of agriculture was beginning to create labour scarcity in some areas, especially during the critical period of the harvest, which enabled those who remained to bid up the price of their labour. Farm workers, therefore, seem to have been less 'pushed' out of agriculture by the lack of employment opportunities, than 'pulled' into the towns by the more attractive prospects offered there. The towns were able to provide a wider range of jobs, with competitive wages, and less exacting hours. Moreover, urban life stood for freedom and lack of constraint. If the streets were not paved with gold, at least a man was more the master of his own destiny and was not rigidly bound by the constraints of the rural class system. For women, too, domestic service in the towns or a factory job offered an escape from the drudgery of work in the fields and a means of self-improvement. It was scarcely surprising that many of the youngest, brightest and most enterprising of both sexes moved off the land to establish 'a new frontier' in the towns. But not all migrants were opportunists—some indeed were victims. These were the men and, to some extent, women employed in rural industries and handicrafts. The new industrial technology gradually undercut and eliminated the markets for village-made products, and in the second half of the century many village industries collapsed or were relocated in the towns. Rural depopulation and the agricultural depression of the eighties and nineties served to accelerate this process. There were, of course, countless individuals who stayed and who, by dint of hard work and the development of special skills, prospered exceedingly. Yet the overall result of migration was a less diversified rural population, better off because smaller, although more susceptible to sudden economic disaster because more dependent on the fortunes of a single industry—agriculture.

One consequence of the growth in total population in the nineteenth century was the increased demand for food. At first, this extra demand was successfully met by British agriculture, with impressive gains in output from the 1830s to the 1860s. But thereafter, home produced food was increasingly supplemented by imports of cereals, livestock and dairy products. The old system of protecting agriculture was progressively dismantled from the 1840s, and by 1860 there remained only a few duties, collected mostly for revenue purposes, on sugar (until 1874), wines, spirits, hops, and the manufacture of tobacco (until 1862) and small registration duties on grains and flour (until 1869). Free trade and cheap food became almost axiomatic principles of political life. Cheap imports of foodstuffs, which occurred in bulk from the 1870s, had two important consequences for the British economy. They ruined the prosperity of arable farming and plunged domestic agriculture as a whole into a recession which lasted for twenty years. They also significantly reduced the retail price of food, and thereby the cost of living, and thus enormously encouraged consumption—both of food and other products.

The decades after 1850 saw a distinct improvement in the living standards of the majority of the population. The greater productiveness of industry compared with agriculture enabled money wages to rise steadily until the 1870s. The ensuing general slump in trade brought a halt to this trend, but its effects were offset by the fall in prices. Real earnings, in other words, continued to rise until roughly the end of the century, when prices moved upwards once more. This overall growth in purchasing power created a large and consistent working-class demand for consumer goods, and itself stimulated new techniques of mass production. Fewer goods were produced by specialist craftsmen to meet individual orders, and more by manufacturers in bulk and in anticipation of demand. Mass production, however, required new methods of marketing, and the second half of the century witnessed what has been called the retailing revolution. The existing outlets for goods, through producer-retailers, itinerant salesmen, fairs and markets, were no longer found to be adequate, and they were ousted in importance by co-operatives, multiple shops, bazaars and department stores. These sold an exciting, expanding range of goods designed to meet all budgets and all tastes. Such developments naturally affected the urban consumer before the rural, but cheap factory products began to be available in market towns and in village stores in ever greater quantity, and in this way spread throughout the rural districts, replacing traditional materials and home-made products.

Improvements in transport and communications were vital to the whole process of social and economic change during these years. In the first half of the century, road transport was slow and costly in spite of the turnpike trusts, and canals were used mainly for carrying heavy goods and raw materials. The railway boom of the 1840s was a prime stimulus in promoting further economic growth. The building of the railways provided valuable technical experience for engineers who were later to be involved in the steel, construction and engineering industries, while railway finance and management provided a model for many subsequent industrial enterprises. Moreover, the establishment of a nationwide rail network helped to create a national market for goods and labour by reducing the disparities in regional prices and supplies. The old, intimate relationship between a town and its surrounding countryside, whereby each sustained the other through the exchange of food, commodities and work, was slowly but irrevocably destroyed. The railway provided farmers with new market opportunities beyond the immediate neighbourhood and, at the same time, brought into a region all manner of goods originating outside it. By the 1880s, the virtual completion of the branch line system meant that cheap food imports (in turn made possible by the growth of the steamship trade across the Atlantic), and the products of manufacturing industry were available in even the most remote rural districts. In addition, the railways facilitated seasonal movements of labour between town and country. It was common, for instance, for casual workers to spend the summer as members of a harvest gang and then to move to the towns for the winter to gain employment in the brickyards or gasworks. Similarly, there was an exodus of women and children each year from London to work in the hop fields of Kent and from the Black Country to work in the orchards of the Vale of Evesham.

Towards the end of the century, the penumbra of the towns spread further, as more and more people took advantage of cheap rail and tram fares to commute daily from the still predominantly rural suburbs to the business centres. As the working classes slowly won the right to more leisure, the cheap day excursion to more distant places became increasingly popular. After the Bank Holiday Act of 1870, thousands embarked on annual pilgrimages to rural beauty spots or to the seaside. The invention of the bicycle gave townsmen yet another opportunity to explore the English countryside in their free hours at weekends. At first, bicycles were bought mainly by the middle classes, but by the 1890s they were within reach of the better off among the working classes, and the mass membership of cycling clubs dates from this time. Some, like the Clarion Club, were intended not only to provide a cheap and healthy form of exercise, but also to instruct the rural labourer in politics and to teach the rudiments of socialism. On the other hand, the development of the internal combustion engine brought the wealthier classes into the countryside. The charabanc catered for one type of taste and income bracket, while the motor car was a prized possession of the privileged few, conveying the Edwardian plutocracy from London residences to weekend estates. In 1914, the motor car was still something of a novelty; nonetheless, it was a potent symbol for the future. In all possible ways, the isolation of the countryside was under attack and the survival of a traditional way of life threatened.

The response of the countryside to the challenge of urban culture was never uniform; rather, it was infinitely varied. But insofar as it is possible to establish trends, urban influences were transmitted from the cities to the market towns along the main lines of communication and then rippled outwards into the surrounding village. New products and fashions were assimilated most readily by the well-off and then, depending on cost and availability, were taken up by the subordinate rural orders. The younger generation was more impressionable than the older, and the better educated quicker to adapt than the less so. The introduction of a truly national system of education from the 1870s was of considerable importance, as an increasingly literate population was better able to exploit the stream of information about vacant situations, excursions and consumer goods that was appearing in the popular press by the early 1900s. The penny newspaper and the penny dreadful were both effective agents of urban culture and helped subvert the countryman from his former pastimes. Yet, if what the towns offered in the way of enrichment, entertainment and a greater degree of comparative refinement seemed alluring to some, others still found urban values fickle and rootless. Many countrymen harboured a deep suspicion of 'townies' and retained their insularity and sense of separate identity. It was among such that E.W. Martin found his 'secret people', and in remote enclaves the 'old knowledge' and old customs undoubtedly lingered on. Even as late as 1924, at Clyst St Lawrence in Devon a farmer was summonsed for assaulting an old woman whom he accused of bewitching his pigs, and other examples might be cited for other counties in the inter-war period. It is the very patchwork quality of rural life that makes its study absorbing; its continued difference from urban culture in some respects, its increased compliance with it in others. There is indeed a sense in which the two nations—rural and urban—survive into the present. Nonetheless, the formative period of change—of the integration of rural society within the modern industrial state—occurred in the Victorian and Edwardian period, and it is to these events that this book is addressed.

Landed Proprietors

Country life had long been dominated by the landed aristocracy and gentry. 'The Duke's country', as observed Richard Jefferies, 'encompassed within its bounds the species of a separate nationality, and whole districts continued to be or felt themselves to be under the sway of some great peer.' By 1870, aristocratic England had reached its full flowering; great estates covered a quarter of the entire country and landholding had never been more concentrated. The Duke of Buccleuch, for instance, held estates of over 10,000 acres in four counties, and estates of between 5,000 and 10,000 acres in two more. In total, he held land in fourteen counties, even appearing in the New Domesday Survey of 1872-73 as a yeoman landowner on account of his eight acres in Surrey—evidently building land—and his 60 acres in Fifeshire. At the other end of the spectrum, a few peers were virtually landless, and some were impoverished. However, F.M.L. Thompson notes, the rough rule, established as early as Jane Austen's time, was that an estate of 10,000 acres or an income equivalent to £10,000 a year from land distinguished the landed aristocracy from the gentry, who typically held estates of between 1,000 and 3,000 acres. Commoners were also numbered among the great landowners: of the 363 owners of estates over 10,000 acres, 186 were peers, 58 were baronets and 117 were untitled. But as Thompson also points out, old established families, such as the Chaplins of Blankney in Lincolnshire, who owned an estate of over 20,000 acres, might actually prefer 'to remain great

A squire: William Lambarde of Beechmont, Sevenoaks, Kent.

squires and to furnish a dynasty of county members' exercising their influence in the House of Commons rather than the House of Lords. Even so, the Chaplins finally merged with the aristocracy, accepting a peerage in 1916.

To considerable extent, the landed classes derived their economic strength from the landlord-tenant system; the fact that much estate land was not farmed by the landed classes themselves, but by tenant farmers, increased rather than diminished their influence. They received rents, a major element in landlords' incomes, and exerted the natural authority of lessor over lessee. The great virtue of the system, however, was that it was based not upon exploitation, but upon the establishment of a natural harmony of interests between landlords and tenants. The tenant gained from the landlord's long-term investments in land, and the landlord gained from a productive agriculture which enabled the tenant to pay a high rent.

This economic symbiosis had a political aspect as well. Since both landlord and tenant had a stake in land, they tended to unite to defend property against its detractors—at Westminster and also in the counties. Disagreements were remarkably few. Some landlords might overstretch the bounds of good sense and instruct their tenants to vote in a certain way, but many tenants supported the landlord's candidate out of a sense of loyalty and local feeling, as a matter of inclination rather than obligation. The truly independent tenant, usually a farmer of some substance or long term leaseholder, was more often avoided than evicted. The man most at risk was the tenant-at-will, liable to immediate eviction if he displeased his landlord at election time—yet dismissals were rare. R.J. Olney draws attention to the verdict of a parliamentary committee which reported in 1869 that inducements to vote in the desired way proceeded 'rather from the hope of future advantages to be conferred than from the fear of injury to be inflicted.' Such advantages might include 'a farm rented at slightly less than its full commercial value, fixtures kept in good repair, and consideration if rent day fell at a time of temporary financial embarrassment.'

Indeed, the landlord's choice of tenant was determined more by economic than political considerations, and friction between the two arose mainly from the determination of both to extract the maximum financial advantage from the arrangement. For instance, tenants sought compensation for temporary farm improvements, such as chalking, marling, and the application to the soil of purchased manures, the value of which was not exhausted at the expiration of the lease. They also objected to game preservation—the landlord's right to raise and kill ground game (rabbits and hares)—even on their best land, resulting in considerable damage to growing crops. In the 1840s and 1870s, much was heard at farmers' clubs and in the farming press of the need for legislation on the question of tenant-right. Only in the late 1870s,

Left: the Waters family, about 1870, tenant farmers who bought Northern Wood Farm, Blofield, Norfolk in 1832. On the right are their two horsemen and dairy maid. *Below:* Sussex labourers during their lunch break, late nineteenth century.

NOONDAY REST AMONG SUSSEX FOLK "Tho' we beant afeard o' wark, nary one on us."

Above: well-to-do country family, 1882. *Right:* a family of tenant farmers—John Ward and his wife, with their sons James and John and daughters Cordelia, Freda and Ada. John Ward farmed at Eastacombe, near Inwardleigh, Okehampton, Devon, until 1907.

however, in the face of agricultural depression, did this become a political issue, providing the basis of the programme of the Farmers' Alliance—an isolated attempt to form a farmers' party. But the Alliance failed to unite the English tenantry, attracting support chiefly from the larger farmers in the stricken corn districts of East Anglia and the South East, and not from the small livestock farmers of the western counties, who benefited from cheap foreign grain. By the mid 1880s, the organisation was a spent force; its sole achievement was to give a certain urgency to Liberal legislation. In 1880, the Ground Game Act gave tenants the right to take ground game—it did not otherwise interfere with landlords' sporting rights—and in 1883, the Agricultural Holdings Act laid down scales of compensation for unexhausted temporary improvements. Neither Act satisfied reformers, but thereafter farmers reverted to pressing their claims through the largely non-political Central Chambers of Agriculture, which undertook to initiate debates in Parliament on the welfare of the industry.

The landlord-tenant system was eventually disrupted, not by internal weaknesses in the system, but by the severity of the arable depression in the last two decades of the century. Although landowners, as a class, suffered more, many farmers suffered grievously. They accepted the obligation of reducing rents in bad years as part and parcel of the right to impose high rents in good ones. During the worst of the depression years, from the late 1870s to the mid 1890s, rents fell on average by about a quarter—more in the corn counties and less in the grass ones. This put severe financial pressure on those without alternative sources of income, and even those who were better off were often anxious to get rid of an unprofitable estate. Moreover, by 1900 land prices had plummetted—in some instances to as little as half the 1870s prices, so that not only rental but also capital values were affected. After 1900, prices levelled, but the damage was done, and the choice for many was to quit—to cease to belong to the landed interest—or to remain and practise retrenchment.

Not all great landowners found themselves in this predicament. Some, in fact, prospered exceedingly as a result of investments outside agriculture. Many families had been swift to exploit the industrial potential of their estates early in the century, making substantial profits from timber, quarrying, lime burning, brick making, mining and iron smelting. David Spring

The game wagon at a pheasant shoot, Studley Royal, Yorkshire, 1901.

observes that 'if landowners lacked coal, their agents searched for it, anxious to carve out what a French traveller on Tyneside described as "farms underground".' Others put money into river navigation and port development, while 'a certain type of landowner usually needed no teaching at all that railways were good for him.' Some great Dukes became industrial entrepreneurs in their own right, deriving intellectual excitement as well as a handsome return from their business ventures. The Marquess of Londonderry owned and worked several valuable pits on his Durham estates and built a seaport, Seaham Harbour, for the export of his coal. The Duke of Devonshire was largely responsible for the construction of a railway line, iron and steel works, and docks at Barrow-in-Furness, while in the Midlands Lord Dudley invested heavily in the development of the western parts of the Black Country.

The increase in urban population from the mid century allowed landowners to participate in the building boom. H.J. Dyos quotes a jingle that appeared some decades later in Tarbuck's *Handbook of Household Property*:

> 'The richest crop for any field
> Is a crop of bricks for it to yield
> And the richest crop that it can grow
> Is a crop of houses in a row.'

By the end of the century, the ownership of ground in the metropolis brought huge profits. Those who benefited most were the owners of estates in central areas, notably the Dukes of Bedford, Portland and Westminster, although as London's suburbs steadily pushed outwards, other landed families came to share in the windfall gains provided by rising land values. The same process was taking place in most Victorian cities and on occasion caused resentment even among Tory councillors. T.H. Gill from Devonport, who described himself in 1899 as a 'fullblooded conservative' deplored the fact that the municipality 'lived in the hollow of one man's hand, who received an income of £40,000 a year he did nothing to earn.' Indeed, in the late Victorian period many landowners seem to have retreated from direct involvement in entrepreneurial activity, preferring instead to rely on rental or speculative incomes.

16

Besides returns from land, the stockmarket provided the possibility of a secure income in government stocks and a 'killing' for those prepared to gamble in overseas ventures. Peers who no longer played an active role in industry might still accept directorships, trading the value of their names on the company prospectus for a suitable financial consideration. Lastly, family fortunes could be saved by a successful marriage. This was a time-honoured expedient, and during the late nineteenth century there were many alliances between the heirs to landed estates and heiresses to fortunes founded, for example, in soap, diamonds or newspapers. Not infrequently, the brides and their dowries came from the New World. In the opinion of some, such marriages seemed to jeopardise the traditional values of the aristocracy, but more often they enhanced, rather than diminished, its vitality.

The pre-eminence of the landed classes was founded not only on wealth and land, but also on their long established leadership in government. Olney puts it succinctly:

"The cabinets of Victoria's reign were not confined to the great landed families, but representatives of those families took their place almost effortlessly at the head of affairs. Russell, Stanley, Fitzmaurice, Cecil, Manners, Cavendish, Spencer—no government was formed between 1830 and 1900 that could not boast at least one of these names. By the 1890s the House of Lords, though diluted with landless peers, had been neither ended nor mended, and indeed could still provide a prime minister, the third Marquess of Salisbury. Many sons of peers continued to sit in the House of Commons, and the elected Commons leader of the victorious Liberal Party in 1880 was Lord Hartington, heir to the magnificent dukedom of Devonshire.'

Irresistibly, however, power shifted away from the landed interest. This can be seen most clearly in the changing composition of the House of Commons. The first Reform Act of 1832 and the second Reform Act of 1867 did not decisively reduce the number of representatives of landed families, since these continued to provide a substantial majority in the House of Commons in 1868 and a slight one in 1880. But the third Reform Act of 1885 and the subsequent re-distribution of seats transformed rural politics. The old two and three member constituencies were replaced by smaller single member constituencies, many of which lost their county character, and even in predominantly rural constitituencies, the influence of a borough or market town—with its urban industrial population—was often substantially increased. At the same time, the wishes of peers and baronets, even when they commanded the broad allegiance of their tenants and newly enfranchised labourers, no longer guaranteed the result of parliamentary elections. In 1885, for the first time, the number of professional and commercial men and manufacturers in the House of Commons was greater than the number of landowners, and this outcome established the pattern for the future.

It is a tribute to the landed classes that they relinquished their monopoly of political power peacefully and with fair grace. Astutely, they abandoned the 'commanding heights' at Westminster when these could no longer be defended against the middle classes, only to assert themselves more strongly in local government. Here the aristocracy joined forces with the gentry, who had long made local administration their special sphere of influence. Individual involvement varied considerably, but an energetic man might leave his mark on every aspect of rural life. In 1861, Professor Von Holtzendorff visited England from Germany to attend a meeting of the

Social Science Congress, and stayed with the local squire, Barwick Lloyd Baker of Hardwicke Court in Gloucestershire. He recorded with amazement the Squire's list of engagements:

'...when most days of the week were filled with county or parochial business—Board of Guardians, Grand Jury and Quarter Sessions, police business, inspection of prisons, workhouse, reformatory schools, parish schools, and lunatic asylum, Petty Sessions, Local Board of Health, Hospital Committees, Savings Bank, Artisans' Building Society, Provident and Friendly Societies, School of Art, Volunteer Drill, and Rifle shooting, and one week every year in camp.'

Such unremitting and unpaid labour was often undertaken for the best of motives, from a sense of 'duty', philanthropy, and a simple desire for useful employment. There was also a sound appreciation of the fact that the preservation of the landed interest as a ruling class depended on such control, and from the mid century attempts to democratise local government met with increasingly bitter resistance.

The creation of new elected authorities from the 1880s seemed to indicate that this struggle too was lost. In the event, landowners had no difficulty in being returned to either the County Councils, formed in 1888, or the Parish and District Councils, formed in 1894. There was some diminution of landed authority as tenant farmers, small property owners and professional men gained election to the new bodies, but the threat of a labourers' victory never materialised. Some labourers—chiefly those with a background in trade unions or non-conformity, which bred an independent frame of mind—put themselves forward as candidates, but the majority were politically apathetic. In fact, many labourers voted for the aristocrat against the ratepayer or their own man, either because they considered that such support reflected 'the proper order of things' or because 'His Grace had always been a fair man.' Thus the population of Stoke Gifford in Gloucestershire approved the appointment of the Duke of Beaufort to the chairmanship of the new parish council on the grounds that he 'is a good landlord, pays 12s a week to the labourers, with half-pay when they are sick, and pensions off his old servants at from 5s. to 8s. a week.'

Eventually, the landed interest was ousted from its dominating position in local government, not as a result of any class struggle, but as the result of the increase in the numbers of trained administrators. An oligarchy gave way to a meritocracy—amateurs to professionals. Thompson has traced this process in the spread of county police forces from the middle decades of the century. These might be led by chief constables drawn from the gentry class, and be under the financial supervision of magisrates in quarter sessions, but they 'were rapidly establishing an autonomous code of conduct and a degree of control over their nominal masters which is exhibited by all bodies of permanent and professional public servants.' This trend was also apparent in poor law administration, public health and schools, and once landowners had lost control over these areas the end of the old order was well nigh accomplished.

Nonetheless, it still seemed appropriate to many to defer to the nobility and gentry. There was respect for great wealth and possessions, certainly, but also for birth and breeding, and what these entailed in terms of superior education, manners, taste and style. The attraction of the aristocracy was compelling. Petty landowners, country doctors, solicitors, local business-

18

Shooting at Berrington Court, Tenbury, Worcestershire.

men and their wives awaited the invitation to attend the county ball with keen anticipation, and gladly obeyed its summons to keep up the hierarchical dance. Those farmers who could dissociated themselves from the 'dull clods' below them and sought to acquire a degree of comparative refinement. Jefferies's 'man of progress' dressed with 'the carelessness of breeding, not slovenliness' and disdained to work alongside his men—'the frame was well-developed, but too active, it lacked the heavy thickness and the lumbering gait of the farmer bred to the plough.' His leisure interests were intellectual, 'His mind is full of art—look at those glasses—of music and pictures. Why he has just been reading Cleopatra—and now he's gone to look after the reapers.' Such a man was a revolutionary only in his enthusiasm for scientific farming, not in his politics.

Yet the carefully measured moments of social intercourse achieved by the tenantry and the rural professional classes with the aristocracy lay outside the common experience of the labourer. Wingfield Stratford recalls that 'It

19

A ladies' archery club, about 1900. (The photograph was used to advertise lawn seed for Sutton's Seeds of Reading.)

used to be said of the first Marquess of Abergavenny, as absolute a *grand seigneur* of the old school as ever walked, that his undergardeners were in the habit of conversing with him on much more familiar footing than they would have dreamed of assuming with the head gardener,' but such freedom was possible only within narrow bounds and by those fully aware of the rules that governed such conversations. Indeed, the great landowner might insist on a show of social respect—the men touching forelocks and the women bobbing curtsies—even when he was prepared to tolerate the expression of political differences. Geoffrey Robinson recalls one such incident in his book *Hedingham Harvest*, when the joiner's wife refused to curtsy to the Rector:

'He—the Rector—complained to the Duke, who summoned the joiner to see him. The man said that his wife did as she pleased and that he could not control her genuflexions. So the Duke had a word with the woman, who not only flatly refused to curtsy to the Rector but to the Duke as well. She would, she said, "only bow her knee to her maker". This religious zeal commended itself no more to the Duke than it did to the Rector, and the joiner was obliged to take his family and his stiff-legged wife out of the village again, because the Duke owned the roof over his head and the roof over the head of everyone who might give him employment.'

Such a show of independence was perhaps less exceptional among rural craftsmen than among day labourers; among the latter, especially the older men, to defer to the nobility was largely a matter of habit. This attitude is caught beautifully by Jefferies in the meeting between Hodge and the Marquis's wife at the agricultural show, when the old labourer steps up to receive some small tribute for 'sixty years of ploughing and sowing, sixty harvests':

'The old man is frosted with age, and moves stiffly, like a piece of mechanism rather than a living creature, nor is there any expression—neither smile nor interest—upon his absolutely immobile features. He wears breeches and gaiters and a blue coat cut in the style of two generations since… He puts forth his arm; his dry horny fingers are crooked and he can neither straighten nor bend them. Not the least sign appears upon his countenance that he is even conscious of what is passing. There is a quick flash of jewelled rings ungloved to the lights, and the reward is placed in that claw-like grasp by the white hand of the Marchioness.'

Some feeling of affection, however, was not altogether missing from Hodge's attitude to his masters. He was not unappreciative of the benefits of paternalism, and his deeper bitterness was reserved, not for the landlord, but for his harder taskmaster, the farmer. The Duke, whose existence generally impinged little on his own, he often wished well. It was after all 'his Duke', and the great man and his family represented a focus for local patriotism and loyalty. Even occasional eccentricities might be regarded with rude good humour. Yet, beyond the yarn-swapping and assumed familiarity of the ale-house, there remained a fundamental awe of the way of life enjoyed by aristocracy and gentry alike. Their very splendour set them apart from ordinary people. As Jefferies noted, the Duke rode to hounds 'as his ancestors rode to battle, with a hundred horsemen behind him. His colours are like the cockades of olden times.' In the eyes of a child, even splendour on a smaller scale was impressive. In response to a question posed at a Sunday School at Aberavon in South Wales, late in the century, 'Well boys, can you tell me who is the prince of this world?' The answer was made by a small boy in a feeble voice, 'Please Mum, Mr Biddulph.' He was referring to the local squire.

The seat of landed authority, the country house, continued to command admiration for its occupants and their way of life. In fact, as the century wore on, country house living tended to get grander. In early Victorian times, standards in many stately homes had been primitive, but by 1900 the keynote was comfort and easy living. The Industrial Revolution brought with it gas, electricity, central heating and modern plumbing. Yet technical advance before 1914 entailed no general reduction in the size of domestic staffs. While labour was cheap, large staffs were retained, chiefly for show. The opulent style found in the town houses of the new plutocrats was increasingly imitated by the landed aristocracy. Furniture and furnishings became more sumptuous, and a certain degree of 'vulgarity' was fashionable. As their political responsibilities waned, some peers, taking their example from the Prince of Wales, now devoted the greater part of their time to pleasure. If, characteristically, the beginning of the century witnessed the addition of libraries to country houses, the end saw the addition of gun-rooms, billiard rooms and smoking parlours within, and tennis courts and croquet lawns without. Previously, sport had been a way of life for a minority of passionate enthusiasts; now it provided a welcome distraction for those too busy to do more than 'weekend' on their estates, and for those too idle to find any other way of occupying their time.

Not all families, however, could afford to live in such a style, and the very fact that keeping up a landed house was now a 'rich man's luxury' increased

Advertisement for lawn tennis fencing, late nineteenth century.

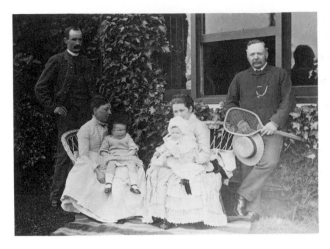

the pressure to sell. Some attempted economies, not always successfully. Thompson notes that the 2nd Earl of Verulam made an effort to reduce household expenditure, restricting the size of his cellar:

'Drinking habits had been tempered to the times: against the 590 bottles of sherry and 255 bottles of brandy drunk in 1870 the consumption in 1880 was down to 298 and 75 bottles; the consumption of champagne, however, had only fallen from 161 to 126 bottles, and of port from 101 to 83 bottles, while in recompense the quantity of claret drunk had risen from 687 to 740 bottles.'

This sort of pruning, Thompson considers, was perhaps as much as could be accomplished by an old man of settled habits, but it was still not enough to enable him to live within his income, and his son, the 3rd Earl, who inherited in 1895, was forced to let the family seat until 1901, when he returned 'to resume some of the former way of life.'

   In the late nineteenth century, a division opened up generally between the very wealthy families who could adjust to altered circumstances and their poor relations who could not. As the effects of depression rippled through the ranks of the land-owning class, the traditional squirearchy became more and more of an anachronism. To some extent, their place was taken by commercial magnates, although as Wingfield Stratford observes, there was no marked discontinuity between the two groups, partly because the process had been going on for decades and partly because the new men were often careful to accommodate themselves to the ways of county society:

'The new arrivals were apt to cherish a secret inferiority complex that made them nervously anxious to avoid the least suspicion of "showing the cloven hoof" by deviating in the least degree from the meticulous performance of "things that are done" by people who count.'

   Nonetheless, conformity to country customs was less obligatory after 1880 than before. The ownership of land was no longer seen as an essential qualification for those hoping to take up a Parliamentary career or to gain access to the peerage. Wealth now spoke for itself. It was often the aristocrat who sought to cultivate the plutocrat rather than the reverse. For the latter, buying an estate no longer involved any traditional social obligations—to serve as a magistrate or County Councillor—but could be enjoyed as pure recreation. Wingfield Stratford notes that the Edwardian 'arrivistes' often

22

Start of the 'Red Van' campaign, 1896, launched by the English Land Restoration League to advertise to rural labourers its aim that landlords should be subject to the imposition of 100% taxes on rents. The theory was that this single tax would provide enough money to pay for social reforms.

treated their estates 'in the light of pleasure grounds, to which they imported large house parties of opulent and up-to-date friends of their own kidney for weekends, or special occasions such as racing or shooting parties.' The trend for landed estates to be increasingly used for sporting purposes was encouraged by the aristocracy, since the lease of sporting rights provided a valuable additional source of income, especially where it helped to forestall the greater evil of having to part with an estate. Ironically, it was Andrew Carnegie who pointed out that the prices paid were 'absurd': $25-50,000 per annum 'for the right to shoot over a few thousand acres of poorly timbered land, and a force of gamekeepers and other attendants to pay for besides.' But it was a price that many English and foreign plutocrats were willing to pay, and by 1900 three million acres in Scotland had been given over to the cropping of deer and grouse. This fact gave ammunition to radical reformers who argued that the displacement of agricultural labour caused urban unemployment and who rejected the assertion that the land would support only game, not men.

Landlordism, threatened in so many other ways, increasingly came under attack at the turn of the century from militant liberalism and the urban labour movement. This reached serious proportions with the return of a Liberal government in 1906, which had openly touted for working class votes in a virulent, anti-landlord election campaign. Lloyd George's land taxes, imposed in his notorious budget of 1909 were modest in themselves, but they alerted landowners to a new trend—that landed wealth might henceforth be regarded as a bottomless pit out of which revenue might be drawn for social reform. With such a prospect, it was small wonder that many landowners, especially those whose margin of income over expenditure was small, decided to sell up and embark on a new career.

To the agricultural workers, however, the new squires were not always unwelcome. They had more money than the old, and as Wingfield Stratford comments:

'In his realistic way, Hodge touched his hat and pocketed his takings without the least tincture of those feelings of loyalty and respect he might, in former days, have entertained for the "family", and perhaps might still evince for such of its members as chanced from time to time to revisit the "thanedom once their own".'

So the bonds of dependence were broken. Such in any case had been the

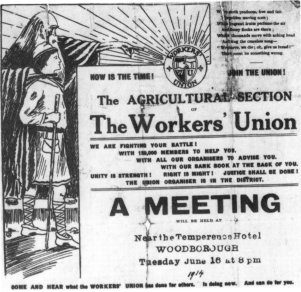

emerging pattern after 1870. Individual cases of want might continue to be relieved with a gift of money, clothes or food, and for some landowners visiting the sick and needy remained an injunction they could not ignore, but economic pressure, changing public opinion and the slow growth of state welfare eroded old habits of paternalism. This fact was not regretted by the younger generation of labourers, who preferred to chance their arm and improve their lot by hard bargaining. Liberated by improving educational standards and the greater scarcity of labour, they breathed a freer atmosphere than their fathers and were able to negotiate a price for their allegiance to the land. They might still lose most of the disputes they undertook, but now they were better prepared to fight, and with newer weapons, which included agricultural unionism. Joseph Arch's National Agricultural Labourers' Union, founded in the early 1870s, did not survive, but George Edwards's Eastern Counties Agricultural Labourers' and Smallholders' Union, set up in 1906, grew into the new National Union, which was to have a long history.

In the final analysis, the landed interest was not replaced by the commercial interest, nor frightened out of its heritage by a reforming government. Many landlords sold out, quietly and without fuss, to their own tenant farmers, for reasons of economic expediency. What was achieved in the process was nothing short of a social revolution, since, besides the diminished form of the old landlord-tenant system, there arose a new class of yeomanry to replace that which had become almost extinct during the course of the eighteenth century. This process was not completed by 1914; the numbers of owner-occupiers continued to increase in the inter-war period, bringing a further weakening of the old hierarchical structure of rural society. But the landed interest endured, and enjoyed great prestige where formerly it had exercised great power and privilege. Even in the latter respect, all was not lost, as some peers, baronets and squires joined the new governing elite, drawn from commerce, industry, the universities, and the professions. Great landowners still had an important contribution to make to national and local life in the twentieth century, but as talented and wealthy individuals rather than as representatives of their class.

Left: members of Joseph Arch's National Agricultural Labourers' Union being evicted from their cottage at Milbourne, Dorset in 1874. *Right:* poster advertising a meeting of the Agricultural Section of the Worker's Union at Woodborough in Wiltshire; this was an alternative to the National Union of Agricultural Workers, and in many ways more successful until the Great War.

Tenant Farms, Tied Cottages

The two largest classes in rural society were the farmers and the agricultural labourers. In 1851, there were about 250,000 farmers in England and Wales, and just short of a million labourers. They led very different lives, the labourers being generally among the poorest in the village and the farmers among the better off. The contrasts between the two groups were not always so stark, however; although there were farmers on the Lincolnshire Wolds who were tenants of as many as 2,000 acres—as much land as some squires might own—small farmers a few miles away in the Isle of Axholme might have no more than twenty acres at their disposal. The labouring class was made up mainly of general labourers engaged in field work, but it also included those with special skills required for work with livestock—shepherds, horse-men, carters and cow-men—who received the higher wages which gave them a standard of living comparable with that of the small farmer. But, in the main, the lifestyles of the farmer and his man were widely disparate.

One thing that set the two classes apart was the quality of their housing. With the exception of those attached to the smallest of occupations, farmhouses were substantial in construction and size; indeed they were frequently the object of surprise to visitors from abroad who took them for the houses of gentlemen rather than farmers. Some were old and rambling, built of local materials. Over much of the North and West, stone was used for building, but in other areas, notably the South East and parts of the Midlands, a tradition of timber-framed building had evolved. Then there were the newer Georgian and Victorian houses, more likely to be built of brick and slate, and owing less to tradition than to current architectural fashion. They could be found in most parts of the country, but perhaps most especially in areas of Parliamentary enclosure, where the layout of farms had been completely reorganised and new farmsteads built to match. Old or new, farm houses were usually of generous proportions, with a whole range of service rooms for brewing, baking, cheese and butter

Below: stone-built farmhouse in the West Country, photographed about 1912. *Right:* a traditional style farmhouse of Cotswold stone, probably dating from the late eighteenth or early nineteenth century. The building on the right is a malt house.

making and washing. The farmhouse kitchen was the hub of activity and the place where the household usually met, but most farmers liked to have a parlour as a 'best room'. Many of the newer farmhouses included a drawing room, a dining room, and sometimes a library. These generously proportioned farmhouses were well populated; besides the farmer and his family, there were domestic servants, and, in northern counties, young unmarried farm workers living in, who slept in attic bedrooms. Mid nineteenth-century census returns for some parts of Yorkshire show as many as twenty people living in a farmhouse.

While farmhouses were roomy and well filled, labourers' cottages were cramped and overcrowded. A report by H.J. Hunter in 1865 showed that 40% of country cottages had only one bedroom, while fewer than 5% had more than two. Many cottages were damp and ill-ventilated. Even where stone and brick were readily available, the dwellings were often cheaply and badly built with mud walls and thatched roofs. They were still being built

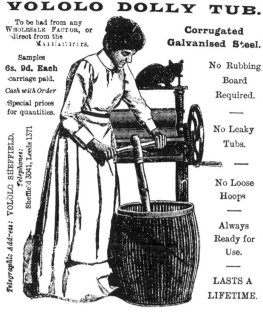

in this way in the 1850s and 1860s; a few still survive. The worst were usually those built by freehold squatters or owners of small amounts of land which might even be along roadside verges. Windows were not plentiful—some houses even had the back wall built directly into a bank—and gardens non-existent. Even on the large estates where the cottages had been better built, many were too old to be adequate dwelling places. Landowners were making strenuous efforts to remedy that situation during the nineteenth century for a variety of reasons. The desire to maintain a well-kept estate, a real concern for the welfare of labourers, and the need to keep labourers on the land in the 1850s and 1860s, when migration to the towns was causing a labour shortage, led to the building in the villages of many solid cottages, usually of brick, in semi-detached pairs, with two or three bedrooms and an ample garden.

Despite these efforts, investigations in the early twentieth century found the labourers' housing conditions little different from those of fifty years earlier. Most cottages were too small, many were insanitary, and modern estate cottages formed only a small minority. The landowners could not keep pace with the need for housing. Greater investment was required than they could muster. The Duke of Bedford quoted £100 as the cost of the cottages he was building at Woburn in the 1850s, and they were by no means extravagant in their construction. Cottage building was not a productive investment; landowners usually subsidised cottage rents, charging one shilling or one and sixpence a week compared with the economic rent of about two shillings and sixpence.

In the mid nineteenth century, labourers' cottages were generally bare and scantily furnished. Many had insufficient chairs for all the family, some did not even have a table, and bolsters were as likely to be slept on as beds. Often the cottage would be too cramped to accommodate much furniture and what little the labourer did possess (apart from the occasional family heirloom) was mostly of cheap pine, spartan in design and limited in durability. However, contemporary reports suggest that all but the poorest

labouring families contrived to create an air of decency and cheerfulness in their homes with rag rugs and cushions, and perhaps a small collection of brass candlesticks and crockery displayed on the mantelpiece.

The interiors of farmhouses in the mid nineteenth century offered a scene of comfort and plenty. The farmer bought most of his furniture from the local joiner. Using traditional techniques, country joiners made simple, durable pieces in native woods, such as oak, elm, ash, yew and the fruit

Left: an old stone and thatch cottage at Upton, Berkshire, about 1900. *Above:* a mid nineteenth century cottage on the Bearwood estate in Berkshire, where the whole village was rebuilt in the 1860s by the owners, the Walters family, who were the proprietors of *The Times.* Houses in estate villages of this sort were generally well designed and constructed.

PLANS AND ELEVATIONS FOR LABOURERS' COTTAGES.

SIX WITH THREE BED-ROOMS EACH.

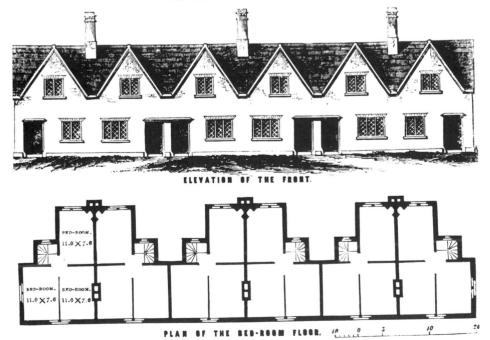

ELEVATION OF THE FRONT.

PLAN OF THE BED-ROOM FLOOR.

Plan and elevation of cottages built by the Duke of Bedford at Woburn in the 1850s.

A cottage interior in Gresham, Norfolk, in the 1860s. It is moderately well furnished, with a set of candlesticks and various mementoes on the mantelpiece.

Below: a settle made around 1880 for a farmhouse kitchen in Chard, Somerset. *Right:* a beehive chair of wickerwork, a type mainly from Gloucestershire and neighbouring counties; a Windsor chair; a simple chest made of elm planks.

woods. Styles changed slowly, and the farmer was satisfied with furniture that was functional rather than fashionable. Some pieces of furniture clearly evolved to suit the particular needs of the farmhouse. For example, the settle, a hearthside seat with a high back, acted as a screen against the draughts in the kitchen, and also contained space for storage. Corner cupboards were useful because they were capacious without occupying too much space, and dressers, which had shelves for the display of household

pewter or earthenware, usually also had cupboards and drawers. The durability and usefulness of such furniture meant that the farmer was often content to be surrounded by pieces which were generations old, acquired by inheritance or bought secondhand. In addition to the practical furnishings which served the basic needs of life, farmhouses often contained a few modest luxuries; long case clocks supplied by the local maker were commonly found, and most farmers owned a little silver—typically spoons, jugs and tankards.

As the nineteenth century progressed, new forces started to influence the lives of country people. The growth of the industrial economy, and closer contacts with urban culture brought about by the railways introduced new goods and new ideas into the rural world. New, cheap factory-made household goods were available to both farmer and labourer. There were new fashions to be followed, most obviously perhaps in dress, for both the farmer and his men discarded the old smocks in favour of manufactured coats, and even the poorer girls did their best to wear dresses in the latest London styles. Education, cheap newspapers brought out from the towns, and more travel brought rising expectations to the rural population, and many of those expectations were fulfilled, even amongst the poorer sections of society, as low prices and higher incomes raised the labourer's standard of living.

Although labourers' wages rose across the country, they varied considerably from region to region, being generally much lower in the south than they were in the northern counties. In the mid nineteenth century, the weekly wage paid to ordinary labourers in some southern counties, such as Wiltshire or Devon, was only seven or eight shillings. In northern districts, such as Cheshire and Lancashire, the rate could be twelve to thirteen shillings a week, while in Lincolnshire it was about eleven shillings a week. The upward progression was not smooth: increases in wages during the 1860s and early 1870s were followed by reductions in the 1880s. But that loss was later recovered, so that by the beginning of the twentieth century the range was from sixteen to seventeen shillings a week

A long-case clock made by John Player of Reading (active 1830-77). Almost every market town had makers who produced such simple and attractive clocks.

Late nineteenth century kitchen interior with open hearth for cooking.

30

Watercolour of a tastefully furnished Essex farmhouse of the 1860s.

The smock, an item of workaday clothing that had largely gone out of use by the end of the nineteenth century.

in high wage areas to about twelve shillings a week in low wage counties, with those in the middle range at fourteen or fifteen shillings. To these basic wages could often be added extra payments for piece work, the largest of these usually being about £5 earned at harvest time, and the family income could be augmented by the earnings of the labourer's wife and children. The labourer's advancement was furthered by the general fall in prices during the last two decades of the century, which meant that he could buy better food and clothes and travel more. He also could make provision for old age or sickness by subscribing to one of the many benefit and friendly societies active in the villages. Of course, fourteen shillings a week did not mean great riches, and several social investigators, such as Seebohm Rowntree, concluded on the eve of World War I that a large proportion of the rural population still lived a life of economic stringency and under-nourishment. Even so, the labourer's standard of living had risen substantially since 1850. By the turn of the century, many could afford several pieces of furniture, often shoddily made of cheap pine at a local factory, but with a modern and fashionable appearance. Usually it was the younger generation that first acquired this new furniture as they set up their homes after coming into contact with urban fashions during their spells of work in the town.

The furnishings of the farmhouse, too, exhibited a rising standard of comfort during the period. At the topmost rungs of the farming ladder, the change was perhaps less marked; the richest farmers, the men with the thousand-acre farms, had always been able to live a life of comparative luxury. They rode to hounds with the gentry, dressed elegantly and furnished their homes with tables of mahogany, sideboards of rosewood. When Richard Jefferies complained in the 1870s that farmers were living pretentiously and aping their superiors by buying paintings and having

31

their daughters taught French and piano-playing, he was saying nothing new. Arthur Young had used almost identical terms a century previously, and similar views were expressed in earlier centuries. But there were new elements in the later nineteenth century. First among them was the influence of urban society, whose lifestyle came to replace that of the squirearchy as the model that farmers wished to emulate. The traditionalists thus came to complain that farmers were becoming indistinguishable from city bankers, which was not altogether surprising, for the closer contacts between city and country meant that some of the farmer's sons were becoming bankers, and some of his daughters marrying stockbrokers. The working life of the farm was also changing. More farmers were tending to withdraw from work in the fields alongside their men to become overseers and to attend business at the markets. Even the upsets of the agricultural depression in the last quarter of the century did not reverse this trend. Indeed, it reinforced it by forcing the farmer to become a better business manager and spend more time on his account books. The work of the farmer's wife became easier; bread and beer were more often bought than made at home, the dairy could be left in the charge of servants, and there were fewer labourers living in to be catered for.

Most factories turned out cheap furniture which labourers could afford, but they also produced more elegant styles to suit the pockets of the middling farmers. This meant that fashionable furnishings ceased to be the preserve of the wealthiest, but permeated lower down the farming ladder. The pieces that the lesser farmers could afford were not always of the best mahogany—they might be imported deal with a veneer, or English beech— but at least they looked smart, and more and more farmers came to furnish their houses in up-to-date style. New items of furnishing fashion, such as the chiffonier, the chaise longue, fitted carpets and curtains, were introduced into the farmhouse.

Not all farmers set out to furnish in the best fashion. Some could not afford to. Some did not want to and, with traditional caution about spending, bought the replacement furniture they needed secondhand at farm sales. There were still farmers in the remoter parts of the countryside and on small farms who led a peasant-like life, at times harder than that of

Below: traditional means of lighting—brass candlestick. *Bottom:* iron firedogs (from Pangbourne, Berkshire) to support a wood fire on an open hearth; cooking pot of a type dating at least from the fifteenth century.

Above: rush light holder. *Centre:* paraffin lamp of a type common in farmhouses. *Right:* open fireplace with firedogs and a chimney crane to hold cooking vessels, from a farmhouse at Woodley, Reading, Berkshire.

the labourer. It was observed of Buckinghamshire farmers in 1892: 'The smock-frock farmer has almost ceased to exist, but some still survive and hold small occupations of from fifty to a hundred acres, leading an industrious, hard-faring life, living oft times more frugally than their labourers and going on as the saying is on the Chiltern Hills "from cherry time to cherry time" and getting no forrarder.'

There were other changes which affected the domestic life of both farmer and labourer. Cheap forms of lighting, heating and cooking became available. In the 1860s, rush lights and candles began to be replaced by paraffin lamps, which were cheaper and gave better light. At first people were rather afraid of the new fuel; the introduction of the new lamps was therefore a slow process, but once this distrust had been overcome they became common in the homes of all classes. They had a great effect on the lives of the labourers. 'Cheap lamps and cheap paraffin have given the villagers their winter evenings', wrote George Sturt, 'at a cost of a few halfpence earned in the course of a day's work a cottage family may prolong their winter's day as far into the night as they please; and that without feeling that they are wasting their store of light.' And this meant that the labourer could stay in at night instead of going to the public house as the only alternative to an early bed-time.

Cooking and heating also became easier. The traditional wood fire which burned on the open hearth came increasingly to be replaced by coal-burning grates. Although wood gave a cheerful fire, it was not well suited to cooking; it produced an uneven heat and the fire died away quickly unless large stores of fuel were to hand. Coal presented none of these problems and was usually burned in a cast iron range with attached oven and boiler, which united all the cooking operations in the kitchen. The range made it possible to bake, roast and stew with a single fire and at the same time

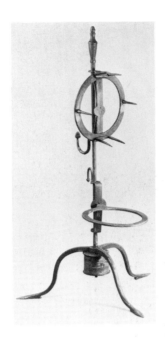

Open hearth cooking apparatus. *Left:* wrought iron trivet/toaster. The circle of spikes, on which meat was impaled, is adjustable in height, as is the carrier for a plate to catch the dripping. *Centre:* ratchet hanger for suspending utensils over an open hearth. *Right:* bottle jack with clockwork mechanism to rotate meat during roasting; type in common use from the early nineteenth century.

provided a constant supply of hot water was available. The advent of the kitchen range greatly simplified cooking apparatus. The age-old method of suspending a pot by a hook or chimney crane over the fire was replaced by the hob or hotplate which was a feature of most ranges. Cooking became not only easier but cleaner, since the cooking vessels did not become blackened with soot.

Kitchen ranges had first become common in manufacturing districts towards the close of the eighteenth century. They spread much more slowly into the rural areas, their use being dependent on coal supplies, which were not readily available until after the railways were built. Many country

Left: trivet, on which kettles and pans were stood at the side of the hearth to keep warm. *Below:* Dutch oven or reflector oven.

Traditional kitchenware: beaker made of bullock's horn and large turned wooden mixing bowl made of ash.

people, therefore, did not use a kitchen range until well after 1850. Ranges were made in all sizes; in the 1880s a small one with a couple of hot plates and a small oven could be bought for as little as thirty shillings by the labourer, or his landlord, and in many new cottages they were installed as the homes were built. They undoubtedly improved the lives of cottage-dwellers. Few of the older cottages had a built-in oven; the labourer's wife had to take her baking to the village baker once a week. With a range, she had her own oven and could produce a greater variety of hot meals whenever they were wanted.

The kitchen range exemplifies the way in which industrial goods and urban influence spread into the country. The introduction and adoption of

Small kitchen range suitable for cottages, from the catalogue of Barnard, Bishop & Barnards, 1881.

10

IMPROVED

COTTAGE RANGE,

Nos. 730 to 733.

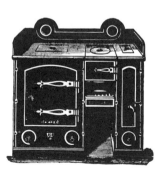

These Ranges are a great improvement on those known as Kitcheners, and they possess the advantages of baking bread and pastry on the bottom shelf of the oven, which cannot be done by any other kind.

Meat roasted by these Ranges is found to be more regularly cooked, and to retain the juices better than when roasted before the fire. The operations of boiling and stewing can be carried out efficiently on any part of the hot plate. The flues are constructed on a peculiar principle, and require less sweeping than any others.

44

BRICKLAYER'S DIRECTIONS

FOR FIXING

THE COTTAGE RANGE.

COTTAGE RANGE

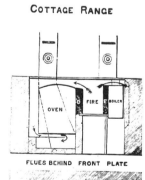

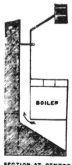

FLUES BEHIND FRONT PLATE

SECTION AT CENTRE OF BOILER

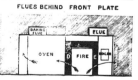

PLAN UNDER HOT PLATE

Unscrew and remove the hob, place the Range in its situation, lay a flooring of bricks **A** under the Oven level with the bottom of the soot door ; build back on edgework **B** from front to back, as high as the plate. Brick on edgework **C** to be carried up as high as the Grate, after which it is to be continued with the fire-brick **D** as high as the lower part of top of Oven. The work behind the small front to be built up solid, and the fire-brick **E** placed above the Grate. The back fire-brick to be fixed between the two side ones, and filled in solid behind. The chimney opening to be enclosed above the bar, and the Register Door fixed so as to exclude all draught.

new equipment was gradual, but the final effect of these innovations on rural society was enormous. Mass-produced earthenware from the Potteries began to displace pewter plates and dishes from the kitchen shelves of farmhouse and cottage at the end of the eighteenth century. Galvanised vessels replaced the bowls and tubs made by the local turner or cooper from the mid nineteenth century onwards. Zinc baths began to be used instead of wooden tubs at about the same time. The result of it all was a society which, although lacking much that was available to town-dwellers, was ready to share in the rise of the consumer society of the twentieth century.

Left: wooden flour tub, mid nineteenth century. *Above:* tinned and enamelled steel utensils from *The Ironmonger,* 1913.

Large, industrially produced earthenware serving dish with transfer-printed Willow Pattern design, probably nineteenth century.

36

Seed Time to Harvest

During the Napoleonic Wars, Britain had enjoyed considerable prosperity, but in the years that followed—from 1815 almost until the accession of Queen Victoria—there was a long period of deflation. Lord Ernle saw this as 'one of the blackest periods of English farming', although historians now consider that the distress was precipitated by plummetting wheat prices, and was largely confined to arable farming in the South and East; within this region, problems were more widespread among those farming the cold, stiff and unproductive clays than among those farming the lightlands, then being taken into cultivation. Indeed, the price fall seems to have caused many lightland farmers to increase their investment in more productive techniques, enabling them to grow more at lower unit costs. James Caird identifies these 'high farmers' as those responsible for increases in output during the worst of the depression years; with the recovery in prices after 1837 productivity shot up even further and agriculture entered its so-called 'golden age' of apparently effortless expansion, which continued for nearly three decades.

By the mid century, British agriculture was almost universally admired: for the excellence of its institutions—notably the landlord-tenant system, its technical accomplishments, its profitability, and, as much as anything, for its general air of well-being and stability. To European observers, familiar with the continental pattern of feudal estates and small-scale cultivation by individual peasants, there was much to envy, and many came simply to look and to learn. In 1855, a Frenchman, Léonce de Lavergne, noted in his book, *Rural Economy of England, Scotland and Wales* that, 'English agriculture, taken as a whole, is at this day, the first in the world, and is in the way of realising further progress'.

One event only disturbed the calm. In 1846, Peel's government repealed the Corn Laws, which had given British farmers security against the import of cheap foreign cereals. Behind this action lay a political consensus in favour of free trade, which, it was believed, would enable Britain to exploit her superiority in manufactured goods to gain new markets abroad, while ensuring a plentiful food supply for a rapidly expanding population at home. It was also argued that cheap food would reduce industrial wages and costs, leading to further economic growth, while farming would be made more efficient by exposure to the chill wind of international trade. Farmers, however, predicted the ruination of British agriculture and campaigned for a return to 'Protection'.

But by the 1850s, the issue seemed to have been a storm in a teacup, and farmers abandoned politics for the more practical business of earning a living. Thus Jones quotes a letter from the notable Squire Surtees, who briefly replied to an invitation to attend a meeting of the County Agricultural Protection Society in Durham in 1851, 'Dear Sir, No more agitation, from yours very sincerely, R.S. Surtees.' Expectations of cheap, easily obtainable food supplies were certainly not fulfilled: other nations were not waiting to pass their foodstuffs on to Britain and, indeed, had troubles of their own. Grain exports from Russia were interrupted by the Crimean War and those from North America by the Civil War, while Denmark's development as a dairy exporter was substantially impeded by the loss of Schleswig-Holstein in the mid 1860s. More significantly, perhaps, Britain was shielded against competition from the Americas and Australasia by prohibitive shipping costs.

By the mid-century, a swelling home demand for foodstuffs was also helping to sustain British farmers. With rising real incomes, the urban working class, in particular, could afford butcher's meat, eggs and fresh milk. Livestock production, rather than wheat, traditionally the 'queen' of the crops, was increasingly more profitable; the demand for bread did not rise significantly and receipts from wheat growing remained static or even declined. Yet the strength of the mixed farming system in the South and East of the country, where grain could be held back as feed for livestock when wheat prices were low, disguised the declining profitability of wheat and delayed a more complete transition to livestock farming. By the 1860s, the basis of the old arable prosperity had been seriously eroded, although all seemed well on the surface and the industry appeared curiously unaware of impending disaster.

The crisis came in the 1870s. The previous two decades had seen the rapid expansion of the US economy; the laying down of thousands of miles of rail track across the interior and the establishment of grain and stock handling facilities at the major distributive centres, such as Chicago, heralded the emergence of America as a major agricultural exporting nation. The decisive factor in bringing grain in bulk across the Atlantic, was the development of a fast, reliable steamship service and a drastic reduction, under fierce competition, of transport costs. The price of wheat fell sharply at European ports and the profitability of arable farming appeared likely to collapse. The response of most countries was to raise tariff walls against the cheap foreign imports; Britain, however, remained firmly wedded to free trade. Farmers might deplore the fact that 'agriculture was being sacrificed on the altar of industrial progress', but protection still remained a lost cause. In the 1880s, Joseph Chamberlain and the Conservatives came to favour the idea of what they called 'fair trade', which was really a system of imperial preference. But the party's adoption of tariff reform in 1903 contributed to its humiliating defeat in 1906: in the public imagination, protection was associated with expensive bread and was regarded by the working classes as a stomach tax. They voted solidly against it and tariff reform remained a dead issue right up to the 1930s.

Arable farmers were hit first and most severely by the depression. Between 1870 and the end of the century, imports of wheat and flour to Britain nearly doubled, while the price was halved. The demand for American wheat easily equalled supply, for it was this hard wheat that yielded the high white flour much prized in bread-making at the time. Even labourers' families ate white bread whenever possible, rejecting other varieties as hopelessly inferior. Thus, Jefferies noted, that even while Hodge was reaping the harvest:

'... huge ships are on the ocean rushing through the foam to bring grain to the great cities to whom—and to all—cheap bread is so inestimable a blessing. Very likely, when he pauses in his work, and takes his luncheon, the crust he eats is made of flour ground out of grain that grew in far distant Minnesota, or some vast Western state!'

The situation was made worse by the inability of many farmers to believe that the fall in prices was more than a temporary matter, brought about by a few wet seasons, which could be ridden out if their courage did not fail. Jefferies observed,

'For some length of time the corn grower puts a courageous face on the difficulties which beset him, and struggles on, hoping for better days. After a while, however, seeing that his capital is diminishing, because he has been, as it were, eating it, seeing that there is no prospect of immediate relief, whatever may happen in the future, he is driven to one of two courses. He must quit the occupation, or he must reduce his expenditure. He must not only ask the labourer to accept a reduction, but he must, wherever practicable, avoid employing labour at all.'

Many arable farmers went bankrupt, and sought new occupations outside agriculture. Others attempted to cut back on the wage bill by laying off men, and it was the threat of unemployment and lower wages that precipitated the formation of the first agricultural trade unions in the 1870s. Many farmers asked their landlords for extended remissions, and this in turn reduced landlords' incomes—forcing those whose estates were already encumbered with mortgages and other burdens, to sell, thus reversing the trend for landownership to become concentrated in fewer and fewer hands.

Not all arable farmers, however, suffered so acutely in the depression. Some found an outlet for their wheat in the confectionery industry; British soft wheats were suitable for making biscuits—an increasingly popular food in Victorian households towards the end of the century. Those who had contracts with maltsters for their barley found that this part of their business was largely unaffected. B.A. Holderness comments that barleys from California or the River Plate were cheaper and of a quality equal or superior to British barley, despite the 'reputation of East Anglian and Scottish malt,' but foreign supplies tended to be infrequent and insufficient. Thus, until the Great War, most of the grain used in brewing and all of that used in whisky distilling was home-produced. Another profitable outlet was oats, since the demand for feed for town horses continued to rise, and those who could supply oats or hay—goods too bulky to import—were assured of a ready sale for all they could produce.

Even in the most stricken areas of the South and East, some farmers prospered. Often these were newcomers; G.E. Mingay points out that:

'Thrifty Scots fleeing from high Scottish rents, and hard-working men from the West Country, were much in evidence. They had taken on bankrupt farms at knock-down prices, and by severe economy in labour and cultivation had made the land pay once more. Mostly they thrived by turning to milk or some other produce strongly in demand in the towns.'

Indeed, the classic response to a decline in the profits of arable farming was to shift into more intensive livestock production: 'down corn—up horn!' What was unprecedented, however, was the size of the arable contraction; Caird commented in the late 1880s that 'in the last twenty years, three million acres, nearly one seventh of the land under rotation, have been added to the permanent pastures.'

Yet livestock farming was not protected from foreign competition either. The sheep farmers of the eastern and southern counties had to face the challenge of increasing imports of wool, which led to a collapse of wool prices almost as dramatic as that of grain, although its effect on agriculture generally was less marked because fewer farmers were involved; the very fine, short staple wool, produced by the merino or merino-cross flocks of Australasia was particularly sought after by the textile industry. More seriously, the livelihood of meat-producers was threatened by the development of refrigeration in the late 1870s; imports of cheap meat trebled in the last quarter of the century. Livestock prices however, did not fall as far as those of grain. The demand for meat continued to rise, and home-produced joints were superior until the Great War. Many butchers would not stock the early refrigerated meat; it was bought chiefly by the urban working class and was not widely available in country areas until the chain butchers invaded the market towns just before World War I. Specialist stock rearers were able to take advantage of the lower cost of imported feed grains to raise larger herds, and in this sense may actually have benefited from the depression. Mixed farmers, too, gained from cheaper imports of seeds and fertilizers. Savings, however, were balanced by the higher wage bill on mixed farms, which required more labour in the various operations of the stock/grain cycle. As wages once again eased upwards in the 1890s, it often became unprofitable to cultivate the lightest soils, which were allowed to revert to rough pasture. Thompson notes:

'Everywhere mixed farming was practised, the pressure of costs and prices produced a decline in the intensity of cultivation, a decline in output, and a decline in income.'

The fall in the cost of imports, therefore, was insufficient to rescue the fortunes of mixed farmers, and it is noteworthy that while the greater part

Supplying milk for the cities. *Left:* the growing demand was at first met by urban cow-keepers, who combined keeping one or more cows with selling other dairy products and sometimes vegetables and other cheap groceries. *Below:* the growth of rail transport allowed milk to be brought in bulk to the cities. Chain retailers, such as the Maypole Dairy, had virtually replaced cow-keepers in the larger cities by 1900.

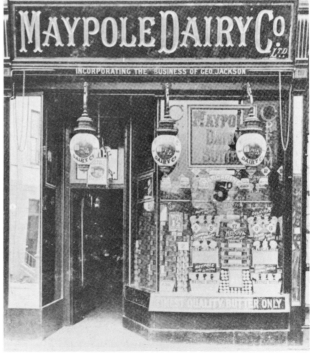

of the increase in livestock production came from within the shifting balance of mixed farming before 1870, thereafter, the increase was achieved mainly by grassland producers in the North and West. The growth in livestock production overall, however, was modest—something like 10% from the mid 1870s to the mid 1890s—and was significant only within the context of a 13% decline in total agricultural output over the same period.

Those who fared best during the depression years were the milk producers and those growing fresh fruit and vegetables. The price of milk showed no tendency to fall during this period. Consumer demand for the commodity had barely begun to be satisfied, and as a perishable product it enjoyed a naturally sheltered market. Improvements in cooling milk on the farm and the spread of the rail network brought relative prosperity to the big contract producers in the areas supplying London and the Midlands. Even small farms in the western counties often did well; Jefferies recorded the transformation that had taken place in one Wiltshire village in a space of just ten years,

'The cows now kept are much too valuable to be treated roughly, being selected from shorthorn strains that yield large quantities of milk. No farmer now would allow any such knocking about. The hay itself is better, because the grass itself has been improved, and it is also harvested carefully... As for the manure, it is recognised to be gold in another shape, and instead of being trodden underfoot by the cattle and washed away by the rain, it is utilised... Sheds have been newly thatched, and generally renovated, and even new roads laid down across the farms, and properly macadamised, in order that the milk carts might reach the highway without the straining and difficulty consequent upon wheels sinking half up to the axles in winter.

'[A newly familiar sound was the noise of] milk tins dragged hither and thither by the men who are getting the afternoon milk ready for transit to the station miles away. Each tin bears a brazen badge engraved with the name of the milkman who will retail its contents in distant London. It may be delivered to the Countess in Belgravia and reach her dainty lips in the morning chocolate, or it may be eagerly swallowed up by the half-starved children of some black court in the purlieus of Seven Dials.'

But as more grassland farmers turned to milk production—the total milk output increased by some 50% between the 1870s and the 1890s—the manufacture of milk products declined. Home-produced dairy produce was replaced by imports, which more than doubled in the last quarter of the century; in fact, by 1900, imports accounted for some 60% of the total consumption of dairy products. Tinned milk came in from the United States, while butter substitutes, another potentially valuable market, were developed chiefly by the Dutch and the Germans. Holderness points out that, like condensed milk, margarine was part of the diet of even the poorest classes by 1900, although British farmers gained little from this, since 'even when manufactured in Britain, margarine was a compound of imported oils and fats, and therefore, if only marginally, it sliced into the traditional market for domestic agricultural produce.'

Fruit and vegetable cultivation and market gardening, however, flourished throughout the depression years. Imports of fresh fruit and vegetables were small because of the problems in transporting perishable goods over long distances, and simply served to whet the appetite for home produce. Large arable farmers turned to the cultivation of field vegetables and vied with small farmers and market gardeners to meet the growing urban demand for fresh produce. The areas to benefit were chiefly the Isle of Axholme, the area around Wisbech in East Anglia, Kent, Somerset, Devon and the Vale of Evesham in the West Midlands.

Another outlet for growers lay in the preserving and canning industries; both of these were still at a relatively early stage of development, although a number of well-known firms, such as Wilkin's of Tiptree, were established at this time. Again, however, British producers faced the problem that many manufacturers were importing raw materials, such as mulches and semi-processed fruit—a trend that was well-established by the end of the century.

Nonetheless, by 1900, agricultural prices were rising and better times were on the way for most farmers—by 1914, gross output was back to the 1870 level. The United States now had an expanding domestic market and was no longer exporting such huge quantities of foodstuffs. In Britain, Canadian and Argentine wheat imports largely replaced those from the United States, although supplies for livestock were not replaced, which resulted in a shortage of meat on the home market that lasted until after the Great War.

By the turn of the century, the fortunes of arable farming had enjoyed a limited upturn, but this was not enough to restore its profitability in relation to livestock farming, and British agriculture emerged from the depression with a substantially altered pattern of production.

The special significance of the Victorian period in the history of modern British agriculture is that it saw the development of a close relationship between agriculture and manufacturing industries. In 1840, most farm produce was still sold fresh or in a semi-processed state, but by the end of the century, all the traditional trades in processing, flour milling, malting, brewing and distilling had become industrialised, and, at the same time, agriculture itself had become a large-scale consumer of industrial goods, a process described by F.M.L. Thompson as the 'Second Agricultural Revolution'.

To Thompson, the First Agricultural Revolution involved changes in crop and livestock rotations, enclosure and an increased intensity of cultivation. Landlords sank more money into the land and farmers became more market orientated, but the concept which lay at the heart of the revolution was that of the mixed farm—a self-contained production unit.

'It produced for sale wheat, barley, meat and some wool: the roots, clovers or other rotation grasses and perhaps pulses, as well as the hay which it grew, were consumed on the spot, and furnished the richer and more abundant supplies of manure from which the larger cereal yields came, as well as supporting the livestock production and the horse-power which worked the farm.'

The essence of the Second Agricultural Revolution was that 'it broke the closed circuit system and made the operations of the farmer much more like those of the factory owner.' The physical changes were associated with field drainage and purpose-built farm buildings, the technical changes consisted of fertilizers and feeding stuffs, the economic changes involved a further increase in the intensity of cultivation, with farmers as well as landlords investing in high output techniques, and the replacement of men by

Above: a Hop Day demonstration in London, 16th May 1909. *Right:* cherry picking in Hertfordshire for the fruiterer H. Aldridge of High Wycombe, Buckinghamshire.

machinery. In brief, farming came to rely on inputs from industry so that it could raise output and feed a growing population; it also needed to offset the decline in the number of agricultural workers by raising productivity.

Fertilizers provided a substitute for animal dung and other natural organic manures, although these continued to be used in large quantities throughout the period. But from the 1830s, a number of other off-farm fertilizers were available—including crushed bones, bone-dust and oil-waste. Bones are a source of phosphate and nitrogen and were applied as a top dressing on light land soils, especially on roots. Lincolnshire was the early home of the bone-crushing industry which later spread to other light land areas. Rag and bone men, who gathered animal bones from the meat consumed by people in the towns, were the chief suppliers of home-produced bones, but from the 1850s, imports outweighed the domestic supply. Thompson also drily reports the comment made a decade earlier by the German chemist, Justus Liebig, to the effect that, 'in their insatiable search for bones, English merchants were rifling the battlefields of Europe and ransacking the catacombs of Sicily: the proceeds of which England then " squandered down her sewers to the sea".'

The idea of using town sewage on the land was much vaunted in the agricultural press in the mid century, although a number of experiments were tried with little success. A more successful, organic fertilizer was Peruvian guano imported in large quantities from about this time. The real breakthrough, however, came with the production of the first truly chemical fertilizer, the superphosphate.

Essential to this was a more accurate knowledge of soil chemistry and the physiology of plant growth. In Germany, Liebig attempted to discover the exact scientific principles at work and published his results in two notable volumes in the early 1840s. But his highly theoretical approach was regarded with suspicion by British agriculturalists: the influential Royal Agricultural Society of England preferred to give credence, instead, to the experiments of J.B. Lawes and W.H. Gilbert, carried out at Rothamstead in Hertfordshire. In the course of these, Lawes discovered a process of producing superphosphate of lime, which gave good results when applied to root crops. By the 1850s, bones were increasingly treated with sulphuric acid—an industrial process—before being applied to the soil. At about the same time, deposits of coprolites—the fossilised remains of bird and animal bones—were discovered in East Anglia, a chance which led to the setting up of new processing plants—including that of Joseph Fison & Co at

Ipswich. Towards the end of the century, however, these resources had been largely exhausted and cheaper supplies of phosphate rock were imported from abroad.

Nitrogen, another important element in plant growth, was available in the form of nitrates, imported from Chile from the 1850s. But a more abundant source, found nearer to home, was ammonia, a waste product of the gas industry, produced in commercial quantities as sulphate of ammonia from the 1860s. Another industrial waste product—basic slag, a residue from open-hearth furnaces, was discovered to have beneficial effect on grassland towards the end of the century, although it, like industrially produced potash, was only used in limited quantities before the Great War.

Purchased feeding stuffs were to provide an important substitute for home-grown fodder throughout the nineteenth century. Oilcake was first used as a manure in the form of rape dust, but after 1815, was more widely adopted as an animal feed—chiefly by arable and mixed farmers, who valued it for the superiority of cattle-based dung over ordinary farmyard manure. But as meat consumption increased from the 1840s, oilcake was more and more sought after for the greater weight that it produced in livestock, and grew in popularity amongst livestock farmers. The rising demand for oilcake was reflected in the development of the seed compounding industry after the mid century. In 1850, Joseph Thorley of Hull began to manufacture 'Thorley's Food For Cattle', which mixed ingredients in a special formula which, it was claimed, would produce 'the very largest beasts in perfect health for the market at the earliest date'. In the next two decades, a growing number of millers, maltsters and seed crushing firms diversified into making their own cake and sack seeds for cattle, sheep, pigs and poultry, although they were eclipsed towards the end of the century by the emergence of the big industrial compounders such as Bibby's, R. & W. Paul, Silcock's and B.O.C.M., who were to dominate the market. The large concerns survived the depression years better than many of their smaller rivals, some of whom failed, and in the opinion of one historian, B.A. Holderness, 'Bibby's Cakettes and Paul's Kosito's (cooked, flaked maize) at least were roaring successes in Edwardian England.'

The application of fertilizers and the use of seeds as fodder were both land-saving innovations—they enabled land to be used more intensively so that a smaller area was required to produce the same amount as before. The success of this phase of the Second Agricultural Revolution may be judged from the fact that rising output between the mid 1830s and 1860s almost kept pace with the growth in population, and indeed, even on the verge of the agricultural depression, when the cultivated acreage was to fall sharply, Britain was still meeting something like three quarters of its basic food requirements. By the last third of the century, however, relying on industrial resources to raise agricultural output was no longer enough, and Britain began to import a growing percentage of bread, meat and dairy products. The country was effectively purchasing additional land abroad, without investing in it.

The last phase of the Second Agricultural Revolution was the adoption of labour-saving devices, namely, the substitution of the toil of machinery for the toil of men. Mechanisation was dependent on two factors—the emergence of the agricultural engineering industry and the positive response of farmers to the new tools and techniques which became available.

The agricultural engineering industry in England had its first period of development during the Napoleonic Wars. From the 1790s to 1815, high cereal prices and an increasing cereal acreage meant an expanding demand for cultivation equipment. Among the firms established at this time or just before were Ransome's of Ipswich in 1789, Garrett's of Leiston in 1778, Bentall's of Maldon in 1805, Howard's of Bedford in 1811 and Hornsby's of Grantham in 1815. Some attempt was made at mechanisation, but the demand was largely for traditional equipment: modern labour-saving devices were expensive, often unreliable, and unpopular with the work force. Most of the early implement makers were located in the great arable areas of East Anglia, although the coming of the railways in the 1840s enabled them to create a network of agencies throughout the country.

The second period of development occurred from the mid 1830s to the 1850s, as agriculture recovered from the post war depression and expanded to meet the requirements of a growing population. Many new firms were established during these years, while the older companies took on new employees and diversified into non-agricultural work. Ransome's, for instance, made railway parts and benefited enormously from the railway building boom.

The application of steam power to agriculture around the middle of the century provided new opportunities for engineering firms. It had been used to drive threshing drums since the late eighteenth century, but it was not until the invention of the cheap, portable engine in the 1840s that steam power became a useful adjunct to animal and human power on the farm. It was first used for threshing and barn work, largely because of its high work rate. Labourers had opposed the introduction of horse-powered threshers earlier in the century, because flailing the corn had provided valuable, if exacting, winter work, but by the 1860s there was no longer such an acute shortage of employment, and the machine was often welcomed for taking much of the toil out of the threshing operation. Firms such as Clayton and Shuttleworth of Lincoln, Fowler's of Leeds, and Burrell's of Thetford in Norfolk became leading manufacturers of steam engines, while Ransome's and Garret's were also important.

The Great Exhibition of 1851 was a showcase for Victorian industrial achievement, and the links which had been forged between agriculture and

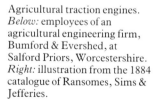

Agricultural traction engines. *Below:* employees of an agricultural engineering firm, Bumford & Evershed, at Salford Priors, Worcestershire. *Right:* illustration from the 1884 catalogue of Ransomes, Sims & Jefferies.

industry were revealed in the large number of agricultural engineering firms—over 300—exhibiting. Most firms produced special catalogues listing the articles that they were manufacturing or selling for the occasion. Thus, William Dray and Co. of London, not one of the biggest concerns, could still offer an impressive range of goods, including 'Barley Hummellers, Bean and Pea Mills, Corn and Cider Mills, Cesspool and Tank Cleaners, Chaff-Cutters, Corn and Seed Drills, Clod-Crushers, Dairy Utensils, Emigrants' Tools, Fire-Engines, Hand-Threshing Machines, Hay-Makers, Horse-Hoes, Machines for Rolling Malt, Ox-Chains and Yokes, Manure Carts, Portable Steam Engines, Stable Furniture, Sheep Racks, Steam Threshing Machines, Tile and Pipe Machines (for field drainage), Weighing Machines, Wrought Iron Hedge-Fences, Gates etc.'

By the mid century, exports of agricultural equipment were becoming increasingly important. Some firms had supplied goods to colonists from the 1820s, but steam engines, railway parts and machine tools now made up the greater part of the trade.

By the 1860s, however, the home market was beginning to show signs of being over-supplied. Farming was no longer able to absorb the continually rising output of so many manufacturers. It became difficult for blacksmiths and ploughwrights to make the transition from a workshop trade to a small manufactory, and small local firms tended to concentrate on a small range of products for which they had established a reputation for quality. Such firms might continue to take on 'special' foundry work, but on a more discriminating basis; many directed their attention to the agency and service sides of their business, which had the effect of helping the larger firms to penetrate into the more remote areas of the country. As Collins points out, 'By 1862, the most common ploughs used in Devon and Dorset were those manufactured by Suffolk, Lincoln and Bedford firms.' Factory-made parts became standard fittings even on locally-made equipment.

The depression in arable farming in the 1870s led to a further contraction in home demand. The big companies, especially those concentrating on steam engines and threshing machine production, looked instead to the export trade. Ransome's, for instance, opened up valuable new markets in Russia, Eastern Europe, South Africa, South America, and even, to some extent, India. Small ironworks, without strongly developed export outlets, faced fierce competition at home and found survival difficult. Some responded by price-cutting or fixing, some by trying to improve their product technically, a few by borrowing on the bank and investing in new up-to-date plant. But for many the pressure was too great. Among the firms that went under at this time were the Reading Ironworks and the well-known steam-engine makers, Tuxford's of Boston, in Lincolnshire.

Between 1880 and 1914, the British agricultural engineering industry seems to have suffered what Collins has called a 'failure of inventiveness'. He notes that a 'technological plateau' had been reached and that the only new inventions of significance were the milking machine and the fuel tractor. This may have been due partly to the change in the pattern of British farming and partly to the arrival of a new threat: foreign machinery, either imported or made under licence in Britain; North American equipment, particularly, tended to be cheaper, simpler and at least as reliable as British. The decline in the acreage restricted the need for new cultivation equipment, while the switch to more intensive livestock farming offered only limited opportunities for mechanisation. British

ЗАВОДЪ

РАНСОМЪ, СИМСЪ и ДЖЕФЕРИСЪ

ВЪ ИПСВИЧѢ АНГЛІЯ.

RANSOMES SIMS & JEFFERIES Lᵈ

Представители въ Ростовѣ на-Дону

ДЖОНЪ МАРТЫНЪ и КО

Малая Садовая улица, д. № 78, при чугунно-литейномъ заводѣ „МАРТЫНЪ".

Catalogue for the Russian market issued by Ransomes, Sims & Jefferies in 1895.

manufacturers, confronted with falling demand, hesitated to risk capital in re-equipping their factories, while the Americans, with an expanding economy, were investing large sums in new techniques of mass-production. The Americans, as major corn-producers, made the mechanisation of the harvest their first priority, and were soon heading the market for harvesting machinery, while the Scandinavians, as specialist milk producers, concentrated on dairy machinery. There were some British firms that accepted the challenge of foreign competition and prospered; for example, Lister's of Dursley in Gloucestershire made cream separators, butter churns, milking machinery and later sheep-shearing equipment, for which there was an ever-growing overseas demand. Generally, though, an increasing proportion of total output was made up of steam engines and threshing machines. Rising costs and the fact that the home market remained saturated resulted in more bankruptcies after 1900. Humphries's of Pershore and Brown and May of Devizes failed completely, while Tasker's of Andover were in the hands of the receiver for a year. Exporting firms continued to do well although, as Collins observes, this concentration on steam machinery was to have serious implications after 1920 when the internal combustion engine took command and the traditional export markets declined.

The more successful firms were those diversifying into industrial engineering. Thus the manufacture of oil and petrol engines, and other power-producing machinery gave a new lease of life to Blackstone's and Hornsby's while Petter's of Yeovil is an example of a new firm effectively combining the manufacture of agricultural and industrial engines. The history of such firms, however, really begins after the Great War.

Whether or not farmers decided to purchase the new machines coming on to the market, depended on a whole host of factors. First, they had to find out what was available. Advertisements appeared in the local press, but a more detailed account of inventions and improvements was given in the farming press. From the middle of the nineteenth century, the most important papers were the *Mark Lane Express*, *Bell's Weekly Messenger* and the *Farmer's Journal*, while the *Farmer's Magazine* and the *Journal of the Royal Agricultural Society of England* were high-quality journals, concerned to promote the practice of science in all aspects of agriculture. Later, the *Engineer* and the *Implement and Machinery Review* reported more specialised technological developments. Manufacturers' catalogues also provided a rich source of information, although some designs existed only on paper or as prototypes and were never carried into large-scale production.

Farmers could see the latest machines at agricultural shows of which the biggest and most important was that staged annually from 1839 by the Royal Agricultural Society of England. Each year, it was held in a different part of the country and helped to advertise the products of the leading manufacturers locally and those of local manufacturers nationally, although they were not necessarily promoted as effectively as they might have been. The machinery trials carried out at the shows sometimes exposed the deficiencies as well as the strengths of the new implements. Occasionally, the demonstrations were themselves ill-conducted and might have an adverse effect on opinion. Goddard quotes an open letter to Earl Spencer from a 'Plain Derbyshire Farmer' in 1843, complaining that the ploughing trials had shown crooked furrows of irregular width and depth leading to ridicule by those hostile to improvement:

' "Well, we are satisfied with our old ploughs now, eh, mates?" was a constant question, "Why, I think we shall go home contented," the nearly uniform answer, whilst at every turn some lusty sexagenarian was seen instructing his chubby-faced nephews in the dangers of novelty.'

More often, perhaps, a farmer's mind might be made up by the experience of a neighbour in trying a new technique, by the weighing up of careful pros and cons at the local farmers' club, or, now that he was able to travel freely, by seeing different methods in use in other parts of the country. He might also give some thought to the ability of his labourers to

Stand at the Royal Show, Norwich, 1911.

use or maintain a new piece of equipment, as well as to their attitude to innovation. As Mary Wedlake's catalogue noted in 1851, much depended on 'the habit or fancy of the man who works the plough, for if you insist on your labourer using an implement he has not been accustomed to, you cannot expect the work to be carried out so well as if the common implement had been employed.'

The physical layout of the farm, the size and shape of the fields, ease of access and distance from the implement shed—all these had to be taken into consideration. So also did the sturdiness of new machinery and its reliability. There was great enthusiasm for the idea of steam power, but the problems involved in direct traction, of using steam propelled implements across the field, proved insurmountable. Even the most practical method of winching implements from one side to the other, with steel cable wound from an engine or engines stationed at the headland was far from trouble-free. The early tackle was designed for particular types of soil and surface and did not perform well on the lighter soils then being taken into cultivation. Steam ploughing was most successful on heavy clays in a dry summer, and even then required skilled operators to ensure that all went well. The more restricted but valuable application of steam was in threshing and barn work.

There were technical problems with other types of new machinery as well. Machines for planting and harvesting potatoes tended to plant irregularly or to bruise the skins in extracting the roots from the soil. Machines for harvesting grain crops was more successful, but there was much trial and error in reaper design; even quite late in the century, it was claimed that some machines were unable to cut crops which were badly beaten or laid to the ground by bad weather—when this happened the harvest still had to be gathered by hand, and the machine stood idle in its shedding. Mechanisation in dairying had its pitfalls. Primrose McConnell, an inveterate disciple of mechanical progress, tried three varieties of milking machine on his farm in 1903, but concluded that each had been a disastrous failure. By 1914, many of the defects had been overcome, but the rapid perishing of the India rubber tubes, which carried the milk to the can, remained a problem not solved until considerably later. Indeed, Collins considers that what the majority of farmers throughout the period required was a range of 'simple, mechanical devices offering modest but acceptable savings in time and labour at least cost!' He notes that small farmers could generally justify the purchase of inexpensive machines, but that the outlay on bigger, more sophisticated machines was not worthwhile unless they were frequently put to work, only the 'very largest farmers growing at least 800 bushels of corn would normally have purchased a steam-threshing set for their exclusive use.' More often, they were owned by firms of steam contractors, who hired them out, thus bringing the benefits of the new technology to small farmers at a price they could afford.

The calculation of cost was of paramount importance as long as labour remained cheap and plentiful, but as shortages began to arise, farmers became more interested in mechanisation. What was critical was not the reduction in size of the permanent work force, but the difficulty of obtaining additional labour during peak work periods, especially the harvest. In many counties, harvest gangs were employed—itinerant groups of labourers working under the direction of a 'captain', who would negotiate with the

farmer to cut and gather the crop for a certain price. These groups were practised workers, often expert with one particular tool—sickle, reap-hook or scythe—who would move from district to district, following the path of the maturing corn. Such bands included women and children, and, most characteristically, the Irish single men who combined a migratory existence during the summer with the cultivation of a potato patch at home during the winter. But in the last third of the century, these gangs tended to die out. After the famine, with a lower population, the Irish turned their attention to enlarging their own holdings. Others sought more lucrative employment in the towns, and as men's wages within agriculture increased, women became less inclined to take on the more exacting forms of field

Sheep farming, like beef and dairy farming, offered few opportunities for mechanisation. *Left:* shepherd and his boy. *Above:* Hertfordshire shepherd and his daughter shearing a flock of 200 Southdowns, 1910s.

Sussex turnwrest plough in use at Horndean Farm, Lewes, 1888.

Bottom left: milking was usually carried out by hand until World War I, as here at Amery Farm, Alton, Hampshire, 1910. *Below:* scything team at Spring Farm, Gislingham, Suffolk, 1870s.

Women field workers planting seed, Akeld Farm, Glendale, Northumberland, about 1900.

work and left it to their husbands. As long as gang labour persisted, farmers could make very fine adjustments in their harvest expenditure from year to year. When wheat was high in value, they might employ the Irish sickle to garner as much as possible of the crop, and when it fell back in price, they might switch to the quicker and cheaper reap-hook or scythe. With the withdrawal of this labour, farmers were increasingly tempted to mechanise, to ensure against the possibility of a lost crop if the expected gang failed to turn up.

In the more depressed and remote of the southern counties, labour remained abundant enough until the new century. Sometimes farmers may have continued to employ this force, rather than mechanise, out of a sense of social obligation, since the alternative was the workhouse. But it is more likely that economic considerations were uppermost in farmers' minds, particularly at a time when their own incomes were under threat. The problem of whether to mechanise or not was most acute on the larger arable farms employing a large labour force, and less marked on small farms, particularly those specialising in grass, which could usually be cut by hand or grazed if necessary.

Gleaners. Fewer women were employed in agriculture as real wages rose, particularly after 1880, but their traditional harvest activity of gleaning continued until after 1914.

In the years just preceding the outbreak of the Great War, many of the tasks of the farm were still performed by hand or with horses. Purely traditional implements and techniques survived in some areas: in parts of Kent, the old turnwrest plough (with a number of features in common with the Roman plough) was quite often used; on Dartmoor and Exmoor, the 'velling sull' or paring plough (which was possibly of Saxon origin) was occasionally employed to clean or clear land; in Wiltshire, some farmers preferred to use oxen rather than horses in deep cultivations; elsewhere corn was sometimes cut with the hook and threshed with the flail. The older methods tended to persist on small farms in the more outlying regions, or were adopted on allotments and in market gardens where small scale techniques were appropriate. Overall, however, the trend was clearly established, towards the greater use of manufactured implements and powered machinery and the integration of agriculture within the industrial economy. Mechanisation did not always achieve great economies in man power, or substantial gains in work output, as more men might be required in the linkage operation or to service the machinery. But it did give the farmer the opportunity to show that he, no less than his urban cousin, might become a skilled practitioner of the mechanical arts, and relieved him of some of the heavy physical work involved in many farm operations.

The first task in arable farming is that of preparing the seed bed, and the implement traditionally used for this is the plough. The seventy years before the beginning of Victoria's reign had seen considerable advances in plough design. What remained to be developed, however, were special refinements and adaptations for particular crops and land conditions.

By the early 1800s, two broad types of plough were in use. For autumn ploughing, a plough with a characteristically long mouldboard was used, which turned a whole or unbroken furrow slice, laying it at an angle against the previous slice, and exposing the hitherto buried soil to the action of the weather over the winter. But in the spring the need was to pulverise the soil so that the land was ready for sowing, and to do this a 'digging' plough was used, which broke up the furrow slice and threw it to the ground, at the same time covering the weed growth. This type was also used for ploughing stubble, grass fields and all kinds of green crop.

Within these broad types, ploughs were either wheeled, or of the 'swing' variety—made with a shorter beam and longer handles for use particularly on sticky ground where wheels would not travel well. Swing ploughs required greater skill on the part of the ploughman, since he had no means of regulating the width or depth of the ploughing, except by the handles, which by reason of their extra length gave great command over the plough. Some ploughs had a single (or land) wheel, of small size, which ran on top of the land and controlled the depth of the ploughing. In two-wheeled ploughs, the larger (or furrow) wheel ran in the furrow on a level with the share and regulated the width of the furrow slice. Two wheels were recommended on level ground, and 'enabled boys to do the work as, when once set, the plough will run almost without holding.'

In the first half of the nineteenth century, two significant developments occurred. The life of a plough was greatly lengthened by the use of iron instead of wood in the working parts. Plenty's of Newbury had produced a

A Ransomes & Sims Newcastle plough being demonstrated in the late 1850s.

metal frame with interchangeable cast iron working parts by 1800, although the beam and handles continued to be made of seasoned wood for a long time thereafter. Some firms continued to offer a choice of wood-beam and metal ploughs until the Great War, but metal ploughs were increasingly popular from the 1860s. The other considerable advance, patented by Ransome's of Ipswich in 1803, was the chilled ploughshare: the underside of the iron share was rapidly cooled to make it harder than the upper surface, which wore away more quickly, thus preserving a sharp cutting edge. (This process of toughening metal by chilling extended to the manufacture of other working parts.)

By the mid century, a multiplicity of different types of plough (produced by local ploughwrights and agricultural engineers) were available for every conceivable combination of soil and terrain and type of agricultural operation. Some were designed by rule of thumb and some by the most precise application of what was known of the mechanics of moving bodies and soil science. Yet controversy still raged in farmers' journals as to the relative merits of swing and wheel ploughs, wood and metal mould boards, single and double furrow implements, the use of horse or oxen as a means of draught power. The more 'modern' writers no longer regarded the plough as the best implement for pulverising the soil; C. Wren Hoskyns noted in *Talpa* in 1852 that 'the plough has the sentence of death passed on it because it is essentially imperfect.'

By the 1840s and 1850s, the numerous possibilities of steam cultivation had gripped the imagination of agriculturalists. Wren Hoskyns was particularly excited by the idea of a steam engine substituting for a horse and pulling a revolving clod crusher behind it; such a combination, would, he thought, prepare the soil in the 'most light, compendious and perfect detail'. At this time steam cultivators were divided into rotary cultivators and diggers. The first smashed the soil by a rotary movement of cutters through it. Diggers imitated the action of a spade, and it was this form of cultivator that attracted more attention later in the nineteenth century. Even so, few machines were made or sold: the earlier models were under-powered, generally awkward to get to the fields, and their great weight damaged the soil structure. Indeed, by the end of the century, steam cultivation was chiefly accomplished with implements drawn by cable across the field, with one or two engines located on the edge, rather than by direct traction across it. The method, which Wren Hoskyns deplored, was to employ:

'A steam engine
To turn a Drum
To wind a Rope
To drag a Plough
To turn up a Furrow.'

But this system avoided the hazard of compacting the soil, while the steel cable could be used not only to draw a plough but a whole range of tillage equipment as well as for pulling out roots or boulders, tearing down trees and clearing land. The name most often associated with the development of the art is that of John Fowler of Leeds, who died in 1864, although other firms such as Howard's of Bedford, Burrell's of Thetford, Aveling & Porter of Rochester, McLaren's of Leeds, Savage's of King's Lynn and Marshall's of Gainsborough, also became manufacturers of engines and tackle. Both

the single and double engine systems were well established by the 1870s and continued to be used into the twentieth century.

Steam, however, was less successfully used in cultivation than in other farm operations. The disadvantages were huge. Capital and running costs were high, labour-savings were few, technical defects, such as the tendency of implements to jump out of the ground, persisted and transporting the engines and their tackle from place to place was slow and expensive. Contemporary records are full of accounts of the loss of life and limb that resulted from boiler explosions, cables flying loose in work, and engines overturning. Steam was, in fact, a dangerous technology. By 1914, it had reached its final stage of development and was superseded by the internal combustion engine.

Cultivators and harrows may both be used to break up clods and work the soil into an adequate seedbed. There is little difference between them in function, except that cultivators deal with the heavier work and harrows with the preparation of a finer tilth. They are also used in weed removal, mixing fertilizer with the soil, and covering seed. Harrows used for this purpose are often trailed behind the drill.

Until the second half of the nineteenth century, cultivators tended to be heavy, crude implements, but soon a much improved piece of equipment emerged, with a light metal body and spring-mounted tines with tips curved towards the point of entry into the soil, giving lighter draught and better penetration.

The same degree of advance is also apparent in harrows. The heavy wood harrow still in use was a cumbersome piece of equipment consisting of four to six timber beams held together by cross-members, with iron tines drilled into the main beams. The use of metal, however, made possible the development of the zig-zag frame, trailed in sections, with rigid teeth. Jointed and spring tine harrows gave a free action which could closely follow irregularities in the soil. The points of drag harrows come in a variety of shapes, adapted to different types of soil and terrain. Chain harrows, made up of a network of chain links, were also popular and were useful for rolling up weeds and, particularly, for use on pastures.

Rollers were employed to crush clods, level the surface and consolidate the soil. They might be used after harrowing to produce the smooth surface essential to the reaping machine, or immediately after the seed had been sown. The best farming practice was to use them not only on cereals, but also on grass and clover.

Wood and stone rollers were common throughout the period, but a more durable implement made of iron and steel was being widely marketed by the 1840s. The cylinders might be plain and constructed in one piece or in two or three sections to facilitate turning at the headlands. Alternatively, they might be of the ribbed or Cambridge variety, which had a number of cast iron segments mounted loosely on the axle. This type was heavier and more efficient as a clod crusher. Other spiked and serrated rollers were produced, and even a plain roller which could be filled with water or sand to vary the weight of the implement. But in general, there were few modifications to the basic design.

By the 1860s, the usual method of sowing the seed was to drill it, but it was still frequently broadcast by hand, especially on small farms, hilly or awkwardly shaped ground, or where the soil was very wet. If broadcast by hand, the seed was contained in a sowing sheet, a large shallow basket, or a thin, kidney-shaped wood box. In a broadcast drill made by the Kell brothers at Gloucester by the 1830s, the seed was placed in a long, narrow box. A spindle ran the length of the box and was rotated by gearing from the wheels. Radical pinions or short brushes, set along the spindle, forced the grain through holes in the box to a wooden platform, whence it was broadcast. Iron slides adjusted the holes to the size of the seeds. A further invention was the fiddle broadcaster. This was introduced from America in the late nineteenth century and provided a simple but effective means of broadcasting. A wood box with a canvas receptacle for the seed was carried under the left arm. A stream of seed fell onto a thin metal wheel, revolving on a spindle. A strap round the spindle was pulled to and fro by the action of a 'violin bow', thus causing the wheel to rotate rapidly and cast the seed in all directions.

The seed drill is distinct from the broadcaster in that it deposits the seed in the soil at a chosen depth. Jethro Tull's drill has been regarded as an important innovation, but it was not widely adopted. The end of the eighteenth century, however, saw considerable advance, with a number of makers providing machines of sturdy and effective construction. The Revd James Cooke produced a drill with a spoon or cup feed and gear drive, which was to be a model for later development, while James Smyth of Peasenhall devised a method of adjusting the drill coulters—which cut grooves in the soil—to different widths of sowing. In 1839, Grounsell produced a drop drill with a spacing mechanism to drop the seed and manure at intervals, rather than in a steady flow as previously.

By the 1840s, the two main types of drill—cup feed and force feed—were firmly established. In the cup feed drill, the seed box is divided into an

Below: harrowing with a heavy wooden implement. The man in the background is forking dung from a cart. *Right:* combined cultivating implement, from a Ransome's catalogue for 1908.

55

upper (seed) and a lower (feed) chamber. A spindle runs through the feed chamber and turns a series of discs bearing a ring of cups around the rim. Each cup picks up a few seeds and delivers them to the hoppers at the top of the seed tubes which run down to the coulter. Cups of different sizes are used for different varieties of seed. The rate of seeding is controlled by the size of cup and the rate at which the seed barrel revolves, the drive being provided from the wheels. In the force feed drill, a partially grooved roller draws seed from the bottom of the seed box and delivers it to the hoppers at the top of the seed tubes. When the plain part of the roller is in contact with the seed, none is delivered, and so the seeding rate can be controlled.

Not all forms of seeding could be so readily mechanised. Potatoes were still hand planted by gangs of perhaps five or six people, often women, followed by four or five dung spreaders. Planting machines, though available from the 1880s, were not widely adopted. Weeding and singling were other operations frequently carried out by manual labour, although horse-hoes were increasingly used to save labour until the end of the Great War, when the practice of hoeing corn declined.

With the greatly increased production of artificial fertilizer from the nineteenth century, the combined grain and fertilizer drill was a standard piece of equipment, but separate manure distributors were also produced by specialist drill manufacturers. Many of these were made on the broadcast principle to give a top dressing on the surface of the soil. Some firms, like Reeves of Bratton, achieved fame for the variety and excellence of the machines on offer, including, for example, Chandler's patent liquid manure drill, made for those who preferred to apply liquid manure directly to the seed (often of root crops).

Many of the operations involved in harvesting continued to be done by hand throughout the nineteenth century, although a number of machines were available from the middle of the century to speed up the process and remove some of the drudgery from the task.

Grass mowers for haymaking had been invented before 1850, but the breakthrough came at the end of the decade. Clayton & Shuttleworth exhibited an American machine which incorporated features that were soon to become standard. The 'Eagle' had a frame mounted on two wheels from which power was transmitted to a side cutting bar. This basic design was considerably improved during the 1860s, with several firms producing highly serviceable machines. By 1869, Bamlett's of Thirsk, Yorkshire, for

Left: 'Suffolk' Lever Corn Drill from Smyth's 1882 catalogue, in which it was claimed that 16,000 of the firm's drills were then in use. *Below:* Garrett's Patent Horse-Hoe, from T. McKenzie's *The Rolling Stock of the Farm,* 1869.

Garrett's Patent Horse-Hoe.

Left: cutting hay with a mower made by J. & F. Howard of Bedford. *Right:* Ransomes, Sims & Jefferies swathe turner at work, 1904.

instance, had produced a mower with an efficient device for raising and lowering the cutter bar to adapt it for uneven ground or weightier crops, and by 1875, J.A. Clarke, a prominent writer on agriculture, was of the opinion that 'mowing machines now cut the major part of the clover and meadow on all but the area under small occupations.'

The hay fork continued to be used for spreading grass for drying, though the haymaking machine became popular from the 1850s. The firm of Mary Wedlake, of Fenchurch Street in the City of London, won acclaim for one such machine, although its violent action could bruise the grass and it could not be set close enough to the ground to lift all the mown crop. An ingenious attempt to overcome these problems was the haykicker, invented by J.V. Gibbons of Oxfordshire. This machine was fitted with a series of spring-loaded forks, which worked in a fashion not unlike a steam digger by kicking the grass backwards and into the air. Blackstone's advertised an improved version in their 1892 catalogue; in the same year they also produced another solution to the problem of haymaking—the swathe turner. This consisted of two forks on a frame, which was set at right angles to the axle and turned the swathe over, laying it down lightly so that the heat and air could penetrate. A different type of swathe-turner, made by T.M. Jarmain, who took over from Gibbons, was produced in 1896. The 'Hazeley' turned the swathe by means of two wheels, with six wings or fingers on each, rotating at right angles to the direction of travel. This machine was the forerunner of a range of combined haymaking machines after 1900, and displaced both haymakers and haykickers in popularity until the latter staged something of a comeback afer World War II.

The next stage in haymaking was that of raking. Again, this was often done by hand, although both the American turn-over rake and the English horse rake were available from the mid century. After raking, the hay would be carted and stacked in a barn or in the field. A field stack could be built up either by pitching with hay forks from the ground or from a wagon, or by means of an elevator or simple crane. The latter method became fairly widely used on larger farms from the 1880s, with either a derrick or a swinging boom attached to a vertical mast.

There were many parts of the country where the corn harvest also continued to be gathered by hand until the late nineteenth century. The process of change was complex; in some places, the sickle was replaced by

the reap-hook or scythe, in others, it was retained until the arrival of the reaping machine.

The first patent for a reaping machine was taken out by James Boyce of London in 1799, but the device was impractical. The following decades saw many attempts to produce a working machine, among which the one invented by the Revd Patrick Bell of Carmylie, Scotland, was the most effective. The arrival of two American machines, made by Hussey and McCormick and shown in the Great Exhibition of 1851, marked a new departure. How much they owed to Bell's inspiration is uncertain, although they adopted a similar cutting principle. The new machines were made under licence by several British manufacturers and were adapted for British conditions. The 1860s saw a rapid development in the efficiency and reliability of reapers. At the Royal Show at Manchester in 1869, some 84 different machines were selected for trial. A further advance was made by the American firm of Walter A. Wood, who produced a sheaf-binder that followed the reaper and collected and bound the sheaves, dispensing with the need for manual labour in this task. Not long afterwards, the combined reaper-binder appeared. This was also pioneered in the United States and was available in Britain from the late 1870s. By the 1890s, the reaper-binder had been more or less perfected, with a wide choice of makes available to British farmers. The self-binder, as it came to be called, did not immediately oust the reaper, although it was increasingly popular and was to become the standard corn harvester in Britain between the wars.

Left: reaping an odd shaped corner with reap hooks. Note the crook to hold the corn, which is cut with a slashing action of the hook, 1880s. *Above:* harvesting hay using an elevator powered by horse-gearing.

Reaper at work cutting wheat, Guildford, Surrey, late nineteenth century.

Above: Ransomes, Sims & Jefferies threshing machinery, from the firm's 1860 catalogue.
Right: Hornsby binder, from an 1897 catalogue.

Barley awner, grid pattern. This implement had largely gone out of use by 1900.

Until the late eighteenth century, threshing was normally carried out by flail. With barley, the awns (or spines) could often be removed only by the use of an awner or hummeller. The earliest contrivance for mechanised threshing combined a number of flails; but the threshing drum, produced by a Scot, Andrew Meikle, in the 1790s, had so far been much more successful. At first, the drums tended to be made as a fixed part of the barn and powered either by water or by horses which walked in a circular or polygonal shelter built into the side of the barn. Such installations were more commonly found in Scotland and the North of England than elsewhere. Portable threshing machines, powered by hand or horses, were available after the turn of the century, but, until the 1840s, were relatively uncommon in the southern counties.

The mid century saw considerable improvements in the design of threshers and also of winnowing machines. Winnowing was the process whereby the ears were separated from the husks or chaff and the head grain from the inferior tail grain. Traditionally, this was done by tossing the corn in the air with a shovel or from a large shallow basket. The process had been speeded up by the artificial creation of an air blast using rotating sails of sacks or wood cranked manually, and subsequently by the invention of an actual winnowing machine. The key idea here was the direction of an air blast across the grain, as it fell from a hopper within a boxed framework. By the early 1850s, several threshers incorporated winnowing and dressing apparatus.

The next important step was the application of steam power to threshing. At the 1848 Royal Show at Cambridge, this idea was still a novelty, threshing machines being tested and demonstrated first with horse power and then, if the exhibitors wished, with steam power. By 1867, progress had been so swift that horse gearing was outmoded and no longer included among the equipment that might be selected for trial. By this time too, the threshing machine had achieved most of its characteristic features.

There were, of course, differences in the machines produced by the different makers, and farmers variously favoured those made by Ransome's, Hornsby's, Garrett's and Clayton & Shuttleworth, as well as more regionally based firms such as Nalder's of Challow in Berkshire and Humphries's of Pershore in Worcestershire. The trend over the next two decades was to produce ever more complicated machines, with double and triple air blasts. Self-feed and other devices were also introduced to reduce the risk in manually feeding the sheaves into the machine. By the 1880s, however, only relatively minor improvements remained to be made to the thresher, although the work of harvesting was facilitated by the

The Barford & Perkins hay press, about 1903.

development of linkage machinery. The straw elevator, with its own travelling carriage and powered either by horses or steam, was a well-tried piece of equipment, but the steam hay press, which compressed the straw or hay into bales, was comparatively new. Dederick's Hay Press, an American invention, was introduced into England in 1882. The principle employed was the forerunner of that adopted later, although the machine was not entirely satisfactory, and the power-driven baling press did not displace the old hand presses until much later.

In England, all the processes of harvesting had been mechanised by 1914, although more than one machine was required to cover all the stages. In Australia, a harvester-stripper, which cut the heads from the straw, had been pioneered in the 1840s, while an early combine harvester had been produced in the United States by the 1860s. These harvesters were being made by a number of firms at the turn of the century. First used in California, they were soon in general use on the extensive corn lands of the Mid West. In England, however, the high cost of the machines and the fact that their purchase could be justified economically only on large farms of more than, say, two hundred acres, meant that the self-binder and the thresher were used for much longer. The combine was not to be introduced into Britain until the mid-1920s and was not widely adopted until after World War II.

From the mid nineteenth century, there was a variety of equipment available for preparing food for livestock. Chaff cutters were used for cutting hay and straw into small pieces as a basic ingredient in warm mashes. The old, cumbersome chaff cutting equipment was replaced from the 1840s—by Richmond's machine, for example, which achieved great popularity; several models shown at the Great Exhibition in 1851 could be powered by hand, horse or steam. Later in the century, chaff cutters could be fed directly from the threshing machine. In 1902, Clayton & Shuttleworth advertised a machine 'capable of cutting the straw as fast as it is threshed' which, after removing the dust, delivered the clean chaff via a sacking elevator into sacks, or via a blast elevator to the barn.

Roots were often sliced or cut into strips before being fed to stock. A favoured machine throughout the century was that originally made by Gardner's of Banbury. It could be fitted with different cutting barrels to produce slices of the right size for cattle and sheep. Roots were also frequently pulped and then mixed with chaff, which had the advantage, as J.A. Clark noted, that 'after being mixed with the pulp for over twelve hours, a fermentation commences and this soon renders the most mouldy hay palatable and the animals eat with an avidity that they would otherwise reject.'

Grinding mills were commonly used for crushing or bruising oats for horses and for splitting beans and peas. These changed little in design from the late eighteenth century. The feed was put into a hopper, from which it passed down, by means of a grooved feed roller, to a cutting roller, which could be regulated to split or grind as necessary. Another form of corn grinding mill, used to prepare a finer meal, was fitted with two circular bevel discs as grinding surfaces. As these revolved, the grain, fed in at the centre, was forced to the edges, being ground down in the process. By the early twentieth century, massive combined roller and plate mills were available and could be powered by steam, gas, water, horse power or oil engine. Lastly, it proved useful to devise a machine for breaking up oil-cake (the residue in the manufacture of oil from seed). By the end of the Victorian period, then, the equipment of the barn was extensive, and while hand feeding remained the practice on most small farms, the portable or fixed steam engine driving a variety of threshing and milling machinery had become part of the normal 'rolling stock' of the larger farm.

Dairy farms tended to be small, and the dairy itself, where butter, cheese and liquid milk were produced for market, was often run by the farmer's wife. The equipment had therefore to be simple and low-cost. Improvements were made to equipment for butter and cheese making, but the effect on productivity was not striking. In fact, the increased emphasis on liquid milk after 1880 meant that there was only limited incentive to

Chaff cutters made by J.R. & A. Ransome, adapted for manual or horse power. The hay or straw was pressed forward between toothed rollers and then chopped into lengths by rotating knives—longer pieces for cattle and horses and shorter pieces for sheep.

Above: linseed cake breaker from a Samuelson catalogue for 1859.

Barn machinery driven by a portable engine, 1866.

improve the technical efficiency of existing manual appliances. There was some mechanisation in the town dairies and in the few butter and cheese 'factories' that sprang up between 1870 and 1914. Liquid milk production was aided by the introduction of the cooler, which enabled milk to be carried fresh over long distances, but new milking machines remained too expensive and unsatisfactory to be widely adopted.

In butter making, the initial step is to separate the milk from the cream. The simplest way of doing this is to set the milk out in pans; the cream, in time, rises to the top and can then be removed with a skimmer. The most efficient method, however, is to use a centrifugal separator. The Laval separator first became popular in Sweden, Denmark and Germany, and was then exhibited at the Royal Show in London in 1879. The principle involved was to become standard in butter-making.

The cream was made into butter by agitating it in a churn. The older form of churn, still commonly used in many small dairies before the Great War, was a plunger churn. An advance on this was the barrel churn, which had been available since the mid eighteenth century, while another common form at the end of the nineteenth century was the 'eccentric and over end' churn. Once the butter had formed, it had to be worked into a usable solid on a butter-making table. The worked butter was finally divided into slabs with the aid of butter pats, and the mark of the dairy was imprinted on the slabs with a butter print or roller.

In cheese making, rennet is added to milk to sour it. From the mid-nineteenth century, the milk was often cooled and re-treated before the rennet was stirred into it. Ater the curd had formed, it was broken up by means of a curd breaker, or with knives. To make the curd firmer, it was customary to draw off some of the whey, heat the curd and return it to the tub. By the second half of the century, scalding the small curd pieces had become a regular process in cheese-making. After this stage, the curd was allowed to settle, and the whey was removed. The curds were then broken up once more and run through a curd mill to allow the even salting, cooling and mellowing of the cheese. After the curd had been packed into moulds, it was pressed. Early forms of cheese press consisted of a heavy weight or

Bottom left: butter working table, Durham, late nineteenth century. *Below:* stoneware plunger churn, made in Bristol, and end-over-end churn made by the Dairy Supply Co., London.

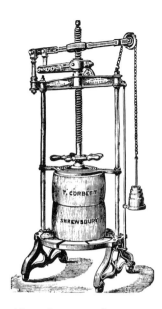

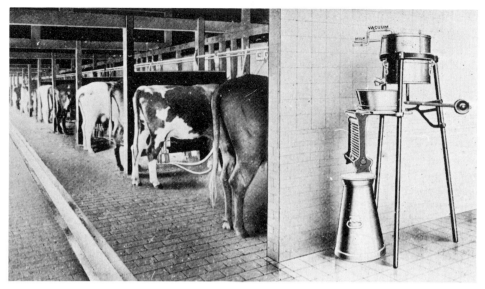

stone built into a strong wooden framework and raised and lowered by means of a steel thread or pulley. Cast iron presses were more generally used from the mid nineteenth century, the pressure being applied by means of a screw thread, turned by a 'ship's wheel'. After pressing, the cheese was left to ripen, a process that entailed turning it every so often on open shelves. Carson & Toone of Warminster in Wiltshire won a prize at the Bristol Royal Show in 1879 for their tumbling shelves, which were turned by a crank handle, but the device, although ingenious, failed to catch on.

The successful transport of liquid milk depended on its having been cooled before it was taken to the railway station. A number of experiments were tried from the mid nineteenth century, but the most effective method turned out to be that of Lawrence's cooler, shown at the Royal Show at Cardiff in 1872 and fairly rapidly adopted thereafter.

There were several futile attempts in the early nineteenth century to devise a milking machine, and it was not until 1862 that an American invention attracted attention in Britain. It used an air pump to extract air out of tubes connected by hollow metal fingers to the cow's teats, and the pressure on the udder expelled the milk. The idea of using a vacuum was a step in the right direction, but the fittings were not airtight, a restive cow could throw the whole apparatus out of gear, and it did not milk cleanly. Other machines constructed on the principle of a continuous vacuum also proved painful to the cow, and milk was often congested with blood. The solution was to imitate the action of a sucking calf, and a pulsator milking machine was produced by Alexander Shields of Glasgow and exhibited as the Thistle Mechanical Milker at the Royal Show in 1895. Unfortunately, the air pump was excessively noisy, and it proved difficult to keep the tubing clean. But an improved version, called the Universal Cow Milker, with a small vacuum pump on top of the pail, was made in 1900 by Lawrence & Kennedy; it was quieter and could be adapted for a single or double bucket system. By the Great War, many of the technical defects in milking machinery had been overcome; firms like Lister's were able to offer a complete milking system, whereby the milk was conveyed from perhaps 50 or 60 cows through tinned copper pipes running the whole length of the cow shed to the dairy, where it was cooled automatically and delivered into railway churns. The cost of such a system, however, put it beyond the reach of most farmers. A cheaper alternative, a mechanical milker which could be taken to the cows in the field, was pioneered by Vaccar of Christchurch in Hampshire and marketed by 1910. But the milking bail (mechanised outdoor milking) was not properly developed until the 1920s, and even then was mainly popular in the South.

Although considerable progress had been made by the late nineteenth century in taking the toil out of farm work, most of the improvements were to manual and horse-powered machines. The steam engine, except in barn work and threshing, ultimately proved disappointing. A new initiative was required, and this was to come in the shape of the internal combustion engine in the 1890s.

A crucial step forward in the development of a new prime mover was the Otto Silent engine of 1976 with its four-stroke cycle. The cheapness and availability of this engine and variants on it in America in the following decade led to early experimental work in the building of tractors, for which there was a huge potential demand. The first practical tractor is usually considered to have been that produced by The Charter Gas Engine Co. of Chicago. Other companies were soon manufacturing crude but workable machines. In England, Hornsby & Son acquired the right to manufacture an oil engine developed by Stuart & Binney in 1890, and this led to the appearance of the Hornsby-Ackroyd Patent Safety Oil Traction Engine at the Manchester Royal Show in 1897. The real breakthrough in tractor design in Britain, however, was achieved by Dan Albone of Biggleswade, Bedfordshire, with the 'Ivel' in 1902. Unlike most American machines of the time, the Ivel was small, compact and intended as a substitute for the horse rather than the traction engine. It could therefore be used for a variety of farm purposes, including direct traction. The Ivel was favourably received by most critical observers and prompted the comment in the *Farm and Machinery Review* in February 1903 that 'the time is not far off when the motor for driving mowers, binders, ploughs and cultivators will be as

Ransomes, Sims & Jefferies tractor with plough, 1903.

The Ivel Agricultural Motor, from *The Implement and Machinery Review*, 1st September 1902.

much in evidence in the field as the mechanical carriage is on the road at the present time.'

Fewer than 1500 Ivels in all were built; the death of Albone himself in 1906 deprived the firm of much of its technical and marketing flair, and it did not survive the Great War. At least a dozen other British firms were engaged in tractor manufacture before 1914; some of their products, like the Sharp, the Ransome and the Petter, promised much but were not produced commercially, while others, like the Saunderson and the Marshall, were made in quite large numbers. Even so, most of the sales were for export, and comparatively few tractors were sold on the home market before the 1920s.

Stationary and portable oil engines were also developed for agricultural work from the 1890s, and their merit was appreciated early in the next decade. The great advantage of the oil engine over the steam engine for barn work was that, once it was started, it could run all day without attention, and its running costs were lower than those of steam. Firms such as Petter's of Yeovil in Somerset were producing over 1500 crude oil engines a year by 1912, but again their real period of expansion lay in the future.

The Marshall Oil Tractor ploughing in stubble from *The Implement and Machinery Review*, 1st November 1909.

65

Industries of the Countryside

When we think of industry today, we are thinking of an urban phenomenon; our view is dominated by great manufacturing centres which are the heritage of the Industrial Revolution. We see the countryside as a place of recreation, leisure, peace. If industry, other than agriculture, exists there, it often appears in the form of a factory brought to give employment to local people, but drawing neither power nor raw materials from the local environment. Yet in the past the countryside has provided workers, power and materials for a multitude of processing and manufacturing trades. Wool was woven and spun, hosiery knitted by hand and on a frame, straw plaited for hats and bonnets, wood cultivated in coppices and shaped into a host of manufactured products, clay dug and made into pots or baked into bricks and tiles, stone quarried and dressed, metal ore mined and smelted. Corn mills, fulling mills and paper mills stood beside remote, fast-running streams. Forges and woodworking shops were found in every village. The pattern of industry was lively and flexible; it differed from region to region and even from to parish to parish. Old industries gave way to new ones, often using the same water-powered mills or the same sort of labour skill.

The period from 1850 to 1914 was a significant time in the history of rural industries. The growth of cities and their industries had greatly increased the demand for rural commodities like timber, underwood and basket willow, and the products worked from them. As agricultural production expanded to meet the requirements of Britain's rapidly growing population, so too did the particular trades which served it: the manufacture of agricultural tools and implements, of carts and wagons, the repair work of the wheelwright, the blacksmith and harness maker. As the rate of innovation rose, new materials were substituted for old ones. Iron and steel became more important than wood, and large urban factories were more profitable than the workshops and foundries of rural and market towns in the early industrial period. In the last quarter of the nineteenth century, many rural enterprises were decaying and, throughout England, factory-made goods were replacing the products of the countryside.

Rural industry was moving from a central role in manufacturing to a position outside the mainstream of economic growth. Indeed, the concept of rural industries did not become apparent to contemporaries until their decay was perceived in the 1890s. Twentieth-century writers sometimes look with interest and nostalgia at pockets of seemingly primitive techniques and methods of organisation in rural areas, but many of these techniques were formerly common to both rural and urban manufacture, and merely survived in the countryside after they had been swept aside in towns and cities. In the pre-industrial economy, a significant proportion of manufactured goods as well as raw materials came from rural areas. The charcoal iron industry operated in sites remote from the centres of population, and the clothing industries of the West Country and East Anglia were associated with small towns and villages. Many enterprises of the early Industrial Revolution were also sited in rural areas, the Shropshire iron industry, for example, and the cotton and woollen mills of the Midlands and North.

It has been pointed out that the location of rural manufacturing industries was influenced by the type of farming practised and by the social structure of the village community. The common-field arable areas were more heavily preoccupied with the daily routine of farming than the dairying and rearing areas. In pastoral districts, less intensive crop husbandry gave the inhabitants more time, and weaker manorial control more opportunity, to follow alternative industrial occupations. Industries often arose as part-time or side employments: West Midland metal workers, lead miners and hand knitters of the Yorkshire Dales, spinners, weavers, tanners, potters and woodland workers combined their occupations with farming in many country districts.

Where goods with a high value-to-weight ratio were manufactured, rural sites were not necessarily a disadvantage, even for distant markets. Transport networks of pack-horses and wheeled vehicles leading from the uplands and other remote areas to the nearest navigable river or canal were well developed by the eighteenth century. It was not normally economic to haul fuel or raw materials long distances over land, and industries tended to spring up wherever wood fuel and charcoal, peat, coal or water power were available alongside a supply of raw materials or mineral ore. The presence of cheap but skilled labour also attracted industrial enterprises to the countryside. Rural workers with smallholdings to supplement their industrial income, and freedom from urban guild restrictions, had long been favoured by the urban bankers, merchants and clothiers who controlled the supply of raw materials and the marketing of finished goods.

Rural industries operated within a framework of a national economy in the pre-industrial era. The London Lead Company invested in mines from the Peak District to Lakeland, the marketing of woollen cloth hinged upon the City factors of Blackwell Hall, and it was London merchants who transferred production from the capital's framework knitters to the cheaper labour force of the East Midlands. Cornish tin was exported, not from Cornwall, but from London. The cutlery of South Yorkshire, the ironmongery of the West Midlands, the malt from the eastern counties all entered London for further processing, consumption or redistribution. In the textile industry, the finishing processes, including dyeing and fulling in water-powered mills, required the most expensive plant, which was usually the property of the clothier, if not provided by the manor. Mining that needed extensive drainage and winding equipment, metal smelting and other highly capitalised industries, such as alkali or alum production, operated on the basis of direct capital investment and control by the entrepreneur. The enterprise of landlords was responsible for developing important coal and metalliferous mines in the North and Midlands, and for the exploitation of estate woodlands and the expansion of the underwood industries, especially in southern Britain.

Where part of the production took place directly in the worker's home, the arrangement is known as the domestic system. Families adjusted their working rhythm so that they could concentrate on their industrial work when agricultural needs, which came first, were at their least pressing. The seasonal nature of production was especially notable in trades that used natural products: underwood cut in winter, bark and osiers harvested in the spring, malting and brewing after the barley harvest. Domestic workers gained a degree of freedom from direct supervision, although financial needs often ensured that they worked long hours in a poor environment. Cottage work by no means created the idyllic existence imagined by craft revivalists

Countryside transformed by industrialisation: steam winding engine hauling up coal in the South Staffordshire coalfield, mid nineteenth century.

of the turn of the century. The advantage to an entrepreneur who supplied the workers with raw materials and arranged for the finishing and marketing of the manufactured goods was that he need not tie up his capital in expensive plant and equipment, for the producers normally owned their own tools, workshops and forges. To increase output, it was necessary only to extend the number of domestic workers, and it was easy to find the growing numbers required for outwork during the early period of the Industrial Revolution. The rural population was growing, and the corresponding scarcity of land lessened the significance of agricultural work. The uneven mechanisation of the textile industry actually increased the need for rural outwork until the 1820s, and the numbers of hand-loom weavers and framework knitters multiplied.

In such regions as the metal-working districts centred on Sheffield and the area that was to become the Black Country, industry became more significant than farming. New industrial villages arose, particularly in the East Midlands, and sometimes grew into towns. In the first half of the nineteenth century, new industry appeared in the remoter rural areas as industrialists established water powered textile mills in the Derbyshire Dales; and mining settlements in the North and the South West expanded as the output of non-ferrous metals reached its peak in Britain. In the early stages of the Industrial Revolution, country-based industries expanded; the dominance of the large urban factory came only after a long period of population growth and technological innovation.

The effective employment of water, the most important power source of the early Industrial Revolution, required a dispersal of industry to sites where a suitable stream gradient was available to drive the water wheels. Although a small corn mill might generate a power of only 4-8 b.h.p., one of the larger and more efficient overshot wheels could provide the 15-40 b.h.p. needed to drive woodworking machinery, and water wheels could provide sufficient power for a mill of up to 400 workers. Lead, tin and copper mines depended extensively on water power for winding and drainage. The Devon Great Consols Mine in the Tamar Valley took its power from 33 water wheels and eight steam engines in 1865. Water wheels were extensively employed in the milling, paper making, textile, edge tool, woodworking and metal smelting trades. There are many recorded cases of the conversion of mills to new purposes. A mill that was adapted from corn grinding to fulling in the Middle Ages and subsequently to paper making or wood turning in the seventeenth or eighteenth century might, with the decline of these industries in rural areas, revert to its original purpose after 1850, and finally fall into disuse after nine or more centuries' work.

Water power suffered the disadvantage of depending on the seasons, with their extremes of flood and drought. In order to provide a continuous source of power, large storage ponds and dams had to be constructed. The limitations of such natural forces as water led increasingly to the adoption of the steam engine, as soon as improvements made it suitable for the powering of complex machinery. The widespread employment of steam motive power stimulated the growth of industries in towns by concentrating a high brake horse power on a single site, usually located on or near a coalfield, with easy access to water navigation or a railway. It became a positive disadvantage for an industry to be located in country areas where the cost of coal was high. The decline of water power after 1850 was a significant factor in the decline

Water wheel at the Finch Foundry, an edge tool and shovel works at Sticklepath, near Okehampton, Devon.

The commercial section of the Stratfield Mortimer entry in *Kelly's Directory of Berkshire*, 1895.

COMMERCIAL.

Attwater George, shoe maker
Awbery Charles, beer retailer
Barefoot Phillip, tailor
Barnard Henry, brewer
Bowman George, wood dealer
Bradshaw George, farmer & assistant overseer, Headlands farm
Brain Sarah Anne (Miss), ladies' boarding school
Burson Henry G. machinist
Clinch Waltr. farm bailiff to R. Benyon esq. D.L., J.P. Butler's-lands farm
Convalescent Cottage Hospital (Miss Susannah Heathern, matron), Wokefld
Davis Charles, butcher, King street
Davis David, blacksmith
Davis John, blacksmith
Davis Rachel (Mrs.), apartments
Dodd Blandy, tailor
Elliott Alfred, farmer, Sheep's grove
Fewtrell John, temperance hotel
Flower Fredk. Anthony M.B. surgeon
Goddard Thomas, Horse & Groom P.H
Gould Nute William (exors. of), brick maker & farmer
Gray Henry, tailor
Griggs David, City of Silchester P.H
Guilding Jn. farm bailiff to R. Benyon esq. D.L., J.P. Great Park farm
Halfacree Charles R. news agent
Halfacree Harold, picture frame maker
Jackson Edwin, shopkpr & post office
King Arthur Michael, grocer
Long James, farm bailiff to R. Benyon esq. D.L., J.P. Little Park farm
Long Richard, saddler
Lovell Thomas, fly proprietor
Lovelock Albert, builder
Martin Thomas, insurance agent
Mason Ellen (Mrs.), Railway hotel
Master George, Queen's Head P.H
May George, fly proprietor
Merrick James, shopkeeper
Mosdell Caleb, builder & contractor, registered plumber & **sanitary engineer ;** special attention given to sanitary work of every description
Mosdell Joseph, carrier
Mulford Frederick William, corn dlr
Parsons Kezia (Mrs.), cowkeeper
Pocock John, builder
Punter James, shoe maker
Roalfe-Cox Walter Jn. L.R.C.P.Lond. surgeon & medical officer & public vaccinator for No. 4 district, Bradfield union, The Laurels
Simpkins William, draper
Smith & Co. shopkeepers
Spratley James, coal dealer
Steel Lewis, shoe maker
Stewart John R. draper &c
Stratfield Mortimer Dispensary, med. officer, Walter Roalfe-Cox, surgeon
Stratford Thomas, butcher
Sweetzer Daniel, wheelwright
Taylor Alfred, mop, broom rake & prong handle manufacturer, timber & underwood dealer & beer retailer
Taylor James, beer retailer
Thorp William Robert, grocer & farmer
Waight Alfred, saddler
Warwick George T. watch maker
Whitburn Charles, oilman
White & Co. shopkeepers
Wilkins Edmund, farmer, The Grange
Wise Mark, farmer, Wokefield commn
Wise William Edwin, coal dealer
Working Men's Club (William Henry Scott, sec. ; Geo. Withey, caretaker)

of country-based industry, although a minority of firms still employed water as the prime source of motive power at the beginning of the twentieth century, and it is not entirely extinct today.

In fact, the decline of rural industry was a varied and often a gradual one. A poem, written by Joseph Mosdell in 1891, surveyed the various non-agricultural occupations of his native village of Stratfield Mortimer in Berkshire; these included wheelwright, blacksmith, machinist (or engineer), harness maker, shoemaker and travelling tinker, carpenter, builder, 'sanitary engineer', painter, plumber, glazier and decorator, bricklayer, coal merchant, brewer, several carriers—of whom the poet was one—a wood turner and a rake maker—who would have obtained his raw materials from the coppice woods of North Hampshire or the Kennet Valley.

Although Mortimer, only seven miles from Reading and linked to it by rail and by several road carriers, was no isolated village, it had a complexity of trades and occupations that would not be found today in a settlement of comparable size; the 1891 population was 1,236. In spite of a century of industrial growth and the availability of a multitude of manufactured goods, Mortimer apparently still possessed a substantial degree of self sufficiency, not only satisfying the domestic and occupational needs of its own inhabitants, but manufacturing for wider markets.

Although their contribution to the country's economy was dwindling by 1900, rural industries remained remarkably diverse. An account, this time in prose, from K.S. Woods's *The Rural Industries* provides a useful classification of the surviving industries in the early twentieth century. Some of them owed their existence mainly to the presence of local materials: quarrying and mining, brickworks, food production and conservation, the underwood and timber industries, osier growing and basket making. Some workers met local needs for services: wheelwrights, carpenters, turners for builders and carpenters, smiths, farriers and agricultural implement makers, saddlers, tinsmiths, halter makers, dressmakers and bespoke tailors. Some industries provided local labour but manufactured for distant markets with their raw materials provided from outside: leatherdressing, glove making, production of ready-made clothing, knitting, lace making, plush making. Some depended on the supply of water: paper mills, cloth mills, blanket mills, carpet manufacture, boat building. Some—brush making, rope making, cooperage—had almost died out in rural areas, but others—weaving, rabbit-skin glove making, rush basket weaving and others—had recently been introduced or revived.

England's geological make-up was sufficiently varied to ensure that few rural areas were without extraction industries of some kind: clay was dug for pottery and brickmaking; limestones and sandstones were the most commonly quarried building stones; coal and iron ore deposits were locally abundant in the Midlands and North. The quarrying of granite and slate and the mining of non-ferrous metals were restricted to the upland zone of the North and South West, and the Welsh borders.

The impact of the extraction industries on the landscape and the local community varied greatly. Metal-ore and coal mining tended to dominate a community. Miners of the Forest of Dean, the Peak District and the Stanneries of the South West still retained part of their ancient rights and privileges. Contracts for work in small partnerships were undertaken under the 'bargain' or 'tribute' system, whereby the miners agreed to work a particular vein at a given rate per amount of ore extracted. Quarrying and

Above: flint knappers striking gun flints at Brandon, Suffolk, 1878. *Right:* breaking and sorting copper ore, 1854.

clay digging generally had less effect on rural societies than mining, but the quarries of Purbeck and Portland in Dorset were among the exceptions to this rule. Other industries that were locally important included china and ball clay digging in Devon and Cornwall, the small gunflint industry of Brandon in Suffolk, rock salt working in Cheshire, the extraction of coprolite or phosphatic fossil material in Cambridgeshire, the digging of fuller's earth—found only in Jurassic deposits and the lower greensand and traditionally employed for the cleansing of cloth—and gypsum mining in the Trent valley of the East Midlands.

Britain's output of non-ferrous metals reached its highest recorded peak in the period 1760-1860, and the country became a net exporter supplying a high proportion of world output. The English mining areas, notably the Peak District and the Pennines for silver, lead and zinc ore, and Devon and Cornwall for copper and tin, reached their highest point of prosperity, creating extensive industrial landscapes with shafts, adits and soughs for drainage, winding gear, engine houses, water wheels and their accompanying dams, reservoirs and leats, in addition to ore dressing and smelting plants; Cornish copper was invariably shipped to South Wales for smelting. Intensive exploitation caused the most accessible deposits to run out; the increase in haulage and drainage costs and imports of richer and more easily worked ores from overseas helped to precipitate a disastrous collapse in English prices which led to the closure of numerous mines in the period 1880-1900. Occasional rich finds left a few enterprises profitable until the Second World War and a switch to arsenic production kept the Devon Great Consols Mine open for another thirty years. The mining centres, however, never recovered their prosperity and their rural populations are today only a fraction of the mid-nineteenth century figure.

Lime burning was found wherever chalk or limestone rock could be quarried. Kilns ranged in size from small parish units providing lime for local farmers to the large kiln banks on coastal sites, such as Seahouses and Beadnell in Northumberland, and in the Tamar Valley supplying lime on an industrial scale. In agriculture, lime was widely used as an agent for soil amelioration, to reduce acidity and improve structure. Chalk or limestone was built up in alternate layers in the kilns with the fuel, furze, wood faggots or coal, as locally available. If the cost of transporting fuel was high, it was advantageous to site the kiln close to the source of fuel and cart the chalk to it from the quarry. In Surrey, limekilns have been found in the middle of coppices.

Lime kiln at Stratford St Mary, Suffolk, on the navigable River Stour.

The manufacture of bricks and agricultural drainage tiles was a widespread clay-using industry. Temporary sites were established where both clay deposits and a supply of fuel were available and bricks were manufactured for local use, and for urban markets, too, if convenient transport existed. Small brickworks would burn their bricks either in small kilns or clamps. The clamps were large piles of bricks with fuel, including household ashes, or breeze, placed around and below them, enclosed by a layer of burnt bricks. In the second half of the nineteenth century, various technical improvements were adopted even by small brickworks. They included the Hoffmann kiln, which allowed continuous firing and hence greater fuel economy, and brick cutting and moulding machines. From the 1880s national output came to be dominated by the companies which produced Fletton bricks containing a high content of oil shale and requiring little fuel in burning.

Brick making in the 1850s. *Left:* pug mill for kneading and mixing clay—the most advanced piece of equipment in most mid nineteenth century brickyards. *Below:* the moulder's bench. Women workers were commonly employed in brickyards in the London area.

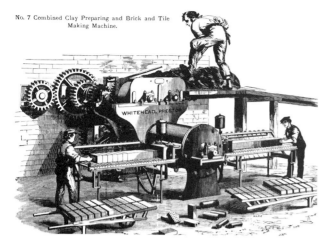

No. 7 Combined Clay Preparing and Brick and Tile Making Machine.

Above: tile making machine advertised by John Whitehead of Preston, Lancashire in 1874. It incorporated both a pug mill and a moulding machine and was capable of producing 20,000 wire-cut bricks a day. *Right:* Wrecclesham Pottery, near Farnham in Surrey, photographed in 1961. The pottery was re-established on this site in 1872 and, like many other country potteries, survived into the twentieth century by reviving traditional wares (in this case, Farnham Greenware) for the luxury end of the market. Production of coarse redwares and roofing tiles continued alongside the making of this 'art pottery'.

The tile drain for underfield drainage was introduced at the end of the eighteenth century. The development of the tile making machine revolutionised Victorian land drainage after 1840; it brought down the price of tiles from 40-60 shillings per hundred to 20 or 10, depending on the local cost of coal, and allowed five men to produce up to 20,000 tiles a day. Numerous small tile works were established in the countryside during the greatest era of public-funded drainage activity from 1840 to 1870.

A pottery in the rural tradition is described by George Sturt, writing as George Bourne, in his biography of his grandfather William Smith (1790-1858), potter and farmer of Farnborough. Smith had bought the pottery in 1819; it produced a lead-glazed ware for the London market, despatched by way of the Basingstoke Canal. He took over an adjacent farm and greatly expanded his business, purchasing a wagon team of his own to carry the ware to London. The farm was always subsidiary to his main occupation as a potter. Clay was trodden by barefoot workers until a horse operated pug mill, manufactured by Sturt's wheelwright father at Farnham, was acquired. The lead purchased from London for glazing was separately prepared. The kiln firing lasted three days producing cooking pots, paint pots, passover vessels for the Whitechapel Jewish community and ware for hospitals and prisons. In the middle of the nineteenth century, the potteries of the Farnham area still obtained their fuel from local sources: turf cut from Frimley Common, and cordwood and bavins supplied from nearby estate coppices. Many such rural potteries had been established in the countryside and in small market towns close to supplies of fuel and suitable clay deposits. By the mid-nineteenth century, their trade was suffering from competition from the mass produced wares of the Staffordshire Potteries; the small potteries responded by substituting coarse products for the tableware now supplied by the Potteries, or specialising in art ware, like the Wrecclesham Pottery at Farnham, or the Barnstaple Pottery, which became famous for Royal Barum ware.

Rural metal working—the primary smelting of iron ore and the subsequent forging of tools and utensils by outwork metal workers—was ceasing to be a vital rural industry by 1860. The English iron industry was being transformed from a largely rural to an urban trade. The charcoal iron industry had existed where coppice woods for charcoal fuel, water power for providing the furnace blast and operating the forge hammers, and iron ore deposits coincided. The new coke smelting industry based on the coalfields was still located in the countryside in the early stages of the Industrial Revolution; Coalbrookdale was a famous example. Eventually the growing coke iron plants with their heavy demand for labour created, as did the collieries and stem textile mills, a new type of settlement essentially urban in character and outlook in spite of its rural location. Those which ultimately failed to develop extensively like Coalbrookdale remained as industrial villages or small towns.

The first stage of ironmaking, smelting in the blast furnace, was the earliest to be affected by the shift in the industry's centre of gravity from rural woodland and riverside sites to the urban and semi-urban coalfields of the Midlands, South Wales, South Yorkshire and Teeside. The second stage, the refining and decarbonising of cast or pig iron which itself cannot be forged or rolled into workable wrought iron, was undertaken at a charcoal fired hearth known as the finery or forge. This was superseded after 1874 by the coal fired puddling process developed by Cort at the rural forge of Funtley in Hampshire. In the charcoal iron industry smelting and refining frequently took place at different sites and the transfer of the forges to coalfield sites sometimes lagged behind that of the blast furnaces.

Rural fineries, like Wortley Forge on the river Don, north-west of Sheffield, supplied bar or rod iron to the secondary metal workers who made it up into a wide variety of products. These industries ultimately derived from the blacksmith's trade, and some blacksmiths continued to manufacture their own nails and tools well into the nineteenth century. In the area centred on Sheffield the rural metal workers produced cutlery, edge tools, razors, files and nails. The local availability of water power, millstone grit for grinding wheels, iron ore deposits and charcoal fuel had favoured the development of a flourishing industry by 1750. In villages like Ecclesfield, Norton and Stannington farmer cutlers and grinders undertook hand forging and grinding in domestic workshops. Throughout the nineteenth century there was a slow decline of these rural metal trades and a tendency for them to migrate to larger centres, although the small manufacturing unit in the cutlery and edge tool trades continued to survive in the city of Sheffield itself.

A similar pattern of rural metal working had been apparent in the West Midlands before the Industrial Revolution. In South Staffordshire, North Worcestershire and the adjoining part of Warwickshire a complex of furnaces, forges and slitting mills developed by entrepreneurs supplied the craftsmen of the villages and market towns with bar iron. The area had plentiful streams to drive water wheels and the easily dug 'ten yard seam' of coal. Like the Sheffield products, the metal ware of the West Midlands gained a national reputation and an early penetration of the London market. The trades had become exceptionally differentiated by 1800, the manufacture of nails, locks, saddler's ironware and agricultural tools all having their particular districts. This particular countryside was becoming heavily industrialised in the eighteenth century, as the originally agrarian based metal trades of the coalfield led to the creation of the Black Country. Domestic manufacture of nails continued in the surviving forges in the nineteenth century but the old dual economy of farming and metal working had broken up. The nailers and locksmiths now worked for the large firms which had replaced the small family units of production. The increasing concentration of metal working in the Sheffield region and West Midlands was accompanied by a corresponding decline of these trades in outlying districts. The

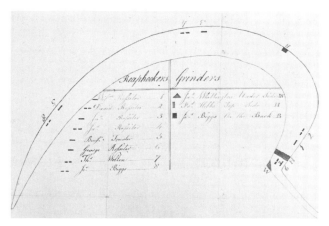

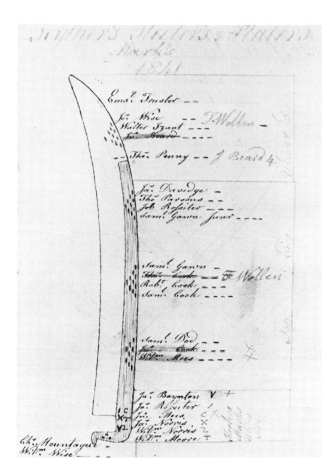

Scythe making. *Above:* two examples of craftsmen's marks from the 1841 pattern book of a West Country edge tool maker, possibly one of the enterprises controlled by the Fussell family in the area of Mells and Nunney, Somerset. *Lower right:* forging scythe blades at Belbroughton, Worcestershire.

isolated needle making industry of Long Crendon in Buckinghamshire, for example, had been established in the sixteenth century and supplied large quantities of needles to London. The horse gear used to provide the power for scouring the needles was replaced by a steam engine in the 1840s but Long Crendon proved unable to compete with the industry's principal centre at Redditch. The cost of transporting coal was high and the factory, which had partly supplanted the cottage industry, closed down in 1862 leaving a remnant of domestic workers who operated independently until the 1890s.

The centralising tendency was also displayed by the agricultural edge tool industry. Scythe forging had always been highly capitalised; it required the use of steel, an expensive material, and water-powered hammers. By the eighteenth century certain areas and individual manufacturers had gained a more than local reputation for their products. One such district on the edge of the West Midland metal working area was centred on the North Worcestershire parish of Belbroughton. Its output has been estimated to be about 10,000 dozen scythe blades a year. In Somerset the scytheworks of Fussell of Mells had achieved a high reputation for the quality of its products by 1830. Members of the Fussell family controlled several production centres in the villages around Mells. The works, which relied chiefly on water power, manufactured reap hooks, scythes, hay knives and billhooks. The businesses of James Isaac and John Fussell were purchased by Isaac Nash & Co. of Belbroughton in 1894 and all production of the Fussell pattern tools was transferred there. Isaac Nash himself had already extended his control over a number of scythe works in the Belbroughton area, owning four and renting seven at the time of his death. Within the Sheffield edge tool district there was a shift from the rural water power sites, like the grinding and forging mill at Abbeydale, to larger works located nearer the city centre. Some outlying firms, including the Finch Foundry at Sticklepath, near Okehampton, Devon, which manufactured special tools for the china clay industry, did manage to survive into the twentieth century, although the agricultural market for edge tools had considerably diminished with the mechanisation of harvesting.

Before the Industrial Revolution, much rural industry was concerned with processing agricultural products: wool, hides and skins, horn and tallow from livestock, grain, malt and straw from corn crops, and the industrial crops, hemp, flax, woad and madder. The trades of clothing, tanning, milling, malting, rope making, papermaking and straw hat making were dependent on the harvest of animal and plant products. During the Industrial Revolution, imported raw materials were increasingly substituted for the native product. Cotton, the archetypal growth industry, was wholly dependent on imports, and those of raw wool generally exceeded the domestic wool clip after 1860. A high degree of national self sufficiency in grains was, however, maintained until the last quarter of the nineteenth century.

Hand knitting was perhaps the most basic of the rural textile industries. The production of stockings, caps and gloves had been common in central southern England and the East Midlands before the eighteenth century. Framework knitting, also undertaken as a domestic industry, then replaced hand knitting in the Midlands, and in the nineteenth century the latter retained its importance only in the Pennines, especially in the Yorkshire and Westmorland Dales; in mid-century hand knitting was already failing as a second means of livelihood for labourers and lead miners and their families. Local mills, such as those at Askrigg, Aysgarth and Sedbergh, sent out work to the knitters and collected their finished stockings, but the majority of these had ceased their connection with woollen cloth by the end of the century.

Tanning. *Left:* general view of tanning yard showing hides being removed from the tanning pits. *Below:* after 9-15 months of tanning, the hides passed to a currier, who undertook the final preparation of the leather for use. Both 1850s.

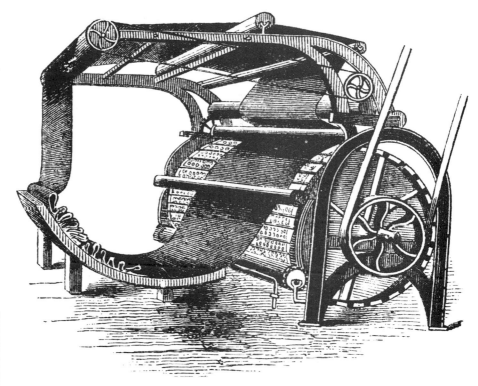

Gig mill, a revolving cylinder fitted with thousands of teasel heads, that had replaced the hand-held teaselling frame. It was used to raise the nap of fulled cloth, one of the finishing processes in the manufacture of woollen broadcloth.

Hand wool comb, used to remove short fibres from wool before spinning into yarn for making worsted cloth. The combing was a heavy task undertaken by domestic workers and was one of the last textile operations to be carried out by hand.

During the Industrial Revolution, certain manufacturing districts took the lead in their industries. The supremacy of Lancashire cotton, West Riding wool and worsted and Nottingham lace became so absolute that the fortunes of region and product became inextricably linked. Their superior resources of fuel, labour and transport assured their successful competition in the mass market.

Among their competitors, the Norfolk worsted industry was an early casualty, the South Midlands pillow lace industry succumbed in the second half of the nineteenth century, and by this time the once supreme West Country broadcloth industry was also in severe decline. A fashion for lighter cloth had superseded that for the traditional heavy broadcloth manufactured in the West Country for the luxury end of the trade, and the Yorkshire mastery of the wool worsted fibre put it in an advantageous position to supply the market. In Gloucestershire, the number of mills fell from fifty to twenty between 1849 and 1901. The outlying river valley sites were the first to go out of production, and the industry contracted to the valleys in the vicinity of Stroud. The West Country woollen industry had tended to be highly capitalised and had not been slow in applying the technological advances made since 1760: hand cards were replaced by carding and scribbling machines, spinning wheels by jennies, teasling frames by gig mills and hand-held shears by shearing frames. New mills incorporating these inventions were sometimes constructed around the old fulling mills.

The introduction of rotary fulling machines in the 1830s condemned these most typical of rural industrial sites to obsolescence. With the effective mechanisation of weaving after 1850, the cycle of innovation was complete. The larger town mills in Wiltshire and Somerset, closer to the Somerset coalfield, went over to steam power and gained a clear economic advantage over the mainly water powered mills of Gloucestershire. Even in the West

Riding, the industry became concentrated in the valley centres, Halifax, Dewsbury and Bradford, when steam became the dominant motive power. There, too, water powered spinning and fulling mills in the remoter upland valleys were abandoned.

The papermaking industry was indirectly based on agricultural products. Its traditional raw materials had been pulped linen rags for fine paper, and discarded cordage, canvas and netting for coarse brown paper. Its need of water to power its machinery, and in the papermaking process itself, led to the siting of mills wherever clear streams, free of suspended clay, could be found. In the Wye valley of Buckinghamshire, and the Maidstone district and Darent Valley in Kent, a particular concentration of mills, serving the London area, emerged and continued to remain centres of the industry. Advanced machinery for pulping was introduced in the eighteenth century, and the Fourdrinier machine, producing an endless web of paper, appeared soon after 1800. The subsequent development of steam powered mills, whose advantages lay in sites with good rail and water communications, gradually reduced the numbers of small rural mills producing handmade paper from one or two vats.

Milling was one of the earliest rural industries to be effectively mechanised. Well over 5,000 water or animal powered mills are recorded in the Domesday Book, and after 1180 they were joined by windmills. In the eighteenth century, a number of technical improvements were made, including iron water wheels of more efficient design, cast iron gearing, automatic governors to regulate the gap between the millstones, and fantails to face a windmill into the wind. From the early nineteenth century, the larger urban flour mills began to install steam engines. Having adopted some of these improvements, the country mill was still performing its traditional functions in 1860. Most millers were content to serve the rural community, deducting their toll from the grain brought to them in individual consignments of a few bushels by farmers and smallholders.

By 1900, this centuries-old pattern of local milling had been substantially overthrown and was being replaced by a new system, based on an advanced technology introduced from Austria-Hungary around 1880. The number of mills had already begun to decline, faced with an increasing output from large urban mills and rising imports of wheat and flour. The arrival of the cylindrical roller mill, which produced fine ground white flour from imported hard wheat on an industrial scale and was most advantageously sited

Interior of a malt house, 1850s.

78

Above: exploded view of a flour mill powered by an undershot water wheel. This 1850s illustration shows the traditional type of flour mill before the introduction of roller mills in the late nineteenth century. *Right:* interior of Hemmingford Grey water mill on the River Ouse in Huntingdonshire.

in ports and large centres of population, hastened the demise of the small local mill.

One of the most famous pioneers of the new technology in Britain was Joseph Rank. Coming from a famiy of millers on the edge of Hull, he rented his first small windmill, Waddingham's mill, in 1875, in an area already over-supplied with mills. He soon entered into a shared venture with West, another Hull miller, running a combined flour and oil-seed crushing mill, the Holderness Road corn mill, powered by a portable gas engine. Rank saw his first roller mill at Tadcaster in 1883, and realising its advantages, built his own steam powered roller mill, the Alexandra Mill, in Hull two years later. The establishment of the quayside Clarence Mills on the River Hull in 1891 indicated new developments in the British flour milling industry.

Not all rural mills gave way to the milling revolution. Some, aided by good communications, were able to adopt the new machinery. Wear Gifford flour mill on the River Torridge in North Devon had by 1889 installed a water turbine driving a modern automatic roller plant supplied by river barges, and W.H. Strong, describing Wear Gifford mill in 1889, praised roller grinding for its removal of the germ flake, forming 'excellent food for horses, sheep and pigs', leaving flour 'of absolute purity'. Other small mills retained their millstones and survived in diminishing numbers well into the twentieth century. Usually aided by an auxiliary oil engine, they concentrated on grinding animal feed for local farmers.

Somerset frail maker plaiting rushes into baskets. These frails were widely used by workers as lunch or tool baskets.

Malting was a major grain processing industry supplying the basic raw material for beer, which formerly held a central place in the national diet. The greatest concentration of barley malting occurred in the arable eastern counties, and it was there that the industry was, and remains, important. The artificial germination of barley, to make the starch contained in the seed available as a source of sugar in brewing, required specially constructed buildings, with ample floor space for spreading the grain, and kilns for the final drying and flavouring. Until 1860, when the malt duty was repealed, every stage of the process was very closely regulated by the excise. There were therefore fewer maltsters than brewers, but small maltings were frequently found in the villages of East Anglia, Lincolnshire, Nottinghamshire and Staffordshire. The London brewers obtained quantities of malt from the Lea and Stort valley maltings of Hertfordshire, processors of barley from the eastern counties. The number of firms declined in the second half of the nineteenth century by about a hundred a year, as the industry became more concentrated in large railside maltings established by the brewers. There were still, however, over 1,200 maltsters listed for England in the *Kelly's Directory of the Wine and Spirit Trades* for 1902.

By 1860, there was a marked disparity in the size of brewing enterprises. The large companies brewing in London and Burton distributed their products nationally, and a multitude of smaller brewers existed in market towns and villages. Nevertheless, by 1835 more than half the malt used was already consumed by the wholesale companies, although publican and retail brewers greatly outnumbered them. The output and numbers of the small breweries diminished steadily throughout the century, and by 1914 they used only 3.3% of the malt consumed in England and Wales.

Even the most seemingly insignificant by-product of wheat, the straw, provided the raw material for a rural manufacturing industry. By 1860, straw plaiting had become an important source of work for women in Bedfordshire, Buckinghamshire and Hertfordshire, and was practised by a few in Essex and Suffolk. In 1822, Cobbett wrote of the trade:

'One of the great misfortunes of England at this day is, that the land has had taken away from it those employments for its women and children which were so necessary to the well-being of the agricultural labourer. The spinning, the carding, the reeling, the knitting; these have been all taken away from the haughty lords of bands of abject slaves, and given to the Lords of the Loom... the crabbed-voiced, hard-favoured, hard-hearted, puffed-up, insolent, savage and bloody wretches of the North have, assisted by a blind and greedy Government, taken all the employment away from the agricultural women and children. This manufacture of straw will form one little article of employment for these persons. It sets at defiance all the hatching and scheming of all the tyrannical wretches who cause the poor little creatures to die in their factories, heated to eighty-four degrees. There will need no inventions of WATT; none of your horse power, nor water powers; no murdering of one set of wretches in the coal mines, to bring up the means of murdering another sort of wretches in the factories, by the heat produced from these coals; none of these are wanted to carry on this manufacture.'

The woodland industries, like the agricultural processing trades, depended on the exploitation of a natural product. In the case of coppice, trees were as systematically harvested as any farm crop. In one of the least wooded European countries, techniques of woodland management had evolved to ensure a continuous supply of wood and timber in pre-industrial England. The Agricultural and Industrial Revolutions stimulated the demand for many types of woodland product: farm tools and implements, carts and wagons, mills, ships, domestic utensils, containers in many sizes and varieties and, initially, industrial fuel. From cricket bats to roof shingles, from the birch twigs used in vinegar brewing to the hornbeam cogs of a mill spur-wheel, woodland products were the most diverse of all the rural industries.

Women straw plaiters at Tring, Hertfordshire. Straw plaiting was a domestic industry, the most significant product of which was the straw hat. The cottagers sold their finished work to dealers in the market towns of the South Midlands straw plaiting area.

A distinction was normally made between underwood and timber. Timber, 'big stuff suitable for making planks, beams and gate-posts', may be considered the product of a tree greater than two feet in girth. Underwood was the name given to the product of coppice, although the same quality of young wood was also produced by pollarding, or the regular cutting of mature tree branches above ground level. This method had ceased to be significant by the mid century, and was abandoned in woods like Burnham Beeches and Epping Forest a hundred years ago. Coppicing was a system of woodland conservation and management which exploited the natural re-growth of trees in order to meet a large, regular and primarily local demand for wood, and had been systematically practised since the medieval period. Young wood was cropped at intervals of between six and twenty-four years, depending on species and usage, the stems being cut back to the stool from which new shoots would grow to form the next crop. The principal coppice woods were hazel, Spanish chestnut, oak, alder, ash and hornbeam. Pure coppice was much rarer than coppice-with-standards, in which coppice and standard trees—that is young wood and timber—were grown together.

The highest concentrations of coppice in the nineteenth century were found in the south-eastern counties of Kent, Surrey and Sussex, extending into Berkshire, Hampshire, Dorset and Wiltshire; in the West Midlands, Gloucestershire, Herefordshire and Shropshire, extending into Monmouth; and in the Furness district of Lancashire. Most other parts of the country, especially the East Midlands and North East, were substantially lacking in coppice. The plantations and natural woods of the Weald, the Forest of Dean, the Wyre Forest on the Shropshire-Worcestershire border, and Furness had been the principal sources of fuel for the charcoal iron industry. The south-eastern and West Midland coppices supplied local farmers with hop poles. It has been calculated that upwards of 2,500 poles per acre were required to establish a hop garden, and 300-400 each year to maintain it. Kent had the largest acreage of both hops and coppice.

Coppice wood being stacked after cutting. The wood was sorted into various stacks: poles for the manufacture of underwood products, pea and bean sticks, and bavins and faggots as firewood for ovens and kilns. A use was found for everything, down to the last twig.

Above: wiring bundles of ash truss hoops in the Midlands for dispatch to the industrial towns where they were used to hoop barrels. *Right:* Cuthbert Westbrook making hurdles from hazel poles on the Herriard estate in Hampshire. Wattle hurdles were used in the South of England as portable enclosures for sheep.

A witness quoted in the report of Mr Vaughan (*Reports of the Special Assistant Poor Law Commissioners on the Employment of Women and Children in Agriculture*, 1843) emphasised the local importance of coppice in the southern counties:

'I am a wood-hoop dealer and farmer, living at Sprat's farm, Capels, in Surrey. I supply the East and West India Docks, the London Docks, and St Katherine's Docks, with hoops for casks and tea-chests. I think that one-third of the face of the country, from Dorking, in Surrey, to Cuckfield, in Sussex, to the east and from Guildford to Petworth to the west, is covered with wood-land. From the beginning of November until the 25th of March labour is employed in the wood-land in cutting wood-hoops and cord-wood to make charcoal. On the poor cold lands of this country little is done in the winter by the labourer in the cultivation of corn, and I think that as many as two-thirds of the agricultural labourers transfer their labour in the winter months to the wood-cutting...'

Thomas Hardy portrayed an entire rural economy based on the under-wood trades in *The Woodlanders* (1887). In the 'wood environed community' of 'Little Hintock' lived the timber and copse ware merchant, George Melbury and the small farmer, Giles Winterbourne, to their mutual convenience:

'Melbury with his timber and copse ware business, found that the weight of his labour came in winter and spring. Winterbourne was in the apple and cider trade, and his requirements in cartage and other work came in the autumn of each year. Hence, horses, waggons, and in some degree men, were handed over to him when the apples began to fall; he in return, lending his assistance to Melbury in the busiest wood cutting season...'

Melbury's homestead contained stacks of timber, faggots and hurdles, a shed for making thatching spars, framing sheep feeding cribs and 'copse ware manufacture in general', and four wagons for transporting the coppice products. He employed top and bottom sawyers to work in his saw pit and travelling spar makers 'who, when the fall of the leaf began, made their appearance regularly, and when winter was over disappeared in silence till the season came again.' Other spar making was performed by outworkers, like Marty South, whom Hardy describes at her fireside wearing a leather apron, with a bill-hook in one hand and a leather glove on the other:

'On her left hand lay a bundle of the straight, smooth hazel rods called spar-gads—the raw material of her manufacture; on her right, a heap of chips and ends—the refuse with which the fire was maintained; in front, a pile of the finished articles. To produce them she took up each gad, looked critically at it from end to end, cut it to length, split it into four, and sharpened each of the quarters with dextrous blows, which brought it to a triangular point precisely resembling that of a bayonet.'

Marty South could produce three bundles totalling 1,500 in a day and half the night, earning, at the rate of eighteen pence per thousand, 2s.3d.

A district in which the underwood industry survived into the twentieth century, and in a highly organised form, was centred upon the village of Tadley on the Berkshire-Hampshire border. The integration of the woodland and farming economies is confirmed by interviews with former underwood dealers and workers. In the winter, the workers cut coppice and timber, and made besom brooms, not only in the locality but in more distant areas, sometimes living rough in the woods. In the summer, they went hop picking in the Alton area and took in a number of corn harvests, taking advantage of the earlier ripening period in Sussex to follow the harvest northwards. Most of the woodmen and their families also occupied smallholdings.

The woods were owned by a number of large estates and underwood dealers who purchased lots of standing wood by tender or public auction, contracting with workmen to cut and work up the coppice in the winter months. The mature or standard trees were normally reserved for the estate and for timber merchants. Coppice products were used in the immediate neighbourhood, but were also sold to distant markets. Hazel hoops were despatched to London by rail or canal from Aldermaston wharf, and used in the manufacture of slack barrels for dry goods such as cheese, cement, apples and sugar. Crate rods went to the crate makers of the Potteries for packing crockery, birch and alder poles to the Thatcham turnery works producing tool and broom handles. Besom brooms were either made up in the woods as furnace brooms for South Wales and the Midlands, or supplied in the form of bavins and handles to be made up locally by village workshops. Other products included poles for gate hurdles and hay rakes, oak bark sold to a Reading tannery, pea and bean sticks, and of course firewood from the residual wood. Charcoal burning was occasionally carried out.

In the Furness district of Lancashire, the exploitation of the coppice plantations was, for the greater part of the nineteenth century, linked very closely to the requirements of local industry. In addition to charcoal, the principal products were barrel hoops for the makers of gunpowder in the Lake District, blocks for mill bobbins, brush stocks, spelk baskets, and bark. Furness saw the last survival of the charcoal iron industry, which had finally died out in the Weald—where all ironworking ceased—and the Forest of Dean—where the furnaces were converted to coke in the nineteenth century. Charcoal was produced by the controlled burning of cordwood in the absence of air to drive off all volatile matter. It has been calculated that an area of 7,000 acres of woodland would have been required to sustain a large furnace in blast indefinitely. In theory, therefore, England possessed sufficient woodland to sustain the charcoal iron industry at its eighteenth-century output, and there is no evidence that the industry ever seriously outran its own fuel supply, although problems were caused by the

Barking. *Above:* bark rick at Bucknell, Shropshire where the bark industry flourished before World War I. After drying, oak bark was crushed and bagged for dispatch by rail to leather dressers and tanners. *Right:* felling and barking team at Brimpton, Berkshire.

limited range over which it was economical to transport cordwood and charcoal; large sheds had to be constructed at the ironworks to store a year's supply of the bulky fuel. The use of coke for smelting had an advantage in terms of immediate availability, and released supplies of underwood for competing domestic and industrial markets.

Traditional coppice work employed a limited range of techniques to convert the poles cut by the billhook. The saw was not normally used, and splitting or cleaving was done along the grain of the wood with a bill-hook or froe—a cleaving axe. Draw knives were employed in barking, shaving and shaping poles, and a side axe for pointing and rough shaping. To support the wood during these operations, it was held in shaving-breaks, cleaving-breaks, or shaving horses. The manufacture of a few products required more specialised equipment, like the tine-former in rake making, the besom grip, and the stock knife in clog sole cutting. Drilling was performed by augers, and bending by heating, steaming, or in a bending horse.

Turnery work, in which cleftwood was rotated as a cutting tool was used on it, utilised both underwood and timber, depending on the size and type of wood employed. Typical products were tool, broom and mop handles, brush backs, chair and table legs, wheel hubs, and domestic and dairy bowls. The survival of the most primitive sort of turnery which employed

Shelter constructed from beech saplings and canvas and thatched with straw, part of a temporary encampment made by chair bodgers in the beechwoods of the Buckinghamshire Chilterns. The bodgers made only the legs and stretcher pieces for chairs manufactured in the High Wycombe furniture factories.

the pole lathe is associated with chair-leg turning in the Windsor chairmaking industry, and bowl turning. The mop stick turners in the Berkshire village of Crookham Common employed the treadle lathe with flywheel, a type also used by the wheelwrights.

The Kennet Valley was an important turnery centre, and K.S. Woods, in 1921, wrote of the time, 'Forty or fifty years ago when Thatcham Broadway used to be filled with cart-loads of rakes and broom and mop handles...' Power turneries were established by the third quarter of the century, and the ones at Thatcham eventually destroyed the trade of small, independent turners on the neighbouring commons. Automatic lathes were extensively used in the fifty or so water powered bobbin mills of the Lake District, which supplied half of the national requirement of mill bobbins around 1850. A large cotton mill might have ten million bobbins in use at one time. The fall in demand after 1870 resulted from foreign competition, the adoption of automatic bobbin turning machinery by the cotton mills, and the advent of metal spindles. The bobbin mills that remained began producing pencils, pill boxes, tool handles, and brush stocks.

The Bradiford water powered turnery in North Devon had produced chairs, rocking horses and later coach wheel felloes, spokes and brushes. It had installed a small stationary engine and the first circular saw in North Devon. After 1869, it was extensively modernised under new owners by the replacement of the wooden water wheel by an iron one and the installation of new gearing, a self acting lathe, circular and hand saws, and a 6 h.p. engine. The turnery produced painted brush stocks, broom heads and handles turned from Devon coppice wood.

Basket willow was cultivated on damp, low-lying land in river valleys. The osier or withy beds were chiefly found in the Trent valley in Nottinghamshire and Leicestershire, the lower Severn valley and Gloucestershire Avon, the Somerset levels, the Thames and Kennet valleys, the Fens, the East Anglian rivers and the Mawdsley area of Lancashire. The various commercial varieties of willow were processed and baskets were made in village manufactories. Urban basket makers purchased rods from country growers. The industry steadily declined after 1900, being particularly affected by European competition, and the substitution of other materials in the manufacture of containers.

It was the decline of markets that was ultimately responsible for the collapse of the underwood industries. As long as the demand for coppice products was buoyant, there was every reason for estate owners to manage their woods efficiently and systematically. Far from destroying woodland, the Industrial Revolution initially preserved it by providing new markets for wood products. By 1900, however, underwood prices had fallen, and coppices were increasingly neglected. There was now little demand for charcoal and firewood, and changes in agriculture had substantially reduced the use of the main coppice products. The old method of cultivating hops on a large number of individual 'hills', each with its own pole, was replaced by the wirework system requiring far fewer poles. The national hop acreage reached its peak of about 70,000 acres in the late 1870s and thereafter declined progressively. As sheep folding on the downlands of central southern England diminished in importance, fewer wattle hurdles and feeding cribs were needed. As machinery replaced hand tools, the demand for scythe handles, hay rakes and other implements constructed of wood fell away. In a free trade economy, there was no protection against the import of cheaper foreign products like barrel hoops, baskets and turned ware.

In the twentieth century, coppice has been consistently neglected in favour of high forest. The first detailed national survey was undertaken in 1905, when the Board of Agriculture returns indicated that in England (which held about 90% of British coppice), the 538,123 acres of coppice formed 32% of the total woodland area. Subsequent censuses of woodlands undertaken by the Forestry Commission revealed the growing insignificance of coppice in England against high forest; in 1921, there were 485,229 acres

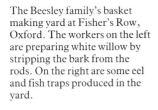

The Beesley family's basket making yard at Fisher's Row, Oxford. The workers on the left are preparing white willow by stripping the bark from the rods. On the right are some eel and fish traps produced in the yard.

of coppice (30% of total woodlands) in 1947, 330,060 acres (18%), and by 1965-67 a mere 72,900 acres (3%) remained, including coppice that had probably gone out of cultivation, so that only about 40-45,000 acres were still regularly worked.

Regular management is necessary for the maintenance of coppice. To end the cutting cycle causes the woodland to close in, destroying the community of plant and animal life dependent on it. Today, the existence of the under-wood industry is tenuous. However, hurdle making survives in Surrey, Hampshire, Dorset and Wiltshire, and coppice is still cut for chestnut pale fencing in Kent, and rake making in Suffolk. The coppicing cycle has remained unbroken in Bradfield Woods, in Suffolk, described by Rackham as 'a living monument of medieval woodland practice', and in the same county, coppicing has been resumed at Hayley Wood.

Village servicing trades, those of the wheelwright and carpenter, the blacksmith and farrier, and the boot and shoe maker, were commonly found in even the smaller settlements. Saddlery and harness making was principally an occupation of the larger villages and market towns.

The market towns also provided a base for the more specialised trades which served their rural hinterland: tailors, millwrights, tinsmiths, ironfounders and agricultural engineers. The range of local servicing trades which tenant farmers could call upon is illustrated by a selection of bills received by an Oxfordshire farmer between 1879 and 1888. William Henman, a newcomer to the area, who had farmed in Bedfordshire until 1860, undertook extensive alterations to his house and farm buildings. The farm was a large one, of 350-400 acres, and most of his dealings were with local tradesmen in Islip itself, in the neighbouring villages of Kidlington, Bletchingdon and Charlton-on-Otmoor, and in the city of Oxford.

Between 1879 and 1888, William Henman had saddle, harness and collar repairs, the provision of gloves, whips, saddle soap, oil, etc., from James Webb, saddler and assistant overseer and assessor of taxes; saw sharpening, supply of plough and mower parts and engine paint from William Allan, wheelwright; cart, wagon and carriage repair from Thomas Hill, wheelwright; cart repair from Henry Stevens, carpenter and wheelwright; manufacture of wheelbarrow, garden chair, ladders, gate, stile, etc., implement repair, window and lock fitting, and carting of coal from Shipley coal wharf, from John Warland, grocer and carpenter; shoeing, plough repairs, supply of cart and engine ironwork and mower knives, and repair of domestic utensils (including a tea kettle) from Mrs Harriet Chamberlain, blacksmith; shoeing and supply of plough shares, repair of plough, horse hoe and cream cistern tap from William Smith, blacksmith; repair and supply of parts to steam engine, threshing machine, mowers, chaff-cutter and bean mill, supply of belting, machine oil, tallow and hemp packing, sale of new Howard plough and winnowing machine from Thomas Warner, agricultural machinist; cart, mower and drill, fitting and repairs, housework—glazing, locks, windows, door, chair mending—making of milking stool, supply of paint, oil and nails from Edward Steele, builder and contractor, English and foreign timber merchant, house decorator and sanitary plumber; pump and iron pump repairs and replacement, window repairs and lead piping from Philip Goddard, beer retailer and plumber; supply of drainage pipes from Joshua Harris, farmer and brickmaker; a supply of drain pipes for the Church Commissioners (the owners of his farm) from Richard, Jesse and Henry Breakspear, brickmakers.

The bills confirm the impression, derived from an examination of crafts-men's ledgers, that the greater part of their trade came not so much from manufacture as from repair and maintenance, and the gap widened as more factory products became available. The changes shown in the craftsmen's recorded (or principal) occupations over the period of Henman's accounts refute the popular belief that these were fixed, if not hereditary. Of the thirteen tradesmen listed, only five list the same trades in both the 1877 and 1887 directories. Two of them had changed their main occupations, and two others had upgraded their descriptions. John Warland is listed as a grocer in 1877 and a carpenter in 1887, and Philip Goddard underwent a transition from beer retailer to plumber. Edward Steele added a large number of functions to his 1877 entry of builder, and there are receipts from James Webb for Henman's house duly signed in his capacity as local assessor of taxes. William Eustace undertook work for Henman in his recorded occupa-tion of shoemaker and in his other part-time trade of rick thatching.

This was a period of transition. The older trades of saddler, blacksmith and wheelwright still flourished, serving the daily needs of agriculture and indeed acquiring additional tasks in the maintenance of new implements. The newer trade of the agricultural engineer and machinist is represented in William Henman's accounts by Thomas Warner, who specialised in repair-ing and supplying spare parts for the complex equipment—threshing machines and portable steam engines—and acted as agents for the large agricultural engineering firms of the eastern counties; this particular firm failed to survive the decade. The activities of Philip Goddard and Edward Steele illustrate the rise of the jobbing builder and contractor. The aspira-tions of this new profession are shown by the employment of such terms as 'gas and water engineer', and 'sanitary plumber', themselves a reflection on the increasing complexity of late Victorian domestic fittings.

By 1850, a number of specialised trades were involved in the construction and fitting out of even the most basic homes. An estimate for estate built labourers' cottages of 1849 mentions diggers, bricklayers, masons, slaters, plasterers, carpenters, joiners, smiths, ironfounders, plumbers, glaziers and painters. New materials—mass produced bricks, roofing slates and cast iron grates—were now widely obtainable, although the local materials, especially stone, were still widely used, where available, and thatching straw survived the competition of machine-made tiles and Welsh slate in some districts.

Walter Rose has provided an admirable account of the activities of a village carpenter and builder in *The Village Carpenter* (1937). Formerly the functions of carpentry, masonry work and the combined trades of plumb-ing, glazing and decorating had been undertaken by different members of the Rose family, although 'in all building and repair work the three separate concerns acted together in unison.' The creation of a single building busi-ness at Haddenham in Buckinghamshire took place in 1893:

'My great-uncle, the masoner, died six weeks before grandfather's death occurred; the way was then open for my father and myself to reconstruct the old carpentry business, which, from that date, was changed to general building, and we then undertook all that came within the meaning of that term... Machine-made panel doors came along at a cheaper price than we could make them: mouldings and prepared sash bars and rails made their preparation by hand expensive in contrast. Each of such changes tended to discount the skill of the joiner. In like manner, the wholesale supply of prepared varnishes, paints, stains, and distemper washes rendered the secrets of their preparation of little further value to the old decorators.'

The powered saw mill and the circular saw were already coming into widespread use by 1860, supplanting the pit saw. Sawyers appear to have been problematic employees without any great affection for their work.

'For a long time my father had experienced increasing difficulty with sawyers. Although the work asked considerable intelligence and skill, the monotonous slog, in the old days, tended to develop a dumb mentality that found its relaxation at the "pub". The sawyers' faith in beer was absolute, doubtless due to the amount of sweat they lost at work.'

Rose added that although 'sentiment continues to incline to the old-folk methods... I have never met a sawyer who has expressed regret at the passing of the work over to the machine.'

George Sturt, writing in *The Wheelwright's Shop* (1923), found the purchase of ready-sawn planks a relief, as well as an economic necessity:

'The sawyers were on the whole so erratic I was always glad to see the back of them. Yet the real trouble was that, as competition grew, a less costly way of getting timber had to be found. At any rate, when planks could be bought in London nearly fit to use, it would no longer do to buy local timber and pay for sawing it, thereby locking up one's money for years while the timber dried. Timber merchants might do some of that. It was for them to employ the sawyers—or to set up the steam-saws.'

The principal work undertaken by the Rose carpentry business before its reconstruction included elm pump boring, house and roof carpentry, furniture repairing, farm carpentry (the making and repair of fences and gates, the maintenance of cow-stalls, threshing floors and granaries and the construction of ladders, rat traps and milking pails), millwrighting (the recogging of mill gear wheels and the construction and fitting of windmill sails) and undertaking.

Rose's account gives the impression of a business well integrated into the fabric of the community that it serves, yet it was a relatively new trade in the family. It effectively lasted only three generations, having been established by Rose's grandfather, 'who commenced his self-taught trade of village

Left: before the introduction of the power saw, the pit saw was the standard method used by rural craftsmen for cutting a tree into even lengths. The top sawyer directed the saw's action and had the hard task of pulling the saw up on every stroke. The bottom sawyer, or pit man, had less responsibility but worked under a constant rain of sawdust. *Below:* sawing timber with a circular saw bench powered by a portable steam engine, New Forest, about 1907.

Above: wheelwright's shop at Heydon in Norfolk, about 1900. *Right:* the interior of Humphries & Son's Wagon Works at Chippenham in Wiltshire.

carpentry' to supplement the livelihood he gained from grazing a few cows. Until the age of twenty-one, he had ploughed his father's lands in the open fields around their village. The enclosure of the fields about 1834 may have stimulated Rose to adopt this new trade. He acquired the means and the premises at the same time by inheriting a small homestead. He certainly continued to combine carpentry with a side-line of grazing. As the greater part of the parish was still arable, 'all carpenters were expected to help over the busy harvest period, an unwritten rule being that any man unwilling should not expect work in the winter.' Rose's grandfather, who perhaps thought of himself primarily as a builder, specialised in the construction of timber-framed farm buildings, a reminder of the carpenter's role as a builder in wood before the development of a separate building trade.

As it happened, the Rose family business never undertook wheelwrighting, although the trade was often combined with that of carpenter in smaller villages. Ledgers suggest that the wheelwright normally undertook a wide range of work, including the manufacture and repair of wood beam ploughs and other implements, millwrighting, and a variety of domestic work. Far more of his time was devoted to the repair and repainting of carts and wagons than to the building of new ones. A wagon had a life span of perhaps a hundred years, replacement was infrequent, and manufacture may have been concentrated in the hands of a few specialist firms in each locality.

One example of these was the wheelwright's business in the market town of Farnham in Surrey taken over in 1810 by George Sturt's grandfather, who had learnt his trade in London. When Sturt commenced work there in 1884, his customers were still 'farmers rarely more than five miles away; millers, brewers, a local grocer and builder or timber merchant or hop-grower' and the business was still unmodernised. Its equipment included a hand drill, a hand lathe, a saw pit, a strake oven and tyring furnace, and a smithy. At about the same time, the range of its work narrowed as the manufacture of wooden ploughs and harrows was discontinued. About 1889, Sturt installed modern machinery—a gas engine powering saws, a lathe, drill and grindstone—and with this equipment the firm survived into the automobile age, undergoing a transition to a 'coach and motor works'. The market of such country town wheelwrights as Sturt of Farnham, and Humphries & Sons' Wagon Works at Chippenham in Wiltshire was further diminished by the output of larger concerns like the Bristol Wagon and Carriage Works. And the falling acreage of arable crops in the last quarter of the nineteenth century lessened the demand for a vehicle principally used to carry the harvest.

The manufacture of wooden ploughs was often part of the wheelwright's work. One craftsman who specialised as a plough-wright was Alec Walter of

Shalbourne in Wiltshire. He started work as soon as he left school in 1899 at the age of thirteen, by helping a carpenter and wheelwright. At nineteen, he had evidently decided to specialise in the repair of wood beam ploughs. There were enough of these still remaining in central southern England to keep him busy. The manufacture of complete wooden ploughs had ceased with the widespread use of factory made iron ploughs. Once, much to his dismay, Walter was requested to construct two new wooden ploughs for use on an exceptionally waterlogged soil and had to obtain disused patterns from a timber merchant: 'I did not know what to say, I think I would rather have had the sack.' Farmers treated their ploughs very badly, Walter observed, leaving them out under a hedge and neglecting to clean them after use: 'I think that the plough most allways had a very rough time.'

Millwrighting was not always practised as a separate trade, and village wheelwrights and carpenters like Rose could re-cog mill gear wheels and make windmill sails. In the late eighteenth century, millwrights had developed a general engineering function; they designed and improved all types of mill, and constructed horse gears and the early fixed threshing machines. This tendency was checked by the rise of foundries, and local agricultural engineering firms began to undertake the maintenance of the cast ironwork that was installed in many mills and the later, factory-made threshing machines. The millwrights who continued to practise their profession had to confine their activities to the surviving wind and water mills of traditional design.

The best mill-stones used for grinding wheat were the imported French burrs. The most important English stones, 'greys', were quarried from the millstone grit of the Peak and Pennines. The stones were cut out and shaped on site for transport out of the upland in carts. The quantity of abandoned stones, including a number only half cut from the rock on the edges outside Sheffield, suggests the sudden collapse of this industry. The periodic dressing of the stones with the mill bill—for the constant grinding wore away the channels in which the flour ran from the centre to the outside of the stone—was undertaken by millwrights or a travelling stone dresser if not by the miller himself.

The saddler and harness maker was more likely to be found, at least after 1850, in larger villages and market towns than in the smaller settlements. Making and repairing the three basic types of draught harness, the shaft and trace harness of the cart horse, and the plough harness, was the most important function of the village worker. The harness and collar maker

Left: sewing leather harness by hand. *Above:* cart harness on display outside the premises of Edward Seymour & Sons, saddlers and harness makers of Minster Street, Reading, Berkshire.

Above: D. Harrison, blacksmith, of Shenstone, near Lichfield, Staffordshire, and some of the men who worked for him. The collection of scrap ironwork and implements awaiting repair is typical of the general smith's business. *Right:* interior of smith's forge at Waterlane, Oakridge, Gloucestershire.

worked with several materials besides leather—metal buckles, hames, hooks, chains and bits, the wooden frame of the cart saddle and the straw stuffing, flock padding and woollen cloth lining of the collar. The harness of draught horse teams needed continual repair, and William Henman called on the services of the Islip saddler, James Webb, every few days for the relining of collars and replacement of cart saddles, cruppers and breechings, as well as the repair of a gig harness or riding saddle made by a town craftsman.

The blacksmith, like the wheelwright and carpenter, provided an essential service for every rural community. He was a worker in wrought iron, and a wide range of agricultural, industrial and domestic items came within his province. The dual nature of his work was frequently indicated by the inscription on signs or billheads: 'shoeing and general smith' or 'smith and farrier'. The ledgers of the Hedges family of Bucklebury, Berkshire, which, untypically, held the business for three hundred years, indicate the range of work undertaken by John Hedges during the period 1736-73: shoeing, the sharpening of wrought iron plough shares and coulters, the sale of new shares and nails, the manufacture and repair of all types of hand tool, including edge tool making, and the repair of cart, wagon and harness ironwork, domestic utensils, locks and guns.

As a farrier, Hedges undertook the veterinary care of horses and was active as a carrier of coal, bar iron, firewood, peat and bricks, both on his own behalf and for others. The ledgers indicate the work of an enterprising blacksmith's business at possibly its fullest extent. A hundred years later, there had been some narrowing of the range of activities—metal was more commonly available, and items would more often be replaced than endlessly repaired. The wrought iron ploughshare was supplanted by the cast iron factory-made product. The chilled self-sharpening edge, patented by Robert Ransome for the cast iron share in 1803, eliminated the necessity for the constant repointing which had been one of the rural smith's commonest tasks. Hand tools were manufactured by specialist firms, although some smiths still possessed a reputation for a locally esteemed hoe or mill bill.

It was in his role as a metal worker that the smith found new opportunities. The mechanisation of British agriculture after 1840 introduced a wide range of implements and machines requiring frequent attention: the replacement of wearing parts, the repair of cultivator tines and drill coulters, and the sharpening of mower knives. Some smiths specialised as machinists, and in time the new profession of village engineer developed.

A jointly run smith and wheelwright's business is described in the re-miniscences of the wrought iron craftsman, Victor Schafer, who was brought up at Ashtead in Surrey, where the Wyatt brothers ran the Forge at the turn of the century, John being the blacksmith and James the wheelwright:

'They were the last link in a continuous chain spanning the whole era of horses and carts. Their fathers made the carts which were used to build the railway, and their neighbours in Leatherhead made four-in-hand coaches for export to America within living memory.'

The yard at Ashtead contained the tyring furnace and plate, 'the inevitable heaps of scrap iron and timber', the traditional chestnut tree and a miller's wagon propped up on chocks underneath it: 'James said that the tree had been planted and the waggon built by his father, about the time that he himself was born.' Apparently, miller's wagons had been a speciality and had been sent all over South East England as far as Portsmouth. Around the yard were the forge, with three hearths, and the shoeing room, the thatched wheelwright's shop, containing a hand operated lathe, and beyond this a shed, housing two grindstones—a large one for garden shears and a narrow one for spoke shave irons, a drilling machine, and a treadle lathe for turning the stocks of barrow wheels. Two adjoining buildings were a timber store and an engine shed with an antique Crossley gas engine, driving a big lathe for wheel stocks, a band saw for felloes, a circular saw, and a grinder for mower knives. In the paint shop were stored the keg of white lead paint and the dry colours that were mixed with it:

'People had been wiping their brushes on the door of this cupboard for generations, with the result that it had become incrusted with paint to a depth of about four inches in the middle, and when you opened it you could feel that it weighed pounds and pounds.'

There were four regular employees: a wheelwright's assistant, a cousin who did tinkering and plumbing work in the neighbourhood, and two farriers who worked from six to six 'with a wash in the hot water from their tue irons before going home'. The tue iron was the pipe directing the hot blast into the furnace. Cooling water, which circulated between a jacket surrounding the tue iron and a tank, was useful as washing water at the end of the day.

Although some new equipment has been installed, the routine of work appears to have changed little. Again there is the implication that repair has largely superseded manufacture, for the miller's wagons are no longer made. References here and in other blacksmiths' accounts indicate that tinkering work was often carried out by the blacksmith. Tinsmiths—or whitesmiths, as they were also known—were sometimes found in towns, and country people would have been familiar with the itinerant tinkers.

Iron foundries for working pig iron were established in some villages and most market towns at the beginning of the nineteenth century. Such a foundry, with two cupola furnaces, was installed by Hedges of Bucklebury next to the blacksmith's shop, in about 1820. Unlike wrought ironwork, which required a separate operation to produce each forging, founding could produce a quantity of identical items: wheels and cogs for mills, cooking vessels, drinking troughs, railings and plough shares. As all foundries would also undertake forging, they came to adopt the more general title of ironworks, taking over much of the engineering work of blacksmiths and millwrights.

F.W. Moore has left an account of the Park Iron Works at Kingsley, in North East Hampshire, during the period 1895-1910. His father, William Moore, is described in the 1890 directory as an 'engineer, iron and brass founder, agricultural machinist, smith and wheelwright', indicating the comprehensive range of functions that the business, established as a foundry in the 1840s, had come to acquire in this village. Clay furnace lining was dug close to the foundry, moulding sand was obtained from a nearby common, and limestone from chalk pits at Froyle, near Alton. The charcoal added to the moulding sand came from local burners, whereas coke and pig iron were bought in from the Midlands. Scrap iron was purchased at auction, from travelling dealers, and from local farmers with old machinery to dispose of. The foundry produced gear wheels, plough shares, drag shoes for horse-drawn vehicles, plough wheels, cart axles, the castings for cooking ranges, and firebars for brick and lime kilns. It no longer made the heavy castings for the wheels and shafts of local corn and paper mills. New wagons were still being constructed at the turn of the century, but the production of other implements had ceased, and the firm now acted as agents for the larger agricultural engineering companies.

Another village engineering firm, Reeves of Bratton, in Wiltshire, had acquired a national reputation for drills and elevators, although output was never large. The Bratton Ironworks prospered because of its wide range of products, and through the sale of other manufacturers' equipment. It had developed from a blacksmith's shop established by Robert Reeves, a new-comer to the village, in the 1770s. The carpentry and implement making side of the business developed, and a foundry was established about 1820. The change from wooden to iron plough manufacture took place in 1846-47. In the period 1850-70, Reeves had to use outside labour from the Midlands, Wales and Ireland. Yet it still continued to serve the local community, as Marjorie Reeves notes:

'They attended to pumps and wells, put in water supplies and heating apparatus, built greenhouses, soldered kettles and pans, and made almost any piece of domestic equipment to specification, even cages for parrots. They made coffins for the village and acted as undertakers.'

The village engineering firm of W.H. Pool in Chipstable, Somerset, was started as a blacksmith's and wheelwright's business in 1847 and later commenced manufacture of agricultural implements on its own account. At the end of the century, it developed a range of oil engines, although the castings were supplied to order. A.J. Pool, who died in 1957 at the age of 93, was one of the two sons of the firm's founder. He kept a diary for 1889, which shows that most of his long days were equally divided between farming and helping in the family firm. After a morning of hurdle making or hauling wood from the coppice, feeding the bullocks, chaff cutting, threshing and winnowing in the barn, haymaking or ricking straw (as the season dictated), Pool would put in an afternoon helping in the manufacture of seed drills or sawing board into planks, grinding paint, repairing a reaper, mending a clock or making a coffin for a local farmer. Thus, on 26th July 1889, he rose at 5.30 a.m.:

'Down in the shop making a frame for Mr Bennett then up about his window home and turned all the sheep down to Bulland to have them dipped finished dipping at 11.15—home and went helping about hay machine till dinner time. PM—down in court helping to cut out timber for A Capels wagon—in the evening we went up and caught 3 rabbits.'

Sometimes Pool would travel out to a nearby farm to repair a threshing machine or horse gear, and he spent the best part of three weeks at the end of the year working on a water mill. He replaced the waterwheel chute and overhauled and tested grinding and chaff cutting machinery and a threshing machine apparently installed in the mill. Pool was considerably occupied in cartage, collecting lime for his fields and ale for his harvest workers from nearby Wiveliscombe, coal from Vernon Cross station, bricks from Croford, supplies from Taunton, and loads of faggots from his coppice. Farmer, woodman, carrier, engineer and millwright, Pool recorded his occupation in one directory entry as 'photographic artist'. Clearly, this versatile and practical man found hard work conducive to the entertainment of new ideas. One diary entry reads: 'whilst plowing I conceived an idea of a scarecrow which was to have a row of barrels...'

The numbers engaged in manufacturing activity in the countryside must have reached their peak soon after 1800. Subsequently, the industrial role of the rural districts diminished in importance against that of the cities, and the countryside became more purely the province of agriculture. The extremely rapid growth of towns and cities in the first half of the nineteenth century

The twentieth century myth of the craftsman. A postcard showing George William Lailey, the bowl turner, at his pole lathe. The primitive hut at Bucklebury Common, Berkshire, became a place of pilgrimage after the Great War following the publicity given to Lailey in newspapers and by H.V. Morton.

Photograph by A.J. Pool of Robert Burge, presumably one of the limeburners with whom he did business

had been fuelled by continuous migration from the country areas, themselves undergoing a massive population increase. By mid century, many rural communities had reached and even passed their peak number of inhabitants and, in the period 1861-1911, the numbers employed in agriculture declined from about a quarter to about a tenth of the male working population. J.D. Saville has provided figures for the county of Rutland, showing the falling numbers of rural craftsmen between 1851 and 1911: wheelwrights from 74 to 40, saddlers from 31 to 24, blacksmiths from 116 to 83, millers from 63 to 22, sawyers from 33 to 10, and shoemakers from 236 to 138. The decline is partly explained by the migration of these craftsmen to market towns. By 1914, however, the servicing trades still had a few decades left in which to perform their supporting role for rural communities dependent on relatively unsophisticated implements and machines, and upon the agricultural draught horse whose peak number of just under a million was not reached until 1910-11.

The decay and near-extinction of certain rural manufacturing industries is demonstrated by the dramatic fall in the numbers engaged in them. The 10,054 women in Bedfordshire and 8,753 in Hertfordshire recorded as employed in straw plait manufacture in 1851 had declined to 65 and 61 respectively in 1911. Another domestic industry of the South Midlands where there had been a continuous decrease in female employment was pillow lace making in Buckinghamshire and Northamptonshire, employing in 1911 only 373 and 219 women respectively against the 10,487 and 10,322 of 1851. By contrast, the lace factories of Nottinghamshire employed 18,109 women and 8,487 men in 1911. In the case of the non-ferrous metal mining of upland England and Wales, employment opportunities had largely been lost to the overseas countries to which many British miners had emigrated after the collapse of prices in the 1880s. The number of lead miners had fallen from 20,030 in 1851 to 2,968 in 1911, of copper miners from 18,449 to 279, with a decline of 70% in the single decade 1881-91, and of tin miners from 12,911 to 7,125. The growth in the number of coal miners in the same period was almost 700,000.

Contemporary observers like J.L. Green quoted many examples of industrial decay, but few effective remedies were forthcoming. Green sets before us a number of idealised labourers' families, apparently longing to take up a home industry and work with their hands in their 'spare time'. 'If only something like that could be done for us labourers, it would be a godsend.' All of Green's solutions have in common the element of imposition from above, whether a class on chip carving undertaken by Miss C. Hayward of Quedgeley, or the establishment of a dye works in Norfolk. There is talk of fretwork and brass repoussé work, of Bavarian wooden toy makers, of the establishment of 'rural jam and pickle manufactories' and of the decentralisation of industry. With the exception of wrought ironwork by rural smiths, attempts to revive rural industries through decorative arts and crafts have failed to benefit rural workers, being generally divorced from the economic reality of their lives. The association with the Arts & Crafts movement has, however, coloured the popular view of what was to become known as the 'rural crafts' ever since.

Rural industries, in their prime, manufactured identical products (with a functional rather than a decorative purpose) by the thousand, and young men regarded the work as routine employment rather than as a sacred calling, and left it when prospects were better elsewhere. Eventually, only a handful of elderly practitioners were left: what had been simple economic activity became mythologised into arcane mysteries practised by an elite few. Romantic images were created by writers, and reinforced by photographers, of aged craftsmen shaping wood in village workshop and sylvan setting. George William Lailey, the Bucklebury bowl turner, was a popular model for this myth. His existing reputation was considerably enhanced by H.V. Morton in his book, *In Search of England* (1927):

'His cheeks were red, and his healthy country face was shaded by a floppy green hat... he was—I looked at his hands—a craftsman... His father taught him to make "treen", and his grandfather taught his father; and so it went back to goodness knows where...'

The idea spread that the rural trades were somehow fixed and immutable, ancient secrets handed down from generation to generation—this was misleading. Bowl turning, for example, was almost casually undertaken and probably occupied no more generations of the Lailey family than carpentry had done of the Rose family. The principal recorded occupation of Lailey's grandfather, George, at the time of George William's birth, was landlord of the 'Old Boot' public house; his father, William, was a farmer. The bowl turner appears to have been for them a by-employment which they combined with the exercise of their commoners' rights on Bucklebury Common. Only George William, the last bowl turner, practised the craft as a sole means of livelihood until his death in 1958 at the age of 89.

It was perhaps inevitable that these last survivors should have inspired so much sentiment. Now that they are gone, we can look back more dispassionately and investigate rural industry, not as a static phenomenon practised by isolated individuals, but as part of a society that was undergoing constant change. In her history of the village of Aldbourne in Wiltshire, Ida Gandy (1975) provides us with a salutary reminder of the dynamic quality of rural industry. Aldbourne's seventeenth-century bell foundry ceased to exist in 1826, when the business passed to Mears of Whitechapel. Its eighteenth-century fustian trade, and the straw plaiting and hat making taken on about 1800, died out soon after 1850. From the late 1840s, willow bonnet making and chair making provided alternative occupations which lasted into the present century. Clearly this was no fixed community of hereditary craftsmen but a mobile and open society, receptive to new opportunities for enterprise when old ones failed.

By 1900, many of these communities were losing their self-sufficiency, and new trades ceased to be adopted. Village men and women now found their opportunities in shops and factories, and in domestic service in the towns. The industries which survived into the new century were declining in vitality. Their products were more cheaply made in factories or imported from abroad. The substitution of new materials for older ones, of inorganic for organic, of iron for wood, of machines for hand tools, of steam power for water and animal power all favoured urban industry against rural. The railway network allowed the distribution of branded and well-advertised goods.

In the main, the rural areas have reverted to the primary production of raw materials, sending their softwood timber and the products of agriculture to the urban centres for processing, distribution and consumption. The countryside no longer earns a significant part of its living by turning its own natural products into goods for the cities.

Water, Road and Rail

By 1850, twenty-five years had elapsed since the opening of the Stockton and Darlington Railway had ushered in the era of public railways. During those years, some 6,000 miles of railway had been opened in Great Britain, sufficient to form something of a national network, with most of the major towns and cities having rail connection by 1850. The next sixty years saw the completion of the trunk routes and the building of cross-country links and numerous branch lines. By 1912, there was a railway network of 23,000 miles. It was a dense system, but unevenly distributed. Lines were congregated around the West Riding towns and the coalfields of Nottinghamshire and Derbyshire, for example, while many parts of rural Northumberland, Lincolnshire and Dorset were some distance from a railway station. Despite this, there was scarcely anywhere in the country where the influence of the railway was not felt. In rural England, it showed first in a reduced flow of through traffic on the roads and waterways. The railway also became the major means of meeting the needs for long-distance transport in the countryside, both for taking away the produce of agriculture and for bringing in fuel and industrial goods. But despite a great profusion of branch lines, railways could not handle all the local transport requirements, and there was an increase in the number of horses, wagons, carts and vans making local trips to the railway station or market town.

By 1850, then, competition from the railways meant that long distance traffic by road and waterway had already entered upon a decline, more or less rapid. Traditionally, the main means of long-distance transport was by water, both coastal shipping and inland waterway. This was simply because transport was so much cheaper by water than by road. Costs of carriage by road were generally three to five times those of water transport, and boats and barges could handle loads in greater bulk than road wagons could manage. Before the railways came, water transport was invaluable to the rural economy in providing the principal means of carrying agricultural produce to distant markets. Vast quantities of grain, wool, hides, cheese and

The opening of the Lambourn Valley Railway, Berkshire, in 1898.

butter were conveyed along inland waterways and round the coasts to reach the main consuming centres, such as London, Newcastle, Bristol, Liverpool and Manchester. Almost every navigable river, from the greatest, the Thames, Severn and Trent, to the smallest, such as the Larke in Suffolk, was used to convey agricultural produce. The traffic was especially great in the southern and eastern parts of the country. The grain surpluses of East Anglia were taken by barge from the granaries, mills and malthouses along the navigable rivers, such as the Yare and the Stour, to the ports, where they were trans-shipped into coastal vessels and taken to London, Liverpool or Newcastle. Yarmouth was the greatest of these ports. In 1840, nearly 200,000 quarters of barley and 43,000 quarters of wheat were shipped out of the port, as well as 94,000 quarters of flour and 78,000 of malt. Similarly, the Kentish hoys brought grain, hops and wool into London from ports such as Sandwich and Whitstable, and vessels plied from southern ports, such as Chichester and Weymouth. Grain from Berkshire and Wiltshire, and cheese from Gloucestershire came down the Thames to London. As well as farm produce, the output of some of the rural industries was sent to distant markets by waterway. The products of many of the wood-using trades of southern England were transported to London by this means. There was likewise a considerable flow of goods into the countryside. Coal, timber and agricultural inputs, such as lime, were among the principal commodities, but household goods, groceries and products of the first factories would also reach the shops of the market town by means of water transport. Passenger traffic on the waterways was slight, but there were some boats which plied, for example, along the Thames from Kent to London, and along the River Witham from Boston to Lincoln.

Although most canals were promoted to transport coal and industrial goods, they did provide valuable facilities for rural transport. Indeed, several of the northern canal companies found the traffic in grain, flour and malt from Nottinghamshire, Lincolnshire and Yorkshire to north western England to be one of the more constant parts of their trade, and substantial enough to be well worth competing for. Mills and malthouses were built alongside canals, such as the Chesterfield at Retford. Some of the canals of the South and Midlands provided valuable links for rural areas. The Oxford Canal, for example, enabled grain from the Thames valley to be taken to Birmingham and Manchester, and coal to be brought south. The Kennet and Avon Canal meant that the millers of Newbury could more readily supply flour to Bristol, and Somersetshire coal and building materials were more freely available in Berkshire towns. But the limited attractions of

Despite competition from the railways, coastal shipping continued to play an important role in the transportation of rural produce. *Left:* grain wharves at Barnstaple, Devon, used by Berry & Sons, millers, at the beginning of this century. *Above:* steamboat on the Bude canal, Cornwall, about 1860.

purely rural trade to canal promoters can be seen from the small number of canals which were built in southern England, even allowing for the greater availability of navigable rivers there.

By 1850, water transport was facing strong competition from the railways, for whom the bulk loads of grain and coal were very attractive freights to be won. The railways set out to gain the traffic by fiercely undercutting the rates charged for carriage by water. In the early 1840s, 10s.10d. per last was the rate charged by the railways for carrying grain from Norwich to London, compared with £1.6s.10d. by coastal vessel. Traffic did not immediately desert the waterways. Wharves and dockyard facilities were often too conveniently placed for traders to abandon them overnight, but over the years traffic slipped away. By the early 1850s, the railways into East Anglia, which had been constructed during the 1840s, had won the major part of the grain traffic to London.

'The point at which the tide of prosperity receded from our port was evidently in 1848', reported the Yarmouth correspondent of the *Norwich Mercury* in 1852. 'The first and chief cause was the transfer of a large portion of the coasting trade of this port to the railway... which has annihilated nearly two-thirds of the grain trade alone of this port.' Declining revenue and traffic forced many river navigation and canal companies to close or to be sold to the railway companies, under whose management the canals were left with small amounts of mainly local traffic. But, greatly diminished though it was, water transport continued to play a role in rural trade. Coal was still brought by sea from Newcastle to east-coast ports. Where facilities were especially suitable, inland waterways could hold their own. This was so of the trade of Ware in Hertfordshire. This little town at the head of the navigable River Lea had for centuries been the centre for milling and malting the grain of the surrounding countryside for the London market. Until 1914, much of this trade continued to go by barge direct from riverside maltings in Ware to the Thames-side breweries in London. However, examples such as this were exceptions in a period of railway predominance.

Long-distance road transport also succumbed quickly to the power of the railways. This was perhaps most dramatically demonstrated in the rapid decline of stage coach services. The stage coach had come to the fore during the last decades of the eighteenth century, stimulated by developments

Canal families and their boats on the Grand Junction Canal.

which enabled coach operators to offer a fast and efficient service. A new network of roads had been built up by improving existing roads and constructing new ones. This network was controlled by turnpike trusts, statutory bodies empowered to levy tolls on traffic in order to fund the maintenance of the roads. The standard of these roads was enhanced by the engineering skills of such men as Metcalf, Telford and Macadam, who constructed surfaces suitable for high speeds, and improvements in the construction of coaches made the ride more comfortable.

The period from 1820 to 1850 was the heyday of the stage coach. There were about 3,300 stage coaches and 700 Royal Mail coaches in operation during the 1830s, offering a wide range of regular services. Many operated on the trunk routes from London; in addition, there was a wealth of cross-country services, including short local routes, such as Pontefract to Knottingley, and Henley to Reading, journeys of five and eight miles respectively. For the country people, the stage coaches, with their stops at market towns, represented an important link with the outside world. Many country places had generous services: Hungerford, in Berkshire, a town of only 2,715 inhabitants in 1831, had a dozen coaches calling on their journeys between London and Bristol, although some, such as the Bristol-bound Royal Mail, calling at 3.45 a.m., were not most conveniently timed for the local population.

By 1850, however, all this was changing, for despite the heroic efforts of several operators, stage coaches could not compete with the railway in speed or in cost. The coaches running on routes that competed directly with the railway disappeared virtually overnight. Those that remained by the 1850s were traversing cross-country routes not covered by railways or were providing feeder services. In Suffolk, for example, there were coaches connecting Halesworth, Saxmundham and Woodbridge with their nearest railhead at Ipswich, and in Norfolk the *Union* coach from King's Lynn to Spalding provided a cross-country link between railway lines. But as the railway network expanded, these coaches, too, ceased to run. The effect of these changes on the life of some country towns was considerable. Hungerford, for example, lost its coaches and ceased to be the 'town of great thoroughfare' it had been known as in the directories, but at least it had a railway service. Others, such as Woburn in Bedfordshire, were not so lucky and rapidly became rural backwaters.

Before the coming of the railways, carriage by water was usually preferred to roads in the transport of goods to distant markets. In areas such as Cornwall, however, which were not so well endowed with waterways, road transport was important; and in parts of the Midlands and eastern England it might be necessary to carry produce long distances to a convenient waterway. Thus grain was brought to Ware from a wide area of Hertfordshire, Cambridgeshire and Essex to be taken forward to London by barges on the River Lea. Road transport was also used when speed was essential; in the early nineteenth century, fish was sent up to London from Yarmouth and Lowestoft in light fly vans.

The one form of agricultural produce which almost invariably travelled by road was livestock. Coastal shipping was also used, but the risks of losing stock on a long sea voyage were sufficiently high for most farmers and dealers to prefer land transport; the animals were entrusted to drovers who walked them to the various cattle markets and fairs where they were to be sold. Cattle reared in Wales were driven to the fattening grounds of midland

Drover and animals crossing the Eden Bridge at Carlisle. Although they were no longer driven long distances, animals walking in to market remained a common sight until the Great War.

and south-eastern England, and Scottish cattle came down to South Lincolnshire and Norfolk. Fat cattle and sheep were driven to London from the Midlands and East Anglia. Even geese marched up from Norfolk for London's Christmas markets. The traffic was extensive, and at times the animals formed a regular procession along the roads. In the early 1830s, about 182,000 sheep and 26,000 cattle each year had travelled the roads from South Lincolnshire to London in the hands of eighty six-drovers. In 1845 some 8,000 cattle and 46,500 sheep passed through the turnpike at Brandon in Suffolk on their way down one of the main routes from East Anglia to London. Besides the main turnpike roads, drovers often took their charges along the 'green roads', ancient trackways, such as the Hambleton drove road across the North Yorkshire Moors, or the Ridgeway through Wiltshire and Berkshire. There were no tolls to pay on these roads, no swift coaches to encounter, and the animals trod more easily on the unmetalled surfaces.

The carriage of livestock was quickly transferred to the railways. This was often more expensive than droving, but had the advantage of being much

Staff at Burnham station on the Somerset and Dorset Railway, one the principal rural lines, about 1890.

quicker—cattle could not be driven at much more than about two miles an hour; the journey from southern Scotland to Norfolk took a month or more. The train could accomplish that in a day or two, and the fact that stock arrived fresh without losing weight on the journey more than offset the higher railway charges. The change from droving to rail transport was piecemeal, as stretches of railways were completed; droving continued to be necessary on the routes not covered by railway until fairly late in the nineteenth century. Many of the railway routes out of Wales were not finished until the 1870s, for instance, and cattle were still being walked round some of the markets of the Midlands then. As the railway network expanded, the distance the cattle had to walk decreased; by the end of the century, droving was confined to short trips to market or railhead.

'No class of the community has received more benefit by the introduction of railways than the farmers.' Thus wrote a correspondent to the *Bury & Norwich Post* in September 1838. Certainly the railway brought the farmer closer to his markets and enabled him to cater more sensitively for their needs. Grain and livestock could be delivered to distant markets more quickly and more cheaply. Moreover, buyers could travel further to sales and markets, bringing with them the prospect of more profitable deals for the farmer. Many of the agricultural developments of the second half of the nineteenth century would have been impossible without the railway, in particular, the expansion of fruit, vegetable and dairy farming in areas remote from the main markets: fruit farming in the Vale of Evesham and Cambridgeshire, broccoli growing in Cornwall, brussels sprouts in Bedfordshire, and potatoes in Lincolnshire, for example. At harvest time for these crops, the railways took away vast quantities of produce, often organising special trains. In 1904 the largest potato farm in Lincolnshire sent out nearly 2,000 wagon-loads from Kirton station.

Perhaps the greatest development facilitated by the railways was the expansion of the liquid milk trade. The Great Eastern Railway was quick to encourage this trade, and by 1868 the company was bringing over 1,300,000 gallons annually into London. Similar developments took place to supply large towns all over the country. The milk platform with its consignment of

Left: Uffington station on the Great Western main line, at the junction with the branch to Faringdon. *Below:* two of the many types of wagons and carts available to farmers and traders, manufactured not by the local wheelwright but by the large firms like the Bristol Wagon and Carriage Works.

The Bristol Wagon and Carriage Works Company, Limited.   33

Milk Van for Station Work.

Crank Axle Cart.
FOR CARRYING SHEEP, PIGS, ETC.

Strawberries being loaded on to the train at Swanwick in Hampshire, with every available road vehicle pressed into service to cope. By the early twentieth century, produce that spoiled easily could now be marketed further afield.

churns became a familiar part of a great many country stations. At the beginning of the twentieth century, almost every station on the Great Western Railway between Maidenhead and Faringdon was served by two milk trains daily, taking the milk to London dairies and the biscuit bakeries at Reading.

The railway could bring further benefits to the farmer by bringing him much-needed supplies in greater abundance and at lower price. Fertilizers—both stable manure from the cities and artificial fertilizers—and imported livestock feeds, such as cotton cake, were delivered to country stations. The farmer's new implements, his Ransome's plough or Hornsby reaper, were also brought in by rail. Then, there were the deliveries of coal to fuel the engine which drove the threshing machine and chaff cutter. It is hardly surprising that farms close to the railway were rented at a premium, while those more than five miles from a station were regarded as isolated. Despite the great gains which railways could bring to agriculture, there were many farmers who remained suspicious of the new form of transport. They were slow to develop their farming to take advantage of the railway's ability to reach new markets, quick to complain of the company's service or charges.

Other rural traders and industries were brought closer to their markets by the railway. The fishermen of coastal villages had their catch sent swiftly to town. Agricultural engineering companies were able to build up national markets through rail transport. Large flour mills and malthouses were built in the grain growing districts; many of them still stand alongside country stations. In the period before World War I, rail-connected creameries were built in dairying counties. Along with this development came some concentration of trade. One large new mill could do the work of several small ones; the building of a new steam powered mill near the station at Hitchin in Hertfordshire, for example, led to the demise of several water and wind mills in neighbouring villages. Rural industries tended to move into the market towns where railway facilities were on the whole better.

The railways brought goods into the countryside. Perhaps the most important commodity was coal, which hitherto had been in short supply and expensive in areas distant from the coalfields. Places with direct water communication had been quite well supplied, but even a few miles' distance from the waterway added greatly to the cost of coal, putting it beyond the reach of most of the village population. The railways brought the price of coal down by about a third in most country districts, and made it accessible to an increasing number of people. All but the smallest of the wayside stations had a coal siding with the yards of two or three merchants. Coal could now be used more often for heating and cooking in the home, even by poorer members of the village, as well as in agriculture and industry: before the railways came, there were few steam powered corn mills, mainly because coal was so dear outside the mining districts.

All sorts of other goods were brought by rail from urban manufacturers. The farmer had long been able to buy his London-made pewterware or his Wedgwood pottery in the market town, but now other items began to follow; the village pub began to serve Bass or Worthington beer from Burton alongside the local brew, and the village shop could receive supplies of chocolate from Birmingham and soap from Port Sunlight. Many of the goods brought into the countryside competed with and undermined rural industries. George Sturt's wheelwright's shop gave up making the old wooden framed ploughs in the face of competition from the cast iron ploughs made by the large engineering firms, and many other rural trades, from soap boiling to leather working, diminished in the same way. This competition was brought right into the farmer's back yard when country butchers began to display New Zealand lamb, and the bakers obtained supplies of flour milled at Liverpool from Californian wheat. There were drawbacks as well as benefits attached to reduced isolation.

The railways, along with the police force and post office, offered employment in the country which was a better-paid alternative to farm work. Although the majority of country railwaymen who remained porters or platelayers throughout their careers can hardly be said to have had easier or more exciting work to do than farm labourers, their wages were a few shillings a week greater, and they had more security. Not surprisingly, quite a few rural labourers took up employment on the railway, but the railway's greater service to the people of the countryside lay in widening their horizons, through newspapers brought out from the towns, or through cheap excursions.

Although the railways took most of the long distance and through traffic away from the roads, local traffic still remained important. There were numerous trips to and from the railway station: the farmer's carts and wagons delivering milk churns or sacks of grain and picking up fertilizer; the coal merchant's wagon on its rounds; the railway company's delivery van. There were the journeys in and out of the market town, farmers going to market, traders delivering goods to the village. Changes in the pattern of rural trade, especially the bringing in of goods from outside and the increasing substitution of purchased bread and beer for that made at home, necessitated many more journeys by delivery vehicles. Indeed, they brought new types of vehicle on to the roads. As George Sturt noticed at his wheelwrighting trade, 'the break-down of village industries was introducing changes which were reflected in my shop in the shape of butchers' carts and bread-carts—unknown of old—and in brewers' drays and in millers' vans, not to mention vehicles for bricks and other building materials.'

While the farmer might ride into the market town, those in the village had to walk or use the services of the village carrier. The carriers provided some of the most valuable transport services in rural England, for they linked

Top: a Wiltshire knife-grinder and his donkey cart in the 1890s, and a butcher's cart, one of the new types of vehicle mentioned by George Sturt. *Above:* a farmer's wagon delivering produce to market. J.H. Knight was a hop farmer at Farnham, and also an inventor. He designed a steam-powered cultivator for his hop grounds, and built one of the first motor cars in this country in 1895. *Right:* a Sussex farm wagon.

country with town. Most carriers were based in the villages and operated regular advertised services into the market towns over fixed routes and with an established schedule. Most ran on market day and perhaps one or two other days in the week; there were some daily services into the largest towns, but these were uncommon. In addition to these regular activities, the carrier might be called upon for other work, perhaps an additional delivery of produce or a house removal.

The services provided by the carriers were varied. They took goods into town, ranging from parcels of linen sent from the great houses to be laundered, to bundles of skins for the tannery and sacks of flour for the baker. An important part of the carrier's load was produce to supply the needs of the townspeople: fruit, vegetables, butter, poultry and eggs were entrusted to the carrier to deliver to the shopkeepers in town. Some carriers took only goods, but most carried passengers as well.

The carrier's cart was usually a small vehicle, seldom drawn by more than one horse. The passenger-carrying capacity was therefore no more than ten or a dozen people. Even so, with the goods as well, the horse could have loads as great as two tons to pull. For the ascent of hills, the passengers would often be expected to get out and walk, or even to give the cart a push; if it was possible to arrange the route so as to avoid hills, this would be done. There are stories of carriers encountering bad weather who would, for the sake of the horse, abandon the cart for the night and walk home.

Most of the routes operated by carriers were short. Fifteen miles was about the limit for most services. There were some longer routes that provided links between market towns: for example, there was a carrier from Farnham to Reading, twenty-five miles distant, and another whose journey

to Reading from Alton in Hampshire covered more than thirty miles when detours to call at villages were taken into account. For the village carrier, fifteen miles represented the maximum distance that could be covered in an out-and-home journey in a day. For the pace was unhurried, with stops around the village and at farms to pick up passengers, parcels and orders. Arthur Randell, in his book *Sixty Years a Fenman*, recalled such features of the journey from Magdalen to King's Lynn in Norfolk and added, 'It took us three hours to do the seven miles journey so we usually reached Lynn just before mid-day and, after driving through Railway Road, Norfolk Street and High Street delivering orders, we pulled up at the Three Tuns where the mare was taken out of the shafts and given a feed and water while we went inside the pub to have our dinner.' After dinner, the carrier would go round the town collecting parcels for the return journey which would start at about three o'clock.

The networks of local country carriers' routes seem to have developed during the later eighteenth century, and far from being killed off by the railways, as were many of the long-distance routes, they remained a vital element in rural life until 1914. True, towns such as Faringdon in Berkshire, once the focus of several carriers' routes, lost many services as their economies declined. But such losses were more than offset by an expansion of carrier services into other market towns. There were 106 services into Guildford in 1854, for example, and 166 by 1914, while those into Reading increased from 205 in 1867 to 238 in 1895. After 1914, however, carrier services dwindled, unable to compete with motor buses.

The operations of the carriers were focused on market towns, and, although many served areas of the country which had no railway, they were

Two of the many varieties of wagon and van used by carriers.

Left: market wagons on the Bath road, 1898. *Below:* a very full load of chairs manufactured in the Chilterns destined for London.

Above: a gig—these light, two-wheeled vehicles were used by many of the better off in rural society, such as farmers, doctors and clergymen. *Right:* a wagonette outside Leeds Castle in Kent, about 1900. Wagonettes were popular with country households as general purpose passenger and luggage vehicles; larger versions were used as private omnibuses by country hotels.

not feeder services to the railway network. There were, however, attempts to establish services to complement the railways. The straightforward reaction from those in country areas without a railway was to build more branch lines, and as the costs mounted in relation to expected traffic, then light railways and tramways were canvassed. And indeed, a great many rural branch lines were built. Even in the 1850s, however, there were those who realised that the traffic on those branch lines was unlikely to be profitable, and alternative means of providing adequate transport for remoter rural areas were considered. One proposal of the 1860s was for a network of steam buses and lorries. Richard Tangye, one of the engineers who produced designs for such vehicles, explained the thinking behind the proposals in his autobiography:

'About 1862 the subject of providing "feeders" in country places for the main lines of railway came into prominence. Branch lines had been proved to be unremunerative from their great cost in construction; and amongst other systems proposed was that of light, quick speed locomotives for carrying passengers and traction engines for the conveyance of heavy produce and other goods. We determined to construct a locomotive of the former class, and succeeded in making a very successful example, with which we travelled many hundreds of miles. The carriage... when travelling at over twenty miles an hour... was easily managed and under perfect control.'

Left: a landaulet. Used as riding carriages by the gentry, light, one-horse landaulets were also used as station cabs. *Right:* Joice of Basingstoke, coachbuilders. Although some of the gentry bought their carriages in London, most rural passenger vehicles were built in the market towns.

Promising though the steam carriages were in performance, they ran into public opposition, especially from users of horse-drawn carriages. They had sufficient power to secure the passage of the Locomotive Act of 1865, which imposed speed restrictions on self-propelled vehicles through the famous provision that they were to be escorted by a man bearing a red flag. Tangye's

prototype was exported to the Middle East; the only steam vehicles on English country roads for the next thirty years were agricultural traction engines, steam rollers and the like—powerful, robust and reliable, but heavy and slow moving.

The aim of developing rural transport services, however, remained unfulfilled. There were some horse-drawn omnibus services, such as the one which had been running from Lambourn to Newbury in Berkshire from the mid 1870s. The bus ran on Monday, Thursday and Saturday at a single fare of 1s.6d. for the twelve-mile journey. Such services, however, were few. The Great Western Railway's timetable for 1902 listed just fifty 'conveyances' which connected with trains throughout the whole of the company's system. It was not until the early years of the twentieth century that rural bus services began to develop. Mechanised transport was now free of many of its legal restrictions, and motor buses were introduced on rural routes. Among the leading pioneers were the railway companies, who saw in buses an ideal means of providing cheap feeder services in areas that could not justify a branch line. The Great Western ran its first bus service in August 1903 from Helston to The Lizard in Cornwall and soon established itself as the main operator of railway buses. By 1908, the company owned more than a hundred motor buses which plied on about thirty routes. Many other railway

Traction engines. *Left:* one of the earliest models, a ten horse-power locomotive built by W. Tasker of Andover in 1869; a steersman is seated in front of the smoke box. Preceding the engine is a man with a red flag. *Above:* the final development—a compound road locomotive built by Marshalls of Gainsborough early in the twentieth century, shown hauling timber.

Opposite page. Top: the motor age reaches Long Handborough in Oxfordshire. *Left:* a motor bus that is effectively a motorised carrier's wagon, and a steam lorry used by a Hereford miller, about 1905. *Right:* car ownership in the early days of motoring was confined almost entirely to the wealthy. These photographs were taken before the law requiring motor vehicles to be registered came into force in 1903. The upper picture shows a White steam car outside Moraston House, Bridstow, Herefordshire, about 1900.

The local coach to Cirencester outside the Bull Hotel, Fairford, Gloucestershire, in the 1890s. The other vehicles are a dog cart and a private omnibus used for taking parties from the railway station to the hotel or country house. Note the bicycle on the inn sign.

110

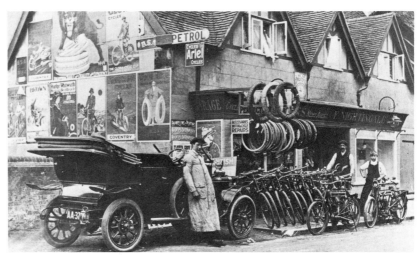

companies followed the Great Western into bus operation, though none on quite the same scale. Most notable among them were the Great Eastern and, with a service beginning just three weeks after the Great Western's, the North Eastern. By 1914, the railway companies and independent operators between them provided a number of motor bus services across the country, though the rural network was far from dense.

Other forms of mechanised transport came on to the roads following the change in the law in 1896. There were steam and petrol driven lorries and light vans for goods haulage. Again the railway companies were among the first to employ these in the country districts, but other traders of the market towns acquired modern mechanised delivery vehicles. Breweries especially found steam lorries and tractors economical for their local deliveries. Motor cars also began to appear on the roads during the 1890s. At first, their ownership was confined to the rich and enthusiastic. The first cars in the countryside, therefore, usually apeared at the great houses, the Duke of Portland, for example, possessing six cars and twelve chauffeurs. By 1914, however, car-ownership was passing down the social scale: there were about 130,000 cars on the roads of Great Britain, and the inexpensive models among them, such as the Morris Oxford and Model T Ford, were likely to be

Left. Above: the penny farthing bicycle, with its advantages in comfort and speed over earlier designs, made cycling very popular during the 1870s. *Below:* the Rover, designed by J.K. Starley in 1885, was the first commercially successful safety bicycle. *Right. Above:* the village baker at Corringham in Essex taking his family out in 1912. *Below:* cycle and motor dealer at Overton in Hampshire.

owned by some of the tradesmen and professional people of the rural areas. Cars were already sufficiently common in the country to prompt the beginnings of modern road surfacing with the laying of tar to prevent the dust clouds which followed in the wake of motor vehicles.

The importance of motor transport was clearly perceived by 1914. In his book, *Highways and Byways*, T.W. Wilkinson declared that the motor car 'has not only resuscitated the whole of our highway system, but strangled the railway monopoly which can never dominate the country again.' The full impact of motor transport, however, did not make itself felt until after the Great War.

Of greater importance to the bulk of the rural population before the Great War was the bicycle. Cycling began to gain popularity during the later 1860s with the development of the 'boneshaker', and during the next two decades became a very popular pastime, especially among the young and athletic who rode the large-wheeled 'ordinary' or 'penny-farthing' bicycles. The smaller, chain-driven safety bicycle was developed in the 1880s, together with the additional comfort provided by pneumatic tyres, invented in 1888. Cycling was a popular leisure pursuit for town dwellers who rode out on excursions into the country. Catering for them brought new opportunities for country business. The sign 'Beds for Cyclists' appeared outside rural inns, local bicycle dealers and repair shops came to the rescue of cyclists in distress. The dealer's main trade, though, was with the local population, for whom the bicycle proved a great boon. For the labourer, especially, a cheap, second-hand bicycle was a valuable acquisition. With it he could travel further afield for work, get into the market town independently of the carrier and even go for a joyride on a Sunday afternoon.

Itinerant sheep shearers leaving a completed job at a farm in Hampshire, about 1900.

In the Market Place

In the late eighteenth century, the range of manufactured domestic goods was still narrow and the demand for them restricted. The low incomes of the majority of the population made this inevitable. In the countryside, the greater part of the ordinary labourer's wages was spent on food. Skilled labourers and those living near to the competitive labour market of the larger towns in the North of England were better off, but they, too, had to practise the most careful housekeeping if wages were to be stretched to cover more than the bare essentials of living. Ordinary country people grew as much food as they could in cottage gardens or allotments; they made at least some of their own clothes and furniture, and made them to last. When they needed to buy something, they usually bought it close to home and often from local craftsmen. Their purchases included a few manufactures: chiefly hand tools, domestic utensils and personal bric-à-brac, slowly acquired out of savings— from the extra money earned, perhaps, at harvest time—or bought on credit. Further up the social scale, farmers and the rural professional classes made more use of the retail market, although their wives were still usually expected to understand the arts of making butter, cheese, preserves, and a good deal else, as well as dressmaking, within the household. Some might choose to adorn themselves and their homes from the more fashionable shops in the country town and nearby cities, but the long distance trade in luxury manufactures was still chiefly conducted with the 'quality'.

The countryside, then, remained self-sufficient to a considerable degree, even though before 1800, it was already being slowly brought within a national pattern of distribution, as the canal system was developed and roads improved. London was drawing cattle along the drove roads from as far away as the lowlands of Scotland to feed its growing populace. Wheat was sent from East Anglia to parts of the Midlands and the North in exchange for cattle and sheep. Manufactured goods, such as Wedgwood pottery, were sent by canal from the factory towns to the larger provincial centres. However, this long distance trading in corn and livestock, raw materials and manufactures did not extend to perishable goods. Flour spoilt easily if sent by water, and, as far as possible, was milled where it was wanted. Cows were kept by cow-keepers in urban dairies to provide fresh milk for city dwellers. Most towns still depended on their surrounding countryside for the purchase of supplies of all kinds, and the countryside still depended on the old forms of exchange—markets, fairs and itinerant peddling. Trading was carried out by large numbers of people engaged in small transactions. The day of the specialist distributor had not yet arrived.

Nonetheless, new forces acting within society were creating new needs and new ways of meeting them. By the first half of the nineteenth century, an enormous growth in population was swelling the demand for goods and services. Then the overall shift in population from South to North and from the countryside to the towns was producing a new working class of town dwellers living in rookeries or back-to-back housing, who were unable to grow their own food and were becoming increasingly dependent on the retail market for their supplies. Demand grew, too, with rising incomes—the result of an expanding economy. This stimulated both the middle class market, looking for choice and quality, and the larger and more stable working class market, looking for cheapness and reliability. Manufacturers' output soared to keep pace with this increase in demand. Improvements in technology brought a whole new range of consumer products, and the spread of the rail network meant that these could be distributed rapidly to all parts of the kingdom, although it led to a greater concentration of markets in a small number of larger centres. The freeing of trade also had its effect. For example, the cheap import of sugar not only encouraged its consumption and turned a luxury into a necessity for working class households, but brought into being new food-processing industries, such as jam and preserve making, which helped to transform the national diet.

The changes in the consumer goods industry and transport, however, required a retailing revolution to make use of them. The old methods, geared to the requirements of a predominantly rural society, were inadequate for the growing industrial society. Moreover, the sheer quantity of produce arriving at British ports from the 1870s was enough in itself to require a new approach to distribution and marketing. The last decades of the nineteenth century saw the acceleration of earlier trends: the growing distinction between wholesaling and retailing, the spread of new forms of retail organisation, and the acceptance of new techniques of advertisement and selling. These changes started in the towns, but steadily spread into rural areas, filtering down through the various strata of rural society, although the old, deep-rooted methods of retailing were by no means to vanish overnight.

In the first half of the nineteenth century, fairs, markets and itinerant traders still provided the chief means by which industrial goods reached the countryside. In the market towns, shops were growing in number, catering chiefly for middle class customers and as yet little patronised by the poorer country people, who could neither afford their wares nor fully understand the jargon of specialist traders. In the villages, shops were less common, except for an occasional chandler, butcher, victualler or general store, or,

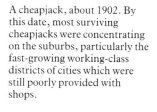

A cheapjack, about 1902. By this date, most surviving cheapjacks were concentrating on the suburbs, particularly the fast-growing working-class districts of cities which were still poorly provided with shops.

more commonly, a beer retailer. Most necessities were made by local crafts-men—the boot and shoe maker, the jobbing carpenter, the blacksmith or wheelwright. Itinerant pedlars or cheapjacks brought with them a wider range of goods.

The cheapjack or johnny was the most prosperous of the licensed haw-kers. He dealt in hardware and other small manufactured items, including crockery and cutlery, pots and pans, tinware, guns and tools, saddles, bridles, whips, watches, pocket knives and other personal impedimenta. Selling his goods from the tailboard of his wagon, the cheapjack made his way through the countryside between spring and autumn, working the local fairs and markets, and calling at the more prosperous villages. When winter made conditions too bad for travel, he stayed in town, where he might own a small lock-up shop or work a bazaar pitch in the market. David Alexander notes that the cheapjack was usually a self-made man who had accumulated a small stock of capital and possessed a shrewd business sense. He quotes Charles Hindley, who recalling his own experiences on the road, observed that 'a Man that travels as a Cheap John is thought nothing of as a master unless he has at least £100 worth of goods... a good horse, and a good carriage.' He would deal only in cash and was a first-rate salesman. The cheapjack who descended on Flora Thompson's Lark Rise one autumn evening flamboyantly set out his stock against 'a backcloth painted with icebergs and penguins and polar bears' and illuminated the scene with flaring naphtha lamps. He then invited his audience to buy such 'alarming bargains' as a tea-set, the fellow of which had been purchased by the Queen for Buckingham Palace, and a job lot of basins, exact replicas of the one the Princess of Wales supped her gruel from when Prince George was born'. The cheapjack got a very small return for his showmanship at Lark Rise and paid no second visit.

At a more humble level came the tinker, who travelled with his barrow, brazier and grindstone, and repaired many of the goods sold by the cheap-jack. Like the cheapjack's, the tinker's arrival was announced by some form of jangling noise or shouted rhyme:

> Any razors or scissors to grind?
> Or anything else in the tinker's line?
> Any old pots or kettles to mend...?

Then there was the pedlar and travelling packman. The pedlar dealt in enticing low-cost goods which he bought in bulk and broke down into the very small quantities that the poor could afford. He sold ribbons, threads, packets of pins and other items of haberdashery, matches, song sheets, and small novelties. Some packmen also sold 'dress-lengths and shirt-lengths and remnants to make up for the children; aprons and pinafores, plain and fancy; corduroys for the men, and coloured scarves and ribbons for Sunday wear'.

The more impoverished families, however, had difficulty in saving even the few shillings to buy things from the pedlar. For them, the tally trade offered a solution, based upon credit rather than cash payments. The Scotch draper travelled on foot, calling from house to house on a regular round, so that he could be paid in weekly or fortnightly instalments. He dealt particu-larly in cheap manufactured textiles, finding his customers in the early nineteenth century among the new factory and mining villages of the North. He was often accused of selling shoddy material at excessive prices and

James Moore, a pedlar from Wadebridge, Cornwall, early twentieth century.

Above: Shropshire tinker grinding knives. *Right:* Knife grinder, Warboys, Huntingdonshire. Both twentieth century.

tempting housewives to buy things they neither wanted nor could afford: nevertheless the system suited the needs of less well off families and was taken up in one form or another in many areas by the end of the nineteenth century. Flora Thompson recalled that, although no Johnny Fortnight or tallyman visited her part of Oxfordshire, a man who kept a small furniture shop did come round selling wares on the instalment plan.

'On his first visit to Lark Rise he got no order at all; but on his second one of the women, more daring than the rest, ordered a small wooden washstand and a zinc bath for washing day. Immediately washstands and zinc baths became the rage. None of the women could think how they managed to exist so long without a washstand in their bedroom.'

Few of them managed to keep up the fortnightly payments of one and six, which dropped to a shilling and then to sixpence, and some defaulted. Lark Rise, however, was a particularly poor hamlet, and enterprising salesmen could fare better elsewhere.

The itinerant trade in general was in decline by about the 1860s. Cheapjacks were never very numerous. Alexander has estimated that there were probably fewer than a thousand substantial cheapjacks in England in any year in the first half of the century. The more common figure was always the pedlar or petty hawker, who often took to the roads, not to make his fortune, but as a stopgap after being thrown out of work or failing in some previous occupation. In fact, itinerant retailing provided a valuable source of employment in the countryside, particularly at times when trade was depressed, and during the period when industrialisation was beginning to eliminate the more traditional forms of rural industry. Its future was strictly limited; the railways at first extended the range of the itinerant, but in the long run acted against him, since their coming meant, as Hindley noted, that wholesalers could 'despatch their representatives to all the principal towns for the purpose of supplying the shops with the very description of goods that Cheap Johns had almost a monopoly in...' and what applied to the elite of the itinerant trade applied to other classes as well.

As late as 1871, the decennial census recorded over 27,000 pedlars and hawkers. However, this figure is deceptively high as it includes the rapidly growing band of urban hucksters. As people moved out of the countryside, the hawkers followed, to ply their trade in the city suburbs, which were still inadequately provided with shops. There is no good statistical evidence to

Peddling family. The husband was a knife sharpener, and his wife was a pedlar. About 1905.

help us to follow the fortunes of rural peddling after 1871, but Flora Thompson's judgement may be regarded as a fair one:

'The packman, or pedlar, once a familiar figure in that part of the country, was seldom seen in the eighties. People had taken to buying their clothes at the shops in the market town, where fashions were newer and prices lower.'

Some survivors continued their solitary journeys into the new century, although increasingly they were reduced to selling novelties at local fairs and markets. Only the tinkers and knife grinders continued to carry out their useful occupations for some decades to come.

In the eighteenth century, the great regional fairs, held on set days in spring and autumn, had performed an important function. Local householders ders stocked up for the coming year, and wholesalers met their suppliers and retailers. Merchants from the larger towns met local itinerants to find an outlet for their goods in the countryside, and farmers arranged to sell their crops, stock and wool to urban factors. The largest of the traditional fairs was perhaps Sturbridge, held just outside Cambridge. It lasted for three weeks in August and September, and dealt in every sort of commodity. Such

Oxfordshire fairs. *Left:* Burford Fair. *Below:* horse fair at Bampton. Both early twentieth century.

fairs, however, were increasingly unable to provide the large and regular quantities of food needed by the growing industrial areas or to distribute the expanding range of manufactured goods that were coming on the market. The eclipse of the fairs started with the improvements in the road and canal systems and was completed by the development of the railways.

The more purely agricultural fair survived longer. The twice yearly livestock fairs continued to enable specialist rearers to sell lean stock to buyers from the grazing districts near the big towns. Thus the famous sheep fairs at Burford in Oxfordshire and at Weyhill in Hampshire retained their importance into the second half of the century, although the cattle fair at Barnet in Hertfordshire, which had drawn cattle from Scotland, Devon and Herefordshire, was already in decline. The new, improved breeds were less able to stand the rigours of droving than the old, and were increasingly shipped or sent by rail to London and the Midlands. In 1868, fifty miles was considered by J. Menzies to be the upper limit that cattle could be sent by road. By this time, only fairs situated near a railway line, such as the Horncastle horse fair or the cattle fair at Hereford, continued to attract stock and buyers in large numbers.

Below: pony sales in the New Forest, about 1905. *Below:* hiring fair at Burford.

119

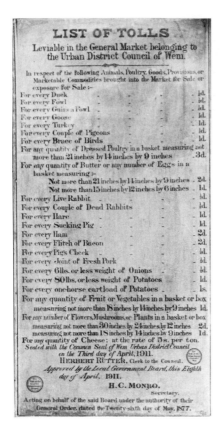

Hiring fairs, at which labourers and their families sought employment for the year or half-year, also endured into the twentieth century. These were always more important in the far North of England and Scotland than in the Midlands and South, where most of the labourers were hired by the week and paid in cash rather than partly in cash and partly in board. In the South, hiring fairs were held regularly in Dorset, and are described by Thomas Hardy in *Far from the Madding Crowd* and *The Mayor of Casterbridge*. In *The Dorsetshire Labourer*, Hardy comments that labour was still plentiful enough in the early 1880s for the farmer to have a choice and drive a hard bargain.

'To see the Dorset labourer at his worst and saddest time, he should be viewed when attending a wet hiring fair at Candlemas, in search of a new master. His natural cheerfulness bravely struggles against the weather and the incertitude; but as the day passes on, and his clothes get wet through, and he is still unhired, there does appear a factitiousness in the smile, which, with a self-repressing mannerliness hardly to be found among any other class, he yet has ready when he encounters and talks with friends who have been more fortunate.'

But thereafter labour was harder to come by, and the men did better. In a letter to Rider Haggard, dated 1902, Hardy observed that:

'I am told that at the annual hiring fair just past, the old positions were absolutely reversed, the farmers walking about importuning the labourers to come and be hired, instead of, as formerly, the labourers anxiously entreating the stolid farmers to take them on at any pittance.'

As literacy gained ground, labourers could make use of advertisements in the farming papers and would travel further afield to improve their position. Hiring fairs became obsolete in the South and continued only in the North, until they were finally suspended throughout the country in 1914 as part of wartime legislation.

Generally, though, by the second half of the nineteenth century the fair had become less a place of business than an occasion for entertainment. Fairs increasingly attracted, not businessmen, but all kinds of showmen—gingerbread sellers, Punch and Judy men, German bands, men with dancing bears, quacks and charlatans. This trend was apparent as early as 1849, when the *Norwich Mercury* noted of the great mart at King's Lynn:

'In days of yore this mart was considered one of the largest trading fairs... and was the resort of traders from all parts of the kingdom, who supplied the inhabitants far and near with every description of goods, useful and ornamental, but of late years its trading character has sunk into comparative insignificance and it is now nothing more than a pleasure fair.'

The decline went so far that in 1871 the Fairs Act empowered local authorities to abolish fairs which no longer performed a commercial function—and this signalled the end of one form of traditonal retailing.

Markets, however, retained much of their importance; their frequency—once or twice a week—allowed large quantities of produce to be exchanged between town and country, at comparatively low cost, conveniently for both buyer and seller. At the beginning of Victoria's reign, William Howitt in *The Rural Life of England* observed the great concourse of people who made their way each week to the market town from outlying districts:

'There are few things which give one such a feeling of the prosperity of the country, as seeing the country people pour into a large town on market-day. There they come, streaming along all the roads that lead to it from the wide country road. The footpaths are filled with a handy and homely succession of pedestrians, men and women, with their baskets on their arms, containing their butter, eggs, apples, mushrooms, walnuts, nuts, elderberries, blackberries, bundles of herbs, young pigeons, fowls or whatever happens to be in season... The carriage road is equally alive with people riding and driving along; farmers and country clergymen, parish overseers, and various other personages, drawn to the market town by some real or imagined business, are rattling forward on horseback, or in carriages of various kinds. There are carriers' wagons, and covered carts without end, many of them shewing from their open fronts, whole troops of women snugly seated.'

Indeed, the market town played a central role in the lives of country dwellers throughout the century; it not only supported its own inhabitants but also the economy and well-being of surrounding villages. Much of the commerce of the countryside was channelled through the market town, since here were to be found many of the rural trades and industries, the professional occupations and, above all, a whole range of wholesale and retail services.

Market towns varied greatly in size, origin and marketing function. They included large county towns such as Lincoln, Northampton or Norwich, typical market towns of moderate size such as Richmond or Banbury and much smaller places which passed muster as towns only by virtue of their possession of a weekly market. Most markets and fairs were of medieval foundation and had been established by royal charter, although a considerable number had come into being illicitly and gained squatters' rights over time. The right to hold a market might be awarded to either private individuals or corporate bodies and this remained the pattern of ownership to 1914. From the 1840s, however, a process of municipalisation took place as local authorities gradually acquired market rights using powers given them in legislation.

Any town might hold a number of different markets, often on the same day. The general market dealt in a wide range of commodities, including locally-made ware as well as cheap manufactured goods, and combined elements of retailing and wholesale trading. Then there were the wholesale markets dealing in agricultural produce. Most towns had their own corn and livestock markets and some held special markets—perhaps for poultry, wool, or leather—or were famous for their fairs; for instance Weyhill near Andover continued to hold a hop fair until 1888.

Corn markets, where farmers sold to corn merchants, millers and maltsters, were usually held once a week. They were all organised in essentially the same way, although some traded in wheat and some in barley. If the farmer took his handfuls of grain to the sample market, the bargain was struck on the quality of the sample, and the bulk of the produce delivered direct from the farm to the merchant's granary. If, on the other hand, the farmer went to the pitched market he took his full wagon-load of grain with him, and one or two sacks were pitched into the market place for the dealers to inspect. Almost invariably, trading was confined to the morning before the market ordinary dinner served by local inns at one o'clock.

Traditionally, corn markets were held in the open market place, in the yard of an inn or under the arcades of a market hall. In the mid nineteenth century, however, almost every town with a flourishing market built a corn exchange with ample covered accommodation for the traders. Stamford's, erected in 1839, was among the earliest; most were completed by the 1870s. With the onset of depression, business was, in any case, much reduced and there was less need for corn exchanges. In areas where pastoral farming predominated, the grain trade was often diminished to a trickle, and in the great corn markets of the eastern counties annual turnover sometimes slumped to half that of the mid century. Even the market ordinary was not what it had been. One 'stalwart old farmer of the old school', giving evidence before the Royal Commission set up to investigate the extent of distress in the mid 1890s, commented that one effect of the agricultural depression was

Left: street market in Castle Street, Farnham, Surrey.
Below: Wisbech market place, Cambridgeshire, about 1900.

to 'make the farmer hasten to catch early trains instead of remaining for the afternoon to open port wines...'

The trade in livestock was very different. There was a much greater variety of produce and market specialisation, with separate markets being held for sheep, cattle and horses, and sometimes for fatstock and leanstock. But here, too, improvements were being made in market accommodation and facilities. Many markets which had long been held in the streets or market places were moved to new, larger sites, often on the outskirts of towns near the railway, with the result that livestock no longer needed to pass through the streets to the centre. Slaughterhouses often became part of the market complex; the carcase trade had increased with the extension of the rail network.

During the depression years, some livestock markets—that for lowland sheep, for example—suffered, but others were little affected. In fact, new markets were being established at this time—by local authorities, like the cattle market at the new settlement at Crewe, and by private companies of auctioneers. Auctioneering was a small trade before 1845 and was subject to taxation, but grew rapidly during the later nineteenth century to become one of the chief means of selling agricultural produce. Many auctioneers set up their own auction marts for livestock—in established markets, in places without a market, and directly off the farm. Sales from the farm, particularly favoured by breeders of pedigree stock, became more widely popular, especially after the coming of the motor lorry.

The development of motorised road transport, however, lies at the end of this period, when improvements in water and land transport, and the spread of the railway system, had already transformed many market towns. The railways in particular vastly accelerated the break-up of the interdependence between the market town and its surrounding countryside. As the urban population and demand for foodstuffs increased in the mid century, farmers adapted their farming systems to meet this need, and the volume of long distance rail traffic in agricultural commodities expanded rapidly. By the 1840s, a greater number of farmers were able to market their produce nationally, some by using a local market as the first stage in the route to industrial towns and cities, and others by forward contracting directly with urban merchants. A significant proportion of foodstuffs, therefore, avoided the market town altogether; this applied to the corn and livestock rearing sectors and, most importantly, to the profitable milk trade after 1880. Moreover, the railways not only took some foodstuffs out of the locality, they also brought other foodstuffs into it. The growth of overseas trade from the 1860s had an adverse effect on many regional markets. Foreign grain was milled at large tide-water sites, depressing the price of home grown wheat; meat and fruit arriving at London or the other principal ports could be directed to the chief provincial centres for resale to distant markets. By the 1880s, foreign foodstuffs, aided by preferential railway rates, were being cheaply distributed to all parts of the kingdom. Farmers complained bitterly that home grown produce was scarcely to be seen in some rural markets, there was such a glut of foreign produce. These complaints were exaggerated (fruit, for example, travelled extremely badly), but they revealed the farmers' awareness that many of their local markets were no longer sheltered.

Traditional retailers, also, were faced with external competition as market towns became centres of redistribution for manufactured products. This reinforced the trend for the various regions, with their different patterns of

prices, to become integrated into a national pattern of distribution with a more uniform and competitive pricing structure. The use of motorised road transport, and of the telegraph and telephone to direct supplies between markets in response to demand, aided these developments. After 1900, some rural areas, particularly those in the far West and North, might still be inward looking, but few, if any, remained self-sufficient.

As markets became part of a more complex system of distribution, some gained in importance and others declined. The influx of goods to the larger market towns drew trade to them. Faster transport meant that buyers and sellers were prepared to go further to attend larger markets, by-passing smaller ones. Thus the market at Bingham in Nottinghamshire faded away after the railway gave the town's inhabitants ready access to Nottingham, while in Derbyshire the coming of the railway reduced trade in Tideswell to such an extent that its previously flourishing market was represented in the early years of the century by a solitary pottery seller. There were of course exceptions. Railways could revive flagging trade in some rural markets, as at Wantage in Berkshire, and Kirton Lindsay in Lincolnshire. Nonetheless, it is clear that the railways considerably hastened a progressive concentration of marketing in the larger centres and a decrease in the number of active market towns. In 1792, Owen's *Book of Fairs* recorded some 550 market towns in England; by the 1880s this figure had sunk to 380—a dramatic decrease.

A further development in the late nineteenth century was for retail markets to become more limited in function. Increasingly, they could not compete with the daily convenience of well-sited shops, offering clothes, household fittings, furnishings and ironmongery—often supplied cheaply from distant manufactories. Only poorer people continued to buy such goods in markets—less because the markets were cheaper than because they held out the prospect of a bargain. By 1900, the retail markets were dealing chiefly in draperies and fresh foods—fruit, vegetables, dairy produce, small livestock and meat. In the latter respect, their vigour was scarcely diminished. Greengrocers' shops remained a rarity until the Great War; even the rich sent their servants to buy fruit and vegetables in the local market. If there was a growing trend to specialisation, however, which lessened the importance of many markets, others continued to thrive. These, sited in the large towns with good communications, continued to offer a wide range of

Bedale market, Yorkshire, about 1904, showing women's market for butter, eggs and poultry, and the sale of fruit and vegetables.

124

goods in a colourful atmosphere, filled with pungent smells and excitement. Clifton Johnson describes the large, vigorous Doncaster market in the 1890s:

'I never was in more of a hurly-burly. The centre of the scene was a low wide-spreading building of dingy gray stone. On the west side of this building was a broad open space full of canopied booths, tables and covered carts arranged in little streets. It was like a small city of shops. There were fish booths, meat booths, sweetshops, and restaurants, and many displays of crockery, dry goods, and hardware. You could even buy a gay-coloured chromo in a gilt frame. Everywhere were people crowding the toy-like streets, buying and bargaining and stowing away bundles in their various-shaped baskets.

'In a lane south of the building were vegetables, fruits and greens in bags, crates and heaps piled along the pavement for disposal a wholesale. In an open space at the end of this lane were the vans and wagons of the farm folk, mostly emptyand without horses, pushed to one side out of the way. Here a gate-way in an iron fence admitted one to the cattle and sheep markets. The sheep pens covered an acre or two, and as much more space was reserved for the cattle. Chipped bark from the tannery vats made its aroma anything but choice.

'Under the edge of a great shed were displays of farm tools and machinery, and in neighbouring vans and booths you could buy harnesses, rope, brooms and other heavy articles.

'Inside the market building, at one end, was the large room known as the corn exchange. Here were many tables strewn with samples of grain and fertilizers, and a crowd of brokers and buyers busy with their bargaining.

'But most of the building was given up to the retail marketers. The part occupied by them was a great, open, high-pillared hall, its floor full of benches with alleys between them for the public. In one section were fruits and vegetables and many flowers, both potted and in bouquets; in another section were a score or two of farmers' wives standing guard over numerous baskets of eggs, butter, cheese, and dressed fowls with their ghastly heads still on their bodies. In another part of the hall were dozens of crates and baskets of live fowls and several cages of timid rabbits, while along the walls were the booths of the butchers—"shambles" they called them.'

Markets such as this served local needs effectively and prospered into the inter-war period.

Doncaster market, Yorkshire, about 1903. Baskets, hampers and craftsman-made barrels are used as containers for produce, although from about 1890 their place was increasingly being taken by factory-made products.

Earlier in the nineteenth century, shops and shopping were undergoing changes which were to bring the products of five continents to the Victorian countryside and to replace much of its traditional material culture.

The number of shops in market towns increased in the first half of the nineteenth century in pace with the growth in population and the prosperity of the middle classes. In 1844, White's *Suffolk Directory* credits Bury St Edmunds with several bakers and flour dealers, booksellers, butchers, cabinet-makers and upholsterers, chemists and druggists, clothes brokers, drapers, fishmongers, hairdressers and hatters, hosiers and haberdashers, ironmongers, tea-dealers, tobacconists, watch and clock makers, wine and spirit merchants, and many other small manufacturers and producer-retailers.

Most shops were run as family businesses to cater for middle and upper class customers. In the grocery trade, especially, most of the commodities on offer remained mysterious and far beyond the reach of the ordinary working man, except as an occasional luxury. Shop-keeping at the time was a specialised art. The grocer had to know how to choose and blend teas, roast and grind coffee, mix herbs and spices, cure bacon, clean and wash dried fruit, and prepare sugar. The chemist prepared drugs, grinding them in a pestle and mortar. The chandler had his own recipes for making blacking and soft-soaps and for mixing up oils for paint. The haberdasher bought cotton and thread by the pound to disentangle and fold into hanks for sale. But even in this period, there seems to have been an increase in small general shops in town suburbs; these sold a variety of low-cost items to working class customers. The *Shopkeeper's Guide*, published in 1853, provides an indication of what a well-stocked shop in a country area should hold.

Grocery: Tea, coffee, cocoa, chocolate, chicory, spices, barley, patent flour, semolina, sauces, pepper, mustard, bird-seed, scent.

Chandlery: Black-lead, paste-blacking, starch, grits (prepared), nightlights, German paste, twine, cord, rottenstone, emery, whiting, putty-powder, oxalic acid, sweet-oil, soda, sandpaper, bath-brick, Fuller's earth, congreve matches, soap, blue, gum, etc.

Hardware: Nails, tools, cutlery, tinware, toys, turnery (i.e. brushes, clothes pegs and other cheap wooden items), garden seeds, stationery.

Drapery: Cheap cotton and woollen piece-goods, needles, threads, wool, beads, etc.

Drugs: (To be compounded by the shopkeeper) purgatives (black-draughts from senna, ginger, etc.), siedlitz powders, adhesive plaster, ginger beer (stone bottles from the Potteries at 10s. a gross), soda-water powders, sherbert powders, ginger-beer powders, baldness pomades, tooth powders, hair dyes, phosphorus paste for rats, inks, bug-poison.

[From *A History of Shopping* (1966) by Dorothy Davis.]

At this time, rural shop-keeping set out to satisfy needs rather than to introduce novelties. Advertising aimed at attracting new customers and informing old ones of what was in stock, not at creating wants in the modern sense. There was comparatively little attempt at window-dressing or at setting up displays of goods, which were often stored high on shelves or in drawers at the back of the shop and had to be asked for by name. The more substantial country shopkeepers prided themselves on the quality of their goods and on the attention they paid to their customers' individual requirements; a good name and a reputation for service were part and parcel of a

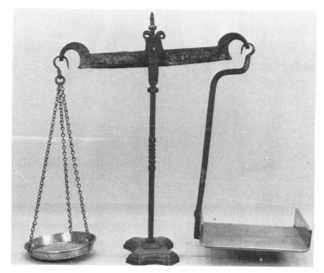

Above: Victorian bushel measure for grain, made in Norwich; tea packing box and mallet. *Centre:* scales—wooden butter scales from Buckinghamshire and a large pair of scales that may well have been used in a small general shop. *Right:* spring balance with two hooks for weights of 0-40 lbs and 20-300 lbs, used in a wide variety of shops; metal can used by grocer for metering out treacle.

'family business' and were tradable assets. Many retailers also had a workshop on the premises and undertook repairs to prolong the life of ironmongery and furniture.

The intimate relationship between shopkeeper and customer meant that giving credit was usual, sometimes over as much as a year, and a certain amount of haggling over the bill was accepted as part of the transaction. This was a period when population growth in itself was enough to provide new opportunities for retailers; before the mid century, expansion typically meant opening other shops in the same town rather than establishing branches over a wider region or experimenting with new selling methods. Monster shops and the early department stores were confined to the very large cities; co-operative and multiple retailing were still in their infancy.

The growth of working class demand in the metropolis and industrial cities, however, inevitably led to new methods of trading, which in the long run were bound to affect country shopping. The obvious way of expanding businesses that dealt with large numbers of people with low, but rising incomes, was to increase turnover by taking small profits on a large number of transactions. In London in the 1820s and 1830s, this meant more vigorous

127

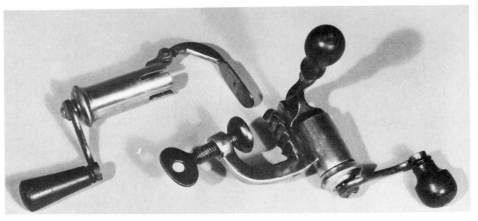

competition between retailers, price-cutting, the ticketing of goods, insistence on cash payments, and the development of advertising techniques. Eye-catching window displays, handbills, and sandwichmen and 'hookers-in' appeared to tempt the passer-by. Personal attention gave way to quick turnover. Such methods, pioneered largely in the metropolis, were to spread elsewhere later in the century.

Another mass marketing venture was the co-operative movement. The experiment was started in the 1840s by the Rochdale Pioneers, and their aims—to provide good quality items at reasonable prices by eliminating the profits of the middleman and the abuses of the truck system—were prompted by ethical rather than by purely capitalistic considerations. The co-operatives were noteworthy for cash dealing as well as for the use of the dividend, but their real innovations were large-scale buying and selling, and the extension of their activities in the 1860s into producing 'own brand' commodities. Although the co-operative retail societies enjoyed a membership of over three million by 1914, their business was predominantly foodstuffs and was limited to the mining and industrial communities of the North of England. They had comparatively little success in the South and in the more agricultural areas.

Left: brass pestle and mortar used by a doctor or chemist for preparing prescriptions. *Above:* apparatus from a chemist's shop at Holsworthy, Devon, said to have been used for making pill and powder containers from paper.

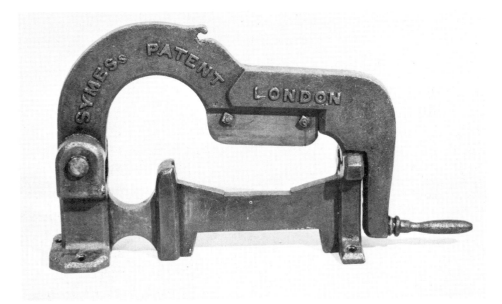

Sugar cutters used for cutting loaf sugar in a grocer's shop.

Ceramic sales pan used in a dairy shop for milk; the metal lid is covered with tin on the inside and brass on the outside. *Right:* sample sauce bottles produced by John & Charles Cocks of Reading, Berkshire.

Below: free sample tin of Huntley & Palmers ginger nuts, made between 1900 and 1914. *Centre:* conical white glazed milk jar used for showing milk in a shop window. *Right:* large decorative milk churn of tinned steel, with the top half covered in brass. It was probably carried on a milk float.

In general, as wholesaling and retailing were developing as separate functions, the place of the old style retailer, who combined production with marketing declined in importance. Technical progress in manufacturing and the mass-production of consumer goods meant, among other things, that makers now assembled, sorted and packed goods themselves. In the food industry, preserving, processing and canning all took place in the factory; by the 1870s, an enormous variety of pre-packed food was on sale, including margarine, meat extracts, relishes, pickles, ketchups, sauces, jams and preserves, the modern forms of chocolate and cocoa, and tinned biscuits. In the household goods trade, lamp-black, brick-dust and oils for colours were replaced by pre-mixed and made-up varieties, while mass-produced ironware—tools and implements, kitchen utensils, fire irons, galvanised buckets, nails and screws—offered cheaper and often more durable alternatives to the products of the carpenter or blacksmith. Men's ready-made clothing was being turned out in vast quantities by the 1890s, while the partial mechanisation of the footwear trade had occurred twenty years or so earlier.

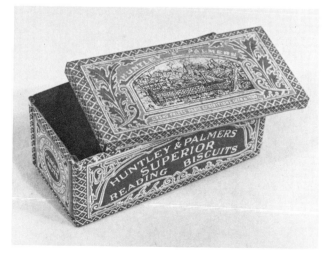

George Oliver's boot and shoe warehouse, Worcester, about 1890.

All of this presented a challenge to the traditional retailer, which he was not always prepared to accept. The high class grocer was often reluctant to make his expertise redundant by moving into pre-packed goods, while the bespoke tailor and city bootmaker spurned the 'inferior' quality of goods turned out by the factories. Old-established butchers refused to sell imported meats, holding them to be substandard and fit only for working class palates. In order to take advantage of these opportunities, both manufacturers and importers were vigorously seeking new methods of marketing their products, and one of the most striking developments in the late nineteenth century was the growth of the great multiple retail chains.

The earliest multiple was W.H. Smith, which won the contract for railway bookstalls between 1848 and 1853; the Singer Sewing Machine Company opened the first of its branches in 1851. By the 1870s, multiples had appeared in most of the main consumer trades, including groceries, meat, footwear, ironmongery, stationery, and circulating libraries. By the 1890s, there were multiples in men's outfitting, confectionery and tobacco, and the chemist's and druggist's trade. The distinctive features of the multiples were

Left: street in Shepton Mallet, Somerset, about 1902. The shoe shop, Frisby's, is a branch of an early multiple. The old established draper is diversifying into ready-made clothing. *Below:* International Tea Co. stores, East Street, Chichester, Sussex, about 1880.

Market day at Sudbury, Suffolk, about 1903. One of the shops is a branch of the International Tea Co.

Pot used for storing cream for sale in a branch of the Maypole Dairy, probably in Dorchester, Dorset.

their low fixed prices, which were displayed on large placards inside and outside the shop, cash dealing and incessant advertising. Their success was founded on buying in bulk, rapid distribution and speedy turnover. The largest firms, with more than 200 branches by 1900, often consolidated their position by expanding into the pre-distributive stages, acquiring, like Lipton's, their own plantations overseas, or, like Jesse Boot, their own factory to supply proprietary articles.

The multiples were established first in the cities, and rapidly expanded into the provinces and the larger market towns. This process can be followed in trade directories, such as Kelly's. Exeter, the county town of Devon, had a number of multiples by 1895. In the grocery and provisions trade, there were branches of the Home & Colonial stores, Lipton's and the International Tea Co. The Maypole Dairy had arrived by 1902. The larger meat importers were represented by Eastman's and the New Zealand Mutton Co. In footwear, three branches of George Oliver's had appeared, as well as a branch of Stead & Simpson's. There was the almost inevitable outpost of the Singer Manufacturing Co., while ready-made clothes were obtainable from Hepworth's. Boots had not yet reached the South-West, and drug companies were represented only by a local chain of chemists, Hinton Lake. Absent, too, and at this time still largely confined to London and the North, were multiples dealing in household goods. The same pattern of trading held true, as might be expected, in Plymouth, the chief port. Elsewhere in the county the spread of the multiples was strictly related to the size of population, the nature of local industries and employment, and accessibility to the railway. The more busy and prosperous towns had acquired a number of multiples by 1902. Barnstaple, for instance, had branches of Eastman's and Oliver's, while smaller market towns, like Okehampton, Tavistock and South Molton, had none at all. Ilfracombe possessed a Lipton's by 1902, and Totnes had an Eastman's, but generally the penetration of rural areas by multiples was slow before 1914, and trading continued to be dominated by local firms until after World War II.

The second half of the nineteenth century saw the appearance of the department store, offering a wide range of goods to the growing urban middle class, who were spending an increasing proportion of their income on household goods and furnishings. Department stores were another outlet for factory-made goods. Initially, they attracted customers by low prices, clearly marked on goods set out for all to examine, but soon the larger city stores were cultivating an atmosphere of luxury, cossetting their customers with the elegance of their surroundings, lifts and restaurants, and the assiduous attentions of large numbers of shop assistants. Where the chain multiples offered low prices without pretensions, the bigger department stores dealt in more luxurious wares and responded to Victorian social and decorative aspirations. Above all, the stores promoted the idea of fashion—of discarding the old for the new and indulging a taste for smartness and modernity. By and large, the growing urban middle classes found this image congenial and sought to give it substance. They tended to regard their country cousins as primitive folk, whose dress and homes were altogether antiquated.

But country dwellers, too, were influenced by changing tastes. At the top of the social scale, Richard Jefferies's 'Grange people' could well afford to import the latest novelties from the city, patronising both traditional retailers and high class department stores. The growth of railways, however, made a day's shopping expedition to the city an increasingly popular pastime for many who occupied a humbler position in rural society. In the provinces, department stores were gaining ground, and by the end of the century they

Left: High Street, Barnstaple, Devon, about 1904. *Above:* the Devon and Somerset Stores, High Street, Taunton, Somerset, early twentieth century.

Bandage, probably about 1910 or later, from the stock of George Senior, chemist, of Holsworthy, Devon. Instructions and diagrams are printed in black on white cotton.

Grocer's advertisement, probably 1880s.

could be found in Reading, Bath, Cheltenham, Southport and Sheffield. In such stores, one department, usually drapery, predominated, and other lines were added gradually. In smaller towns, drapers, such as Badcocks of Newton Abbot, were just beginning to expand into furnishings, floor coverings, lamps and other brass fittings by the 1890s. Other stores, like the Devon & Somerset Stores, based in Exeter and Taunton, concentrated on provisions, but also offered ironmongery, fabrics and furnishings, ready-made clothing and boots. Market town stores tended to be less grand than their city counterparts, offering value for money rather than a heady atmosphere of luxury; many deliberately imitated the chain multiples in their blatant advertising and selling methods. Even so, they did not appeal only to the lower end of the market, but drew their customers from the middle class and the better off section of the working class, providing them with the chance to join in the game of fashion. Jefferies claims that by the 1870s tenant farmers' wives were beginning to insist on silks, satins and kid gloves, while even country girls 'must have a "fashionable" bonnet, and pair of thin, tight boots, let the lanes be never so dirty or the fields never so wet.' The stores flourished because they were more approachable and more enjoyable for these shopping novices that the specialist retailers.

The competition offered by the new multiples and department stores, however, stimulated many traditional retailers in the market towns. If some found their livelihoods taken away by mass production, others were prepared to specialise, diversify or otherwise adapt their businesses to meet the needs of the time. In rural areas, traditional retailers continued to predominate, and many entered a new period of prosperity between the 1880s and World War I. They benefited from the new varieties of goods that were coming on the market, while the influx of population into the more prosperous market towns from the countryside increased overall demand. Drapers still sold mainly piece goods, but also began to stock made-up clothing and in the larger towns some specialised as hosiers, milliners, haberdashers and

corsetières. Gown shops catering for the middle classes grew in numbers after the 1880s. The oil and colour men and chandlers tended to disappear as the trade became more complex and specialised: some retailers concentrated on hardware, while others dealt only in wallpapers, paints, and distempers, and yet others in glass, china and pottery. Ironmongers now sold more and more factory-made goods, and could select their stock from the vast range of items that were illustrated in manufacturers' catalogues and trade journals. Often these ran to nearly a thousand pages of text and ilustration, encompassing stoves and ranges, chimney pieces, baths, brass foundrywork, ironmongery, railings and garden fittings. Indeed, the spread of suburban villas in market towns towards the end of the century substantially increased the demand for products associated with the building, ironmongery and furnishing trades.

Some traditional retailers were forced to adopt the techniques of their competitors—bold advertising, marked prices and cash payments. These

Advertisement in *Kelly's Directory of Norfolk*, 1892, which shows the range of activities undertaken by a late nineteenth century retailer.

Selby Cross and Cowthorpe, Yorkshire, about 1900. Note the meat hung outside the butcher's shop, which also sells groceries.

expedients, accepted by the local townspeople, were often resented by farmers. The problem, as Jefferics noted, was that the old-fashioned farmer:

'...would have such a length of credit—a year at least—and nowadays a shopkeeper, though sure of his money, cannot wait long for it. But to ask for the account would give mortal offence ... "Suppose you thought we was a-going to run away-eh?" and the door would never again be darkened by those antique breeches and gaiters.'

The expansion of trading in market towns between the 1860s and 1914, however, did not necessarily lead to the diffusion of manufactured clothing and goods into the countryside. Men's ready-made clothes were commonly worn by the 1880s—much earlier than women's—since the outer garments were heavier and more difficult to make by hand. On the other hand, the invention of the sewing machine enabled country girls to make their own clothes for longer. Home dress-making saved money, and for the poorer families, extra pennies still meant the difference between sufficiency and dearth; and so old clothes were cut down, altered and refurbished with ribbons and frills, in fanciful versions of 'the latest' from Paris or London. Only when a girl obtained employment in the town could she usually afford to buy any part of her wardrobe off the peg. Similarly, the ill-fitting nature of the first factory boots, which were available only in limited sizes, meant that up to the turn of the century agricultural workers often preferred to buy a stout hand-made pair from the village bootmaker. By the 1890s, the more skilled and highly paid labourers could afford a few pieces of purchased furniture: a table or chest of drawers, and sometimes a cheap matching set, turned out by a factory. Linoleum was also occasionally introduced as a floor covering, but the new manufactured carpets, run off power looms, were an unheard-of luxury. Indeed, most cottages still had home or locally-made

Village shoemaker, about 1909.

furniture and were brightened up by bric-à-brac obtained from markets, shops and itinerant retailers.

More substantial pieces of furniture might sometimes be acquired through sales. A sale at a cottage after its occupant had died or moved away was an occasion when precious savings might well be spent. Pulbrook recounts:

'Numbers attend the sale more for the fun of the thing than a desire to buy, especially when the auctioneer is reputed to be a wag, and most of them know how to bring forth a laugh which helps to increase prices. Treasures may still be picked up at marvellous bargains, especially in out-of-the-way places, but, on the other hand, it is surprising what sums are bid for ordinary articles much in demand, when popular neighbours fall on evil times. After a sale a curious procession wends its way up the village street, women sharing the burden of armchairs and baths, crockery or a bedstead on a wheelbarrow, a piano laboriously carried by two men who put it down every few yards, or a studious young man carrying an armful of assorted books.'

But new commodities were now entering the countryside through the growth of village shops. In spite of an overall shift in purchasing to market towns, there was a rising local demand for provisions and other necessities. In the first half of the nineteenth century, the spread of shops seems to have

136

Beer retailer. Unlike public houses, retailers could not sell beer for consumption on the premises.

been very slow in villages of under 500 inhabitants. Whether or not a village could support a shop depended on a number of factors—size, social class, position, location, availability of employment, and perhaps even the attitude of the local landowner. The low level of incomes, however, was the chief constraint. What could not be made at home might be obtained from local craftsmen—even quite small villages possessed a number of shoemakers, carpenters, blacksmiths, and wheelwrights. The trend away from home baking might also be revealed in the presence of a baker, who besides making bread and some confectionery, would make his oven available to the local cottagers for a small charge. White's *Norfolk Directory* of 1845 reveals that in the village of Tittleshall-cum-Godwick, the baker combined his occupation with tailoring, while the blacksmith kept the local inn, the Golden Wyvern. Such dual occupations were common. Larger villages might support a butcher, a victualler and a general shop—selling hardware, chandlery, cloth, garments, pills and potions, sweets and powders. As often as not, the most patronised establishment in the village was the beer retailer or tavern. The village of Swanton Morley, also in Norfolk, with a population of only souls in 1845 had no fewer than four inns (although one of them, the Angel, was empty) and a beerhouse.

After 1860, however, the provision of shops in rural areas increased greatly. The sub-post office and general shop appeared in quite small villages, which might even possess a range of more specialised shops. For example, Codford St Mary in Wiltshire had a population of only 322 in 1891, but Kelly's *Wiltshire Directory* for 1895 lists a total of two shopkeepers, a baker, a grocer and draper, an agent for W. & A. Gilbey, the wine and spirit merchants, and a combined Post Office and tobacconist. This was not exceptional; even smaller parishes in more outlying locations in Wiltshire had acquired shops by this time. Brixton Deverill, with a population of 112, had two shopkeepers, one of whom was a cow-keeper, while the neighbouring parish of Kingston Deverill, with 234 people, had another two shopkeepers as well as a sub-post office. Multiple occupations were still common. Michael Ashman of Heytesbury, also in Wiltshire, combined keeping the

Bridge Street, Evesham, Worcestershire, about 1910. By this time, many ironmongers were stocking cycles and also often sold motor accessories.

Angel Inn with work as a plumber, glazier, and painter, although carting and haulage were the more usual adjuncts to innkeeping. Women often took on shops to supplement their husbands' wages or to maintain some small means of independence after being widowed. Those who had gone abroad to try their luck and failed, ex-soldiers, and the disabled were all likely candidates to become shopkeepers. Village shops varied considerably in size and contents. Some were very well stocked; others were more modest affairs carrying only a small miscellany of items and trading solely at the whim of the proprietor. Their nomenclature was often confusing, as the description of the trade given on the outside of the shop was by no means, as Pulbrook points out, a guarantee of what was for sale:

'It would be difficult to define many establishments whose proprietors describe themselves simply as "shopkeepers", sweets being common to all, whatever the staple commodities may be. The saddler probably sells fruit and eggs; the butcher greenstuff and dairy produce; the grocer anything in the edible line except butcher's meat, with household materials and seeds; and almost every shop deals in proprietary articles in packet and tin. Some little shops can almost equal the stores for variety, but the sign or show-card is no index to the interior, being perhaps a legacy of a former tenant or merely displayed to attract.'

In the last two or three decades of the century, village shops were dealing more and more in prepacked and branded goods. Shelves were filled with Peak Frean biscuits, Hartley's jams, Tate's sugar cubes, Bovril, Nestlé's milk, Mazawattee tea, Sharwood's pickles and Reckitt's Blue. The new emphasis on advertising was reflected in window stickers and enamelled signs, all provided by the manufacturers. Acrobats, explorers, balloonists, soldiers, sailors, opera singers and society ladies extolling the virtues of this or that proprietary article lent a startling cosmopolitan glamour to the sides of cottage shops. But, if advertising was an increasingly normal part of commercial life, village shopkeepers did not, by and large, engage in aggressive marketing. Many regarded their stores as general social assets as much as money earners. Some shopkeepers were even less alert to commercial possibilities than others; cherishing their goods, says Pulbrook, 'like rare

Village shop, Stratton, Cornwall, 1888.

East Clandon Post Office, Surrey, about 1910. Note the spread of advertising into a small village.

possessions from which they can be parted only by persuasion or guile', and 'Every wise housewife learns to know a shop as intimately as the proprietor, as he is sure to forget some of his wares.'

Certain shops—fruit shops, greengrocers, fishmongers, chemists and ironmongers—were usually found only in market towns. One way, however, in which fresh bread, fruit and fish reached the villages was through the growth of the roundsmen system, at first by pony and cart and later from motorised vans sent out by local retailers. The ice-cream seller was also an increasingly common figure in suburban parishes in the Edwardian period, while the cigar and cigarette salesman catered for more expensive tastes. One such salesman covered over 2,000 miles on his bicycle during the year 1906, and recorded his everyday experiences in a diary now in the Institute of Agricultural History at the University of Reading. A true harbinger of the twentieth century was the newspaper vendor, bringing papers or weekly magazines to the villagers. Richard Jefferies took a jaundiced view of this development:

'Once a week the discordant note of a horn or bugle, loudly blown by a man who does not understand his instrument, is heard at intervals. It is the newspaper vendor, who, like the bill-sticker, starts from the market town on foot, and goes through the village with a terrible din. He stops at the garden gate in the palings before the thatched cottage, delivers his print to the old woman or the child sent out with the copper, and starts again with a flourish on his trumpet. His business is chiefly with the cottagers, and his print is very likely full of abuse of the landed proprietors as a body. He is a product of modern days, almost the latest, and as he goes from cottage door to cottage door, the discordant uproar of his trumpet is a sign of the times.'

The coming of the mass circulation papers, the *Daily Mail* in 1896, the *Daily Express* in 1900 and the *Daily Mirror* in 1903, made possible by the introduction of linotype as well as the growth of literacy, marked the further liberation of the village from its parish pump horizons.

139

Ice-cream man, around 1900.

As the new distributive retail network spread into the countryside, the old trades declined. This process was gradual, although most of the crucial changes had occurred before 1914. Production had shifted decisively out of the villages into the market and factory towns. Marketing itself had become largely a matter of supplying mass-produced commodities, designed to meet urban tastes, to urban markets. Rural customers shared in the benefits of cheapness and reliability, while the sheer quantity of goods to be bought created wants among the labouring classes which rising wages enabled them partly to satisfy. But the improved standard of living in rural areas reflected the diffusion of industrial artefacts, not the survival of thriving village industries. Indeed, it was not until the inter-war period that a limited demand for village-made artefacts was revived among sentimentalists, largely from the urban middle classes, who regretted the passing of what they considered, wrongly, to be 'peasant England', and sought, with comparatively little success, to breathe new life into traditional rural industries. By this time, the modest functional objects previously found in working class homes had become prized rarities in the villas of the comfortably off.

Left: village baker, Corringham, Essex. *Below:* newsagent's shop, Godalming, Surrey, showing the large range of newspapers and magazines that were available by the 1910s.

For the Public Good

In the early Victorian period, many political thinkers believed that governments should intervene as little as possible in the lives of the governed. The political philosopher, Jeremy Bentham expressed the view that things were best 'left-alone', and that the greatest happiness of the greatest number would be secured by allowing each individual to pursue his own self-interest. Disagreement centred mainly around whether a natural harmony of interests could be achieved, or whether the state should act to ensure an artificial harmony. In practical terms, a government's responsibilities were held to extend only to the protection of its citizens against force and fraud; arrangements for general convenience, such as a common currency or a set of standard weights and measures; and the raising of sufficient revenue for the performance of its necessary functions.

Yet, by the 1830s, this concept had already been overtaken by events. The growth of population, towns, industry and commerce brought a substantial increase in national wealth and unprecedented social and economic problems. To combat mass poverty, disease and unemployment in the new industrial cities, the advocates of *laissez-faire* (non-interference) and self-help often found themselves, ironically enough, devising new powers of state intervention. As a result of both administrative exigencies and political conviction, there slowly emerged the highly centralised, bureaucratic and interventionist state of the late Victorian period. New policies, however, were designed primarily to meet urban needs, and often legislation was slow to bring change in the countryside.

At the beginning of Victoria's reign, many of the changes seemed for the worse, for example in the treatment of poverty. From the 1790s, a common form of relief was the Speenhamland System, inaugurated by Berkshire magistrates, in which low wages were supplemented by small allowances calculated in accordance with the size of families and the price of bread. Labourers were entitled to relief in parishes in which they had a settlement, the money being raised by means of a tax levied on local property owners. By the 1830s, however, the Benthamites and other political economists argued that this system interfered with the free working of the labour market and undermined the independence of the labourer, who would abstain from work if assured of an income from the parish. The payment of such allowances, therefore, was not only economically but also morally undesirable. In addition, the Benthamites attacked the central structure of the Old Poor Law on the grounds that it left an enormous amount of discretion to local authorities; instead they advocated the setting up of a centralised administration, which would employ properly trained and salaried officials.

The Poor Law Amendment Act of 1834 embodied much of this thinking. The principle was adopted of abolishing the payment of outdoor relief to the able-bodied, offering instead maintenance in a workhouse, in which conditions were to be sufficiently severe to put off all but the really

destitute. The parishes were to be grouped into Unions, normally centred on a market town or some other prominent place, and the Unions were to be administered by a Central Board, known as the Poor Law Commission until 1847, and thereafter as the Poor Law Board. Many workhouses were built between the 1830s and 1860s, grim, substantial buildings, usually designed to accommodate from 100 to 300 paupers. The aim of deterring labourers from applying for relief was quickly achieved: little more than a quarter of those offered workhouse accommodation had accepted it by 1836. From the 1840s, the occupants of workhouses were increasingly the old, the sick and the very young—often deserted and illegitimate children. Such remained the pattern throughout the century.

The prospect of going into the workhouse was regarded with horror by country people. Digby quotes a Suffolk woman who stated that, 'I'd work the flesh off my bones afore I'd be parted and locked up like a felon in the workhouse.' This was in 1849, but even in the 1890s, the English Land Restoration League found that rural labourers still regarded the workhouse with loathing, not least because they knew that it was a fate awaiting many of them.

What was resented about the workhouse was the stigma of pauperism, the cold condescension of many of the officials, and the general harshness of the regime. Families were segregated by age and sex—a fact which continued to enrage George Edwards, the founding father of the National Union of Agricultural Workers, many years after his young experience of workhouse life. His father was arrested and imprisoned for fourteen days in 1855 for the crime of stealing a few turnips to feed his family. George and

Before the coming of old age pensions in 1908, life for the old was often a constant struggle against destitution. *Left:* stone picking, one of the most back-breaking and least envied agricultural tasks. Photograph by Sir George Clausen, taken near his home at Childwick Green, Hertfordshire between 1882 and 1885. One of the workers is a woman, which was rare by this time. *Above:* John Brinkworth of Kings Stanley, Gloucestershire, late nineteenth century. He was a hedger and ditcher—one of the most skilled agricultural occupations, but even at 81, he was still not able to retire.

142

his mother were taken to the workhouse, where they were kept all winter: 'Although only five years old, I was not allowed to be with my mother.' Segregation was bad enough; even more to be dreaded was what Digby calls the 'tedious purposelessness of existence'.

Workhouses varied considerably in the standard of comfort that they offered. The Andover workhouse became notorious in the mid 1840s, when its occupants were allegedly so hungry that they were compelled to gnaw at the bones they had been set to crush for fertilizer, while others, under more enterprising officers, might offer a reasonable diet, warmth and diverting occupations. Towards the end of the century, conditions improved, but here Jeffries makes the vital point: the workhouse might be the refuge in which Hodge spent his last days, but it was not his home.

'Plain as is the fare, it was better than the old man had existed on for years; but though better it was not his dinner. He was not sitting in his old chair, at his own table, round which his children had once gathered. He had not planted the cabbage, and tended it while it grew, and cut it himself. So it was all through the workhouse life... He knew all the rain that had fallen must have come through the thatch of the old cottage in at least one place, and he would have liked to have gone and re-thatched it with trembling hand. At home he could lift the latch of the garden gate and go down the road if he wished. Here he could not go outside the boundary—it was against the regulations. Everything to appearance had been monotonous in the cottage—but there he did not feel it monotonous.'

Despite the policy of the Central Board, many able-bodied paupers continued to be given outdoor relief. The local authorities—the Boards of Guardians—manipulated their returns to show that outdoor relief had been paid on account of sickness, even though the payment was in fact made to able-bodied workers, temporarily out of work, or low-paid and with large families. Partly, the local boards were influenced by humanitarian considerations—rural unemployment remained high in many areas until the 1850s—and partly by financial ones—outdoor relief was often cheaper than the cost of maintenance in a workhouse. Indeed, the Boards of Guardians—made up largely of tenant farmers and tradesmen—were often accused of meanness, of guarding the rates more effectively than they guarded the poor. Yet, as Rose notes, this parsimony was to some degree attributable to the rating system itself, since:

'Until 1865 each parish (within the Union) remained responsible for the cost of relieving its own paupers, and until 1861 a parish's contribution to the common expenses of the Union was assessed on the basis of its relief expenditure, not its rateable value, on its poverty rather than on its property.'

These failings in the 1830s legislation were acknowledged in the Union Chargeability Act of 1865, which placed the whole cost of relief on the Union rather than the parish, thus redressing 'the inequality of burden between rich and poor parishes within the same Union.'

Nonetheless, the new Act did not fundamentally alter the attitude of many Victorians, who considered that relief had a demoralising effect on the labourer by instilling habits of pauperism, and who argued that private charity should continue to play an important part in the treatment of poverty. One advantage of charity was that it allowed a distinction to be drawn more carefully between the deserving and undeserving poor, and while the worthy cases might be helped back to independence, the others were often abandoned to what was considered to be self-induced misery, caused by idleness, drink or a lack of thrift.

Rural charity was channelled either through endowments or individual acts of philanthropy. Both might provide for the building of almshouses, or for pensions for the elderly of a parish. Doles were also given at certain times of the year, and were a much needed source of clothing, bedding, fuel, food and money to the poor. The inhabitant of the estate or closed village usually did better than the inhabitant of the open village, since he was most likely to benefit from the gifts of a wealthy proprietor, but private charity was increasingly resented by the rural poor. Men and women did not wish to be patronised, but to receive a just reward for their labours.

The mid century, however, witnessed the beginnings of a slow change in the attitudes to poverty. This was largely due to a considerable increase in knowledge of the extent and causes of working class distress. Middle-class Victorians were impelled to investigate poverty with great vigour and statistical exactness, not least because they feared that the constant growth of population might outstrip the nation's ability to support such numbers. Malthus's gloomy prediction that men would multiply more quickly than the means of subsistence—leading to ever greater poverty, disease and civil unrest—still carried weight. Moreover, it was increasingly obvious by this time that the New Poor Law was totally inadequate as a means of tackling the vast problem in towns. Edwin Chadwick, a principal architect of the 1834 legislation, went on to conduct the detailed survey that resulted in his famous *Report on the Sanitary Condition of the Labouring Population of Great Britain* (1842). A host of other investigations followed. In 1849, Mayhew published his four volumes of *London Labour and the London Poor*, a painstaking piece of research showing that 'much destitution was due to the sheer insufficiency of wages, that accidental circumstances like three wet days could bring 30,000 people to the brink of starvation.' Later, Charles Booth's *Life and Labour of the People of London*, published in the late 1880s and early 1890s, and Seebohm Rowntree's *Poverty: A Study of Town Life* (in York) published in 1901, not only added new facts, but provided the new analytical tools needed to create a social science.

What these experts demonstrated above all else was the falseness of the assumption that the poor were poor because of some weakness of character and the truth of the fact that private philanthropy could do no more than touch a small part of the total problem. Sometimes greater awareness of the extent of poverty served only to inspire to greater charitable efforts—as in the setting up of the notable Charity Organisation in Society in 1869. But the overall progress was clear—towards the exercise of more central control and responsibility by the state.

By the 1860s, pressure was growing on the Poor Law Board to make a number of improvements in the treatment of paupers. One advance was the Metropolitan Poor Act of 1867, which enabled separate asylums to be established for the sick or insane poor in London, and dispensaries to adminster outdoor medical relief. But country people who fell ill had few choices. Only the better off could afford a doctor's fees. Many tried to insure against illness by paying in a little each week to a Friendly Society Benefit Club. This was prudent at a time when epidemics of cholera, typhoid and smallpox were not uncommon, when whooping cough, diphtheria and scarlet fever were potential child killers, and bronchitis, pneumonia and rheumatism took a heavy toll in old age. The benefit consisted of the payment of a few shillings a week during illness, and the attention of a Club doctor. For those who could not afford even this modest insurance, there was always the assistance of neighbours, the kindness of hall and church, the doctor who might be willing to forego his fee or ensure free treatment at a local hospital—and a wide range of folk medicines. But if the need were sufficiently great, the sick person might be forced to seek aid from the Poor Law authorities. This carried with it a hated investigation into the family's circumstances and the penalty, until 1885, of disenfranchisement as a pauper. Moreover, the Poor Law medical officers appointed by the local Boards of Guardians were themselves often inadequately trained, over-burdened and underpaid. They were salaried from 1842, but were often expected to provide medicines out of their own pocket—a stipulation scarcely calculated to ensure adequate supply. Indeed, the 1854 Select Committee on Medical Relief expressly drew attention to the fact that expensive medicines such as quinine and cod-liver oil were withheld from patients; instead they were offered the cheaper substitutes of wines, spirits, strong beer and meat. A circular from the Poor Law Board in 1865 recommended that such medicines be given at the expense of the Guardians, but, although the majority of local Unions complied, some continued as before.

Those who could not be treated at home were admitted into the workhouse. In rural areas, however, the general mixed workhouse remained standard and only rarely were there separate infirmaries for the sick. Pamela Horn records that:

'It was to combat this kind of situation that the cottage hospital movement was established in the 1860s. As the name suggests, the hospitals were set up in converted cottages and catered for about six to ten patients at any one time. Medical treatment was provided by a resident nurse and by regular visits from the general practitioner. Patients were usually expected to pay something towards the cost of the scheme, even if that were as little as 2s 6d a week. The remainder of the funds came from charity. Equipment and medicaments were minimal—chloroform inhalers, fracture splints, one ear syringe and a stomach pump being among the modest list of instruments recommended for cottage hospitals in the 1870s—but food was both plentiful and wholesome.'

By 1870, there were about 70 cottage hospitals in the country, although the fact that they imposed some charge on their patients still acted as an effective bar to labourers and their families in those districts where ordinary day wages were not much above twelve to fourteen shillings a week. However, the trend towards more effective state intervention continued to gather momentum. This can be exemplified in the career of Sir John Simon, at the Privy Council Medical Department. Perkin notes that in the 1850s Simon and Tom Taylor of the Local Government Board 'still prided themselves on their "open minds" and their loyalty to the principles of decentralisation and local autonomy', but by 1865, Simon 'had been converted by experience to central compulsion'. Simon wrote in that year:

'I venture to submit that the time has now arrived when it ought not any longer to be discretional in a place whether that place shall be kept filthy or

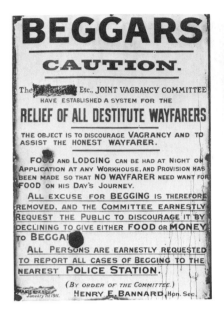

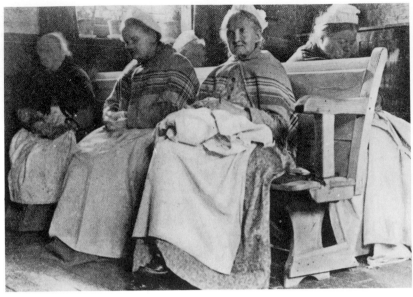

Left: notice cautioning beggars, Maidenhead, 1901. *Above:* workhouse inmates, a photograph from a *Country Life* article, 28 October 1911.

not. Powers sufficient for the local protection of the public health having first been universally conferred, it next, I submit, ought to be an obligation on the local authorities that these powers be exercised in good faith and with reasonable vigour and intelligence.'

Simon was influential in securing the Sanitary Act of 1866, with its enlarged powers of compulsion, and the new dispensation which arrived with the Local Government Board of 1871. The latter took over the work of the Poor Law Board on Public Health and exercised supervision over the local Rural and Urban Sanitary Boards. In 1888, this process went one step further when the county and borough councils assumed the chief responsibility for public health under statutory guidance, and county medical officers were appointed.

By the last quarter of the century, with, as Rose observed, 'its increasing awareness of poverty as distinct from pauperism', the Poor Law was seen as increasingly obsolete and even irrelevant. The attitudes of the Poor Law Board, which was still committed to the principle of deterrence and the restriction of outdoor relief did not help, and other agencies were becoming more important than the Boards of Guardians in dealing with various types of poverty.

Other influences were also at work. The Victorian belief in individualism as a political philosophy was becoming less assured. The old dichotomy between individual and state gave way to a new conception of man in society, which accepted that since it is the community that creates the conditions for an individual's moral and personal development, the best hope for the individual is in the betterment of the community. A corollary of this view was that poverty could no longer be regarded as evidence of individual failure but of some general fault in the fabric of the state. Such ideas were expressed by T.H. Green and the Oxford School of philosophy in the 1860s and 1870s, and provided an intellectual justification for the broadening of state power. They were eagerly taken up by Fabians, Christian Socialists and many other social and political reformers in the 1880s and 1890s, who found a common point in calling for positive rather

Workhouse inmates, from *Country Life*, 1911.

than negative government to defend the weak and helpless in society—the victims of unrestrained competition.

This concerted attack on the old *laissez-faire* philosophy was all the more timely as it was launched within the context of severe industrial recession between the mid 1870s and the mid 1890s, when it became very much more difficult for middle-class employers to preach the virtues of hard work and labour discipline to their employees, many of whom were being thrown out of work by the action of impersonal economic forces. Even Conservative governments were driven to concede that the state might intervene to organise relief for industrial unemployment, and after various measures had been tried, a full-scale Royal Commission on the Poor Laws and the Relief of Distress was set up in the winter of 1905.

The Royal Commission did not report until 1909 and, even then, was deeply divided in its recommendations. Meanwhile, in 1906, a Liberal government, committed to some measure of social reform, had assumed power. Although some Liberals retained a deep commitment to *laissez-faire*, and businessmen and property owners in the party hierarchy obstructed the acceptance of radical policies, the men who now began to acquire ministerial office were influenced by the social ideals of the late nineteenth century, and by the writings of progressive journalists, such as J.L. Hammond, H.W. Massingham and C.F.G. Masterman. By 1908, by-election reverses and the need to outbid the small but rapidly growing Labour Party for the working class vote in a general election forced the Liberals more sharply to the left. Among the piecemeal reforms they undertook were old age pensions in 1908 and National Unemployment Insurance in 1911.

Neither piece of legislation was, in itself, far-reaching. Old age pensions, which had been seriously discussed since at least the 1880s, were to be restricted to the very poor; only those with an annual income of less than £21 were to receive the full pension of five shillings a week. Yet many old people in rural areas qualified for the new statutory pension, and there can be no doubt that for many it made the difference between fragile independence and pauperism. The coming of Unemployment Insurance had less effect on the lives of country people, since the legislation was at first restricted to skilled artisans, who were often already insured through a friendly society.

In 1914, the structure of the Poor Law of 1834 was still intact, but had been considerably eroded by the much broader acceptance of the idea of state intervention in providing welfare services. Country people, though, had not yet escaped from the drudgery of the old system and some, like Joseph Ashby, maintained their sense of fierce independence for a considerable while, as state charity was no more to their liking than private philanthropy. But Ashby, who in the 1890s had heartily disliked the idea of the old age pension, believing that most men should provide during their working lives for their old age, had, ten years later been persuaded of their utility. And when a bonfire was held in his Warwickshire village of Tysoe to celebrate their introduction, 'Joseph said a couple of quiet sentences about the beginning of better times for old folk who had worked hard and lived rightly'.

For young people, however, with their lives still ahead of them, education was the key to a better job and a higher standard of living. Again, the state was to be a principal agent of change, although it was not until after 1870 that it sanctioned the provision of efficient schools for all working-class children.

In 1800, education of the rural poor had depended almost entirely on local benevolence and enterprise, and standards varied a great deal. Some labouring families could send their children to endowed schools, founded under the terms of wills of local benefactors. These included grammar schools in the market towns—usually for boys over eight who had already made some progress in reading and writing, and primary schools, run by countless small charities, in the villages. The most generous parish endowment might be sufficient to employ a salaried master or mistress to teach as many as thirty or forty pupils, and to provide a school house. The smallest allowed only for the instruction of perhaps two or three children by a local person, often in make-shift accommodation, and many teachers had to supplement their incomes by taking fee-paying scholars. The education provided was fairly standard in content, if not in the quality of teaching. Benefactors might express the wish that poor children be taught 'to read, write and to cast accounts', or more commonly, that they be given simple reading skills 'to know the Bible and the Catechism of the Church of England'. The curriculum contained little else, unless it was thought desirable to give practical instruction in the occupations that labouring children were likely to take up. Thus, in the textile district of Derbyshire, the boys at the schools at Walton-on-Trent were 'first to knit stockings, and after they had attained a competent skill therein, then to knit and read.'

In other villages, schools were almost entirely maintained out of the poor-rate by local subscriptions or by patrons—usually the incumbent of the parish church, or local landowner. Where there was no proper school building, lessons took place in the church house or even the church itself, and parsons often took a large part in the management of the local school, sometimes acting as the schoolmaster.

Many villages however, had no school at all, or only a Sunday School or a private Dame school, run by men or women too old or not fit for other occupations, and charging a penny or half-penny a week for each child. At worst, they were little more than a child-minding service and dismal

148

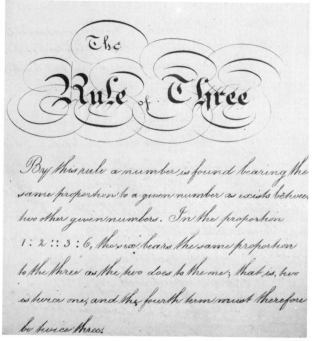

Above: exercise book page written with a quill pen, Oak House School, Axminster, Devon, 1861. *Right:* multiplication sum done by John Reed at Oak House School in 1861. Sums of this complexity would surely have deterred all but the brightest pupils; Reed later became Professor of Chemistry at St Andrews University.

failures even at that. Thus Horn draws attention to a certain Hugh John, who opened a school in Cornwall in the 1830s, while he continued to clean clocks, measure land, castrate cattle and kill pigs—and 'unfortunately, for his pupils, he sometimes returned from his duties rather the worse for wear from drink.' The parish, too, frequently supported incompetent teachers: in the 1840s, the Revd J. Allen found in one school 'a poor lame creature, apparently disabled by paralysis, [who] kept precarious order by hitting the boys on the head with a Testament which he held in his hand', while in another, 'a master made the practice of hiring himself out as a day labourer at harvest-time and at other seasons of the year, *during school hours*, and sent the children to gather sticks for him, or to collect manure from the public roads.'

Unsuitable teachers were not dismissed, Mary Sturt observed, because then they 'would become a charge on the parish: or starve, painfully, in the sight of all'. Small endowments, therefore, were often diverted to become little more than a supplement to the parish poor-rate. Farmers, who frequently had to pay for education, generally resented the expense and the waste of time in providing schooling for the sons of labourers, who were only going to be 'hewers of wood and drawers of water', and among the upper classes, it was commonly held that the education of the poor would induce them to question their poverty-stricken state, and lead eventually to social disruption and even, perhaps, to revolution.

A major obstacle to providing new schools with teachers in the first half of the nineteenth century was the cost. One means of overcoming this—at least in part—was the monitor system: employing the older children to teach the younger ones. This idea was adopted by the British and Foreign Schools Society, which was founded in 1808. The British schools adopted a non-sectarian approach to religion, grounded in the common principles of Christianity, and drew support from dissenters. As a result, they encountered almost immediate opposition from the Church of England, which responded by forming the National Society for the Promotion of the Education of the Poor in the Doctrine and Discipline of the Established Church in 1811. There followed a period of vigorous competition between the two societies, although the National schools, able to command more financial support locally, soon substantially outnumbered the British schools. The two societies were to dominate British education until the 1870s.

Unlike the British and National Schools, which taught little more than the three Rs at a penny a week, the schools that were soon set up by other religious denominations, offered extra subjects for additional fees. In the mid century, the prospectus of the Congregational School at Bakewell in Derbyshire offered a basic course in 'Reading and Spelling, Writing, Slate and Mental Arithmetic, Geography and Natural History' at threepence a week, or three shillings a quarter. If training in 'English Grammar, Entymology [sic] and the Elements of Natural Philosophy' were desired, the fee was sixpence a week, and the Advanced Course, at ninepence a week, covered 'History, Mensuration, Algebra, Geometry, Book-keeping and Drawing.' Such schools were attended by the children of the better-off sections of rural society—the offspring of farmers and tradesmen who could not afford one of the older fee-paying grammar schools.

Pressure for a state system was successfully opposed by supporters of the voluntary system, not only churchmen and the Tory party, but also many Liberals and those influenced by Benthamite ideas—to whom state control was tantamount to the worst kind of tyranny over the freedom of the individual. As late as 1859, John Stuart Mill pronounced in his *Essay on Liberty*, 'A general state education is merely a contrivance for moulding people to be exactly like each other, and as the mould in which it casts them is that which pleases the predominant power in the Government, it establishes a despotism over the mind, leading, by natural tendency, to one over the body.'

Nevertheless, from the 1830s, the government made a grant of £20,000 to the British and National societies in equal shares, to enable them to build more schools. This capital sum was increased in later years, and remained an important source of funding until it was withdrawn as part of the 1870 Education Act.

In the late 1830s, a fresh stimulus to social reform was provided by the discovery that there were some 40-50,000 pauper children in workhouses, whom the Poor Law was failing to protect. Their plight resembled that

School house at Sandford St Martin, Oxfordshire, between 1877 and 1880. The school was founded and built in 1842 by Edward Marshall, FSA, at the expense of himself and his mother. In 1865, an infants' classroom was added. The lady in front of the door is Miss J.E. Marshall, daughter of the founder.

described in Charles Dickens's *Oliver Twist*, published as a propaganda piece in 1839. Sturt notes that:

'Oliver was brought up in an establishment separated from the adult paupers, but, as he was farmed out for seven and a half pence a week, and as there was no selection of his guardian and no supervision, he was maltreated and starved. He received no education, with the result that, at the age of nine years, when the workhouse wanted to get rid of him, no one wished to be burdened with a child lacking all skill and power of work.'

As an Assistant Poor Law Commissioner in the Eastern Division, and then in the metropolis, Dr Joseph Kay (later known as Kay-Shuttleworth) was well-placed to observe the consequences of state neglect: he pointed to 'prolonged dependence and subsequent chargeability as criminals in the prisons and penal colonies'. In 1838, he was appointed Secretary of the newly-formed Committee of the Privy Council on Education. This was to have only advisory powers, but could invoke the authority of the Privy Council 'against the attacks of the Church and Tories' to ensure that its recommendations were adopted.

One of its first actions was to require, from 1840, that all schools receiving a government grant, be open to government inspectors. This directive was bitterly opposed by the Church of England, which promptly appointed Diocesan Boards of Education to inspect and aid Church Schools, but tempers were cooled somewhat when the Archbishops of Canterbury and York were given powers of veto over government inspectors in Anglican schools, and the practice of state investigation was retained. The new inspectors sent out into the countryside in the 1840s were quick to condemn the monitorial system that was used in many of the larger rural schools. Thus one HMI, the Revd Frederick Watkins, noted of the monitors:

'They are in general very young—rarely thirteen years of age. I have found a boy of 9 teaching children of his own age. But the average age in boys' schools is 11. In girls' schools, it is rather higher and may reach 12... They are ignorant of the subjects taught. They go heavily and unlovingly to it. A [teaching] card in one hand, the other in their pocket, they go singly, or in pairs, to their work. What is it? A reading lesson, seldom with any questions, but with spelling afterwards. I have often stood by in silence and heard the grossest blunders made in both—words miscalled—left out—half-said—others substituted for them. The monitor takes no notice. He frequently does not recognise the blunder if he hears it. In general he does not hear it. His thoughts are elsewhere...'

The Education Committee attempted to improve matters by the inauguration, in 1846, of the pupil-teacher system. Suitable pupils were apprenticed between the age of thirteen and eighteen to a teacher—they received instruction and assisted with classroom work. Each year, they were examined by a government inspector and, if successful in a final examination, qualified for a training college. At one of these, both men and women could gain a teacher's certificate, which brought with it an augmented salary. Not only did this system provide a supply of certificated staff to elementary schools, but the pupil-teachers themselves were superior to monitors, since they were older, usually better instructed and under external supervision. They also had the incentive of a small government

Fobbing Church School, Essex, 1887. A parish school was recorded in the Fobbing church rate-book as early as 1810. The master was paid a salary of ten pounds a year, six from the church and four for children from the parish. In 1870, a meeting held at the school after the passing of Forster's Education Act resolved that 'the school be placed in an efficient state'. The photograph of the governess, Miss Milne, and the children was taken at the time of Queen Victoria's jubilee in 1887.

grant during their apprenticeship and had the eventual prospect of entry to a professional career.

Inevitably, not all pupil-teachers proved to be suitable candidates, and Horn notes the example of one distraught Head in Somerset in the late 1890s, who listed a whole catalogue of offences against his charge:

'1.Absenting himself from his duties without permission. 2.Sending scholars during school hours for Whiskey. 3.Drinking Whiskey in the presence of his class. 4.Taking and claiming for his own a book belonging to Sidney Rossiter. 5.Being in possession of, and using, duplicate keys to School Cupboards and Sunday School Harmonium. 6.Breaking open a cupboard in the School from which a Missionary Box was lost (contents included).'

The Education Committee, however, was sufficiently encouraged by early reports submitted by its inspectors of the success of the system, to offer a capitation grant in 1853 based on average attendance for adequately maintained schools with certificated teachers. Yet, as Sellman points out, the Committee's action often tended to increase disparity in rural areas since it was only the better schools, which were under the management of a progressive Head, and in a parish willing to pay augmented salaries, that benefited. Nonetheless, he also observes that for the fortunate few the effect could be 'revolutionary', as is shown in the HMI's report on Holberton in Devon in 1855: 'where a few years ago the people had no desire for education, the attendance has become so good and regular that the capitation grant was made for 40 boys and 39 girls.' The problem of attendance, however, was to bedevil attempts to improve rural education throughout the century. Even where adequate provision existed, there was no guarantee that country children would attend regularly. Margaret Ashby commented that by the 1850s 'a Bledington boy could not hope to get work on the railway or a girl in any but a rough farmhouse kitchen, without the power to read.' The problem was that many labouring families could not survive without every member working. Usually, boys had started working by the time they were ten, and some began at five, six and seven years old. Girls were needed at home to help their mothers. As Ashby remarks, 'such a state of affairs was incompatible with education, and literacy under these conditions was a miracle.'

Besides the children who missed school altogether, very many more took time off to assist with seasonal agricultural activities. Then there were wet days, when mothers kept their children at home to conserve precious clothes and shoes, days off for illness and for special occasions, such as Club Day, a traditional feast day, a church outing, or a family excursion to a fair, circus or racecourse. Such interruptions meant that a child often made little progress, accumulating only a jumble of half-understood facts.

Nonetheless, the number of rural schools with certificated Heads and teachers which could command reasonable attendances increased steadily through the 1850s until the infamous Revised Code of 1862 was introduced in an attempt to reduce the growing Education budget. This abolished government grants for pupil-teachers, augmented salaries for certificated teachers and grants for 'inessentials' such as books and scientific apparatus. State funding was to be confined to a single capitation grant based on average attendance and passes in an annual examination in the three Rs. The result was a tremendous drop in income for many rural schools, which obliged them to dismiss qualified staff or to appoint those who would accept the lowest remuneration.

The Code also introduced a curriculum for the schools under inspection arranged in six standards for each of the three Rs, beginning above infant level. The standards in reading, for instance, ranged from 'a narrative in monosyllables' to 'a short ordinary paragraph in a newspaper or other modern narrative'. But Sellman indicates that most rural children got no further than standard four, 'which required only reading from a book in use in the school (with which they were already familiar), the writing of a sentence dictated from a school book, and a sum in compound rules [simple weights and measures].' He adds that the standard system was 'devised for large town schools where each standard could form a separate class', and 'lay heavy on a village school where several, and often all, standards must be taught together by one teacher.'

Some teachers, even in country districts, did go further than the three Rs and, from 1867, grant-earning extras included Geography, History and Grammar. But the teaching of these subjects could be reduced to such a level of monotony as to render them almost useless. Sturt quotes an HMI who reported that 'at the end of such a course... the children knew nothing, not even the name of their own country.'

It was the very fact that the schools' grant depended on success in the yearly examination that deterred the majority of teachers from departing from the strict letter of the curriculum. It has been generally recognised that the Revised Code ensured that the minimum required standard became the maximum attained. Before, the visit of an HMI had been welcomed—his role had been to give advice and encouragement. Now such visits were dreaded—a bad report might lead to closure. As examination time approached, teachers attempted to cram their pupils and were frequently reduced to writing frantic notes imploring parents to send their children to school to keep the attendance figures up.

By the 1860s, indeed, there was increasing national concern about the problem of poor attendance. Despite the provision of generally better schools in urban areas, neither the Poor Law nor the various measures enacted by the education departments had touched the hard core of urban poverty. All the major cities contained their legions of waifs and strays—their street arabs and mudlarks condemned to live in misery and ignorance. Sturt notes that, towards the end of the decade, a survey carried out by government inspectors in Birmingham, Leeds, Liverpool and Manchester indicated that of some four million children of the poorer classes only one and a half million were on the registers of schools, and that of these only just over one third were offered for examination.

At about the same time, the Report of the Royal Commission on the Employment of Women and Children in Agriculture revealed the unsatisfactory nature of rural education, while other investigations indicated that the Workshops Act of 1867, which was intended to restrict the part-time occupation of children in industry, including such rural industries as straw plaiting, lace and glove making, was largely ignored.

There were increasingly urgent reasons why a good school should be within the reach of every child. The most obvious was the enfranchisement in 1867 of the lower middle classes and urban working classes. 'Now,' said Robert Lowe, the President of the Education Department, 'we must educate our masters.' Yet literacy was not only desirable in political terms to ensure that voters should choose their government in an informed, rather than ignorant way, but also from an economic and practical point of view. The ability to read was an established condition of employment in quite humble work, and was increasingly necessary for making sense of the new industrial society. People needed to be able to decipher a railway timetable, to look at the Situations Vacant column in the local newspaper, and to understand what they were buying, as goods had begun to be sold in branded packs, with printed labels and instructions for use.

In 1868, the electorate returned a Liberal government committed to educational reform. Forster's Act, passed in 1870, required that all children should receive adequate elementary schooling. Parishes were to assess their existing provision and, where necessary, form a School Board to build and maintain a suitable school.

In the countryside, the parson, squire and local farmers often joined forces and managed to fight off the establishment of the School Boards for several years. Churchmen objected to the fact that religious instruction was to be on a non-sectarian basis, while farmers still tended to be against education, believing that too much learning would encourage labourers to rise above their station and that, 'the younger the child was started on agricultural work, the better for everyone'. Their main concern was, however, economic—to keep the rates down, particularly after the start of agricultural depression. They could not see why they should have to bear the cost of rural education, which enabled labourers to leave the land and get a higher-paid job elsewhere.

Government inspectors were only too well aware of the likely reception of the legislation in country areas. Bellairs, an HMI in Oxfordshire in 1872, remarked, 'The Act of the last session, so far as the rural parts of this district are concerned, will be, for many years at least, almost wholly inoperative'. Thus, as Sturt observes, by 1878, 'in Berkshire there were only seven [School Boards] covering a population of 40,000, and three had been formed by compulsion: and in rural Buckinghamshire, of 23 Boards covering 36,000 only eight were voluntary formations.'

But such hostility was not universal. Ashby reports that the farmers of Bledington in Gloucestershire were in favour of having a Board at the earliest opportunity, as they wanted a school for their own children as well as for those of labouring families:

'In early days, the Board showed a natural understanding of their teachers' and children's needs for encouragement and help. One member would go to school to play accompaniment to the children's singing, another brought his magic lantern to entertain and inform the children. Farmers' wives came and helped with the needlework when the Master's wife was ill. On May Day, for some years, after the chldren had sung their songs at every house in the village, "friends and lovers of children" provided them with "a plentiful tea" served by the Board's ladies.'

The Act tended to be most unpopular with the labourers themselves, because of the loss of potential earnings if their children had to attend the Board School. B.J. Davey, in his study of the village of Ashwell in Derbyshire, notes the reaction of a Mr Flitton expressed in a letter to a local newspaper:

'Permit me to offer a few remarks on one of the most inequitous and oppressive acts of parliament ever entered on the statute book, namely, the Education Act in its amended form. How on earth are its penal clauses to be enforced in a purely agricultural district? Look at the state of a Poor Man's wages –barely sufficient to supply the common necessaries of life and forsooth this Act is to stop channel wherewith this scanty pittance may be augmented. Let us take a labourer's family of seven children, and there are many as numerous as this, most likely there will be three boys under 14 earning in the aggregate ten shilling per week. If this is stopped, and the labourer is thrown on his weekly wage, I ask, how on earth is he to live or keep his children in the bare necessaries of life and pay the school's fees ? I think it incumbent on employers to agitate for a reduction of the standard age as it is altogether unworkable and impractical for rural districts. I am a member of the Ashwell School Board, and I feel it impossible to enforce this most oppressive and abominable Act.'

Among many labourers, Davey comments, there arose a sullen resentment of the imposed system alien to the old village ways and because the Act did not abolish school fees. The argument was that free education would pauperise the labourer: he would not value something he did not pay for. Each Board, therefore, was allowed to set its own fees, and those where farmers were strongly represented often increased the cost of schooling above standard four, arguing that if a labourer could afford to keep his children from work, he could afford to pay fees.

As there was no provision for compulsory attendance, Forster's measure did not solve the problem of absenteeism. Further legislation in 1876 and 1880 attempted to remedy the situation: attendance was made compulsory up to the age of ten, and special committees were set up to enforce the new regulations. The Attendance Officers, however, were not very vigilant, and magistrates were usually reluctant to convict in non-attendance cases. Sometimes, even the members of Attendance Committees and School Boards were themselves guilty of employing children who should have been at school. Seasonal agricultural work continued to interrupt schooling, although the employment of children probably declined with the reduction in arable acreage during the depression, with the mechanisation of certain farm tasks and with the rise in agricultural real wages from the 1890s. It was certainly much diminished after 1902, when the responsibility of enforcing attendance passed to county councils.

The period between the Education Act of 1870 and the Act of 1902 witnessed the growing importance of Board Schools in national education, while many voluntary schools were in financial trouble, with their income falling short of expenditure. Indeed, by the 1890s, such schools were almost entirely maintained out of public funds. The quality of education also tended to be lower in Church Schools, as the state schools attracted a higher percentage of certificated staff. With the abolition of the set examination in the 1890s, some of the pressure on teachers to adhere rigidly to the three Rs was relieved, and schools generally were encouraged to widen their curriculum to include special industrial and rural subjects, among them cottage gardening, dairying, land-surveying and a variety of rural crafts. A further advance was the abolition of school fees in 1891, and their replacement by a state grant, much to the relief of both parents and teachers, who no longer had cause to dread the annual visit of the government inspector. They could see him once again as a source of valued aid and expertise.

Nonetheless, disparities still existed between rural education and that provided in the towns, which had benefited more from the 1870 Act. Rural supplementary teachers were usually unqualified, while pupil-teachers in country districts largely lacked the stimulus of the training centres that were open to their urban counterparts from the late 1890s. Attendance, comments Sellman, was more strictly enforced in urban areas, and the mechanisation of industry lessened the demand for young child labour.

The 1902 Act was the essential preliminary to a levelling-up of standards. The miscellany of independent School Boards was placed under the authority of county councils, who became wholly responsible for the maintenance of all day-schools within their areas, so that the village schools benefited by being under the same authorities as those in the towns.

Schoolboys helping with the harvest at East Kent Hop Gardens, about 1901.

156

By the outbreak of the Great War, education was free and compulsory for all rural children. Tenant farmers, however, still often chose to send their sons to fee-paying schools to acquire a superior education, which included Latin and French in the curriculum. This 1916 photograph shows one such boy, John Kingdon Ward, who attended Hele's School, Exeter, Devon. With him is his sister, Sadie.

The county authorities were not only responsible for elementary education, but were also empowered to establish rate-aided secondary schools. Here the inequality between rural and urban districts remained, since secondary provision was to be limited to children of exceptional ability and to those who could pay a fee, usually of not less than three pounds per year per child. This barred the entry of many urban working class children, but the consequences were even more serious for the children of agricultural labourers whose wages, despite their upward drift, still remained substantially lower than those of their urban counterparts. Horn points out that 'even in 1924, it was estimated that only about 5% of the entrance to secondary schools in rural areas were the offspring of agricultural labourers'—a reflection not of their intelligence, but of their economic circumstances.

Nonetheless, a considerable advance had been made. Sellman concludes:

'The combination of state aid and initiative with local effort (even if this was compelled) had revolutionised rural education by comparison with the standards of thirty (and particularly of sixty) years before. For the great majority of country children, the result was probably little more than some grounding in social discipline, the ability to read the less demanding newspapers, to write (if with a limited vocabulary), and to do simple sums: but this in itself was a great step forward.'

Such an achievement paved the way for many to leave the countryside and to seek their fortunes elsewhere. Education thus did much to break the insularity of the village and, in Davey's words, 'must be recognised as a major factor in the destruction of the old community.'

Another facet of change was the growth of public order in the countryside, with the introduction of professional police forces in some counties from the late 1830s and the gradual reduction of many of the worst types of violent crime.

The establishment of a professional police force had been advocated by the Benthamites earlier in the century on the grounds that the prevention of crime was better than punishment. Sir Robert Peel had established the Metropolitan Police in 1829, and the Royal Commission on the Rural Police, set up in 1836, had reported three years later, recommending the setting up of a single police force for the counties, with the same principles of training and management as the Metropolitan Police. The County Police Act of 1839, however, was a permissive measure, in which magistrates in quarter sessions were empowered, but not required, to establish a police force, either for the whole county or a division of it. Thus there was to be no centralisation of police powers or interference with those of local magistrates.

It was not until 1856 that it finally became obligatory on all counties to establish a paid force. The principle of central supervision, however, was combined with local management by magistrates, leaving considerable powers of control in the hands of the rural establishment—an arrangement that endured into the twentieth century. In practice, though, the local chief constables soon acquired a degree of autonomy which enabled them to create their own standards of efficiency and professionalism.

From the outset, the intention was that the rural police, like the Metropolitan Division, should form a highly disciplined, educated and loyal body of men. But the job was not easy and the rewards were not substantial. A constable's pay varied between 15s. and 21s. a week (after 1886, it was raised to 30s.). For this, he was expected to work seven days a week, with a rest day only every four to six weeks. The average day's duty was some ten to twelve hours, usually in two shifts, the longer—up to seven hours—at night. All patrolling was on foot—up to twenty miles might be covered in a day—and no boot allowance was paid until 1873. The policeman was expected to attend church on Sundays, usually in uniform, and was discouraged from entering a pub or beer house unless on duty. Even so, the police force was often an attractive opening for young labourers since it offered, as Critchley observed, 'respectability, warm clothes and the opportunity of self-improvement', with promotion to Sergeant after four or five years, and to Inspector after eight to ten. There was also some prospect of security in old age, as a small pension might be paid at the discretion of the Chief Constable; the pension was automatically awarded after 1890.

But on their first appearance in the countryside, the new policemen were often assaulted, and indeed, violent crime continued to worry county authorities until a turning-point was reached in the mid 1860s. Important changes were taking place in the nature of rural crime. In particular, as Jones points out, 'crimes of assault and stealing which had once constituted about a half of all petty session proceedings, lost much of their prominence.' Newer categories of crime, such as breaches of the Education and Highway Acts, began to take their place. On the other hand, villagers still continued to be arrested in large numbers for drunkenness and disorderly conduct, while poaching remained common. Over 2,000 poachers were fined or imprisoned in Norfolk in the years 1863-71. Many were young labourers, although there were also the more feared gangs of night poachers, whose activities gave rise to the hated Poaching Protection Act of 1862 which enabled the police to search any person on the road or in a public place whom they suspected of poaching. As Horn comments, 'what was disliked was the increased right of search the Act gave to the police, and also the way the legislation could be turned to obtain convictions for minor thefts.'

Other factors apart from the increasing efficiency of the police contributed to the fall in the crime rate. One was the improvement in wages and employment resulting from the high rate of migration to the towns. Another was the appearance, towards the end of the 1860s, of the agricultural trade union movement, which provided a more effective channel for social protest than the sporadic and spontaneous acts of vandalism which had marked the earlier phase of agrarian unrest. Gratuitous acts of violence and instances of agrarian outrage, of course, did not disappear entirely. Horn records that at Carlton Curlieu and Kibworth in Leicestershire during 1870, threatening letters were found tied to the hedge near the scene of rick fires. One of them noted in tones reminiscent of the 1830s and 1840s:

'If you don't raise wages this week, you won't have a chance next. If there is any Irish left here after this week they will have to have a fresh gaffer. This is the last week of low wages.'

By this time, however, recorded instances of arson seem to have been carried out chiefly by vagrants.

The second part of the century also saw changes in prosecution policy. Jones comments that 'the coming of the new police made prosecutions cheaper, commitments more certain and punishments less severe.' The result, however, was that 'villagers, especially juveniles, were taken to court for petty theft and minor breaches of the peace that had once been ignored.' Horn records that, in July 1864, two boy labourers from the village of North Stoke in Oxfordshire were convicted of stealing 'four pounds of Bacon and one four pound loaf in Bread of the value of three shillings and sixpence' and were sentenced by the Henley bench to twenty-one days' imprisonment with hard labour; later, at the Oxford quarter sessions, in April 1874, a female labourer, who had stolen a bushel of oats and two pecks of barley was sentenced to four calendar months' hard labour. Such examples are not hard to find, although prosecutions and the severity of the sentences passed depended greatly on the character of the local bench.

In late Victorian England, however, the community was becoming more respectable and law-abiding. Such values were being constantly inculcated by almost all levels of society, Dunbabin notes, 'by radicals and non-conformists as well as by Tories and a revivified Established Church'. At the same time, the police themselves had become integrated into village life, as Critchley observes that this had been largely accomplished by the 1890s:

'When half the force turned out for the annual sports and the police band played waltzes at the summer fête or carnival, even the older generation, brought up in the 1830s and 1840s, would realise that the modern policeman represented a complete break from the watchman and parish constable of their boyhood.'

By this time, the country bobby on his bicycle had become a familiar and comforting sight.

In the course of the century that preceded the Great War, the administration of the countryside was completely reorganised. At the outset, authority had been exercised by the unpaid Justices of the Peace, comprised almost entirely of the landed interest and the clergy, qualified by the virtue of their property and status. The change was brought about in the interests of efficiency—made necessary by a new magnitude of urban crime and poverty. New administrative bodies were created: the Poor Law Boards, Burial Boards, Highway Boards and later School Boards. Each was composed of elected representatives with power to levy rates, under central supervision. In the short run, the landed aristocracy and gentry often gained entry to these bodies and their influence as petty monarchs was sustained and in some cases even enhanced. But as much of the work was performed by paid officials, the actions of the latter tended, in the end, to 'circumscribe the area of independent local judgement'. The constant stream of new statutory regulations from Westminster had much the same effect. This process reached its apogee in 1888 when most of the magistrates' administrative responsibilities were transferred to the county councils. As Moore concludes, 'when their leadership was challenged, many of them [the gentry] simply left the game.'

The result of what has been termed 'the nineteenth century revolution in government'—the creation of a centralised interventionist state—reached into every corner of rural life. The practical gains may have been small and urban areas were often the first to benefit, but the countryside was not entirely left behind. Education provided the children with new opportunities and, for the majority of the older generation, life after 1900 was no longer so harsh, and, with old age pensions and other welfare benefits, the future seemed secure.

The Labourer's Leisure

As urban and industrial England advanced steadily in power and influence, rural England both contributed to this process and was transformed by it.

The loss of numbers to the towns in the second half of the nineteenth century was less significant than the depletion of these special skills and experiences that had blended together to create intricately balanced and self-sufficient communities. Economic independence was sacrificed and also a sense of corporate identity. Before 1800, folk customs were not antiquated curiosities, but the customary way in which the common people marked the events of the rural calendar. Holidays were regular occasions for intensive enjoyment, when the pleasures of the table, of singing, dancing and sport could be indulged, and when seasonal rituals and recreations were observed. Many such diversions had survived attack from medieval times, and most fell into disuse in the nineteenth century as they lost their relevance within an industrialising society. Technology and capitalism, education and religion eroded them and substituted new recreational forms. As early as 1840, Howitt could write: 'In my own recollection the appearance of morris-dancers, guisers, plough-bullocks, and Christmas carollers, has become more and more rare, and to find them we must go into the retired hamlets of Staffordshire, and the dales of Yorkshire and Lancashire.' By 1880, such activities were memories to most old men, to be recounted over a pint of ale, and of little interest to the younger generation, who were enthusiastic for more urban pastimes.

The Horn Dance, Abbots Bromley, Staffordshire, 1899. The characters include a clown or fool, a hobby horse, a musician and Maid Marian.

160

Tipteerers' Play, Chithurst, West Sussex. A form of folk drama extant at least until 1912. The characters included Father Christmas, Jolly John, Gallant Soldier, King George IV, Turkish Knight, Noble Captain and Doctor Good. All carry swords painted with blue spiral stripes, except Father Christmas who, as usual in West Sussex, carries a holly bush on a similarly painted staff.

Indeed, the reigns of Victoria and Edward saw a reshaping of popular culture so profound that its extent can only be appreciated by a review of the place of leisure in pre-industrial England.

In 1808, there were forty-four official holidays when the Bank of England closed. By 1834, these had shrunk to four—Christmas Day, Good Friday, May Day and the first day of November. The 1808 figure was itself a reduction from earlier times, when the principal holidays were derived from the realities of the farming year. Bouts of intensive effort—ploughing, sowing, lambing, sheepshearing, the hay and corn harvests—were followed by slack periods, not exactly of inactivity, for the land was a demanding mistress, but times when ease and merriment were possible. The great Christian festivals, Christmas, Easter, St John's Day and All Souls, framed the seasons, and behind them lay an older pagan calendar dominated by the two great agrarian cycles which related to the preparation of the crops and their harvesting. Many of the customs associated with these festivals had their origins in prehistory. Mumming plays, traditionally performed at midwinter before the spring sowing, symbolised at their deepest level the pagan supplication for the regeneration of the earth and return of the sun. Guising, or the wearing of animal masks, which again took place in winter, recalled a belief in sympathetic magic. May-time ceremonies were intended to aid the coming of spring and linked human fertility with the increase of nature.

With the coming of Christianity, the old pagan festivals were taken over and adapted to new purposes. Over the centuries, they lost much, although not all, of their original content and meaning. Primitive superstition would remain a force as long as dearth and the possibility of harvest failure continued to dominate the lives of the majority of the people. At the same time, new ecclesiastical customs came into being. The church wake—often a week-long celebration—commemorating the founder or patron saint of a parish church was a typical medieval mixture of religious festival and secular event, marked by a temporary surfeit of eating and drinking before the grim task of wresting a living from the soil was resumed. By the end of the Middle Ages, the common people were in possession of a rich, if not

The Padstow hobby horse, Cornwall.

always well understood, orally transmitted culture, made up of custom, song, dance and popular drama—to which was added an expanding repertoire of indoor games and outdoor sports.

Certain aspects of popular recreation had always attracted the opposition of Church and State, but from the seventeenth century there developed a series of more determined attempts to reform the leisure habits of the labouring classes. At first, the onslaught was launched by an aggressive Protestantism. The puritan outlook has been succinctly described by Malcolmson:

'For these "preciser" sort of people the traditions of popular leisure were objectionable on a number of grounds: they were thought to be profane and licentious—they were occasions of worldly indulgence which tempted men from a godly life; being rooted in pagan and popish practices, they were rich in the sort of ceremony and ritual which poorly suited the Protestant conscience; they frequently involved a desecration of the Sabbath and an interference with the worship of true believers; they disrupted the peaceful order of society, distracting men from their basic social duties—hard work, thrift, personal restraint, devotion to family, a sober carriage.'

The force of puritan indignation was largely spent by the end of the Stuart period, but the religious outcry against popular recreation revived with the rise of the evangelical movement in the early eighteenth century. To Hannah More, her play-writing days behind her, true religion involved a turning of the whole mind to God; recreation was at best a distraction and at worst, where pagan elements were concerned, a device of the Devil. The effects of evangelicalism were far reaching. The more exclusive sects, such as the Primitive Methodists or the Bible Christians, prohibited members who took part in popular pastimes. *The Primitive Methodist Magazine* in 1815 asserted that 'No person shall be continued as a member of our society who visits public or worldly amusements; nor those who waste their time at public-houses.' And evangelicals re-stated the old puritan insistence on the holiness of the Sabbath and the necessity of devoting it to spiritual rather than worldly pursuits. The movement also contributed, towards the end of the eighteenth century, to building up public opinion against the pastimes of bull and bear baiting, cock-fighting and badger hunting, and attracted some support from labouring men themselves.

A different development, which had similar consequences, was the growth of rationalism and the cultivation of moral sensibilities. This was particularly evident among the more educated classes and revealed itself in a concern to 'improve' the poor. Superstition was deplored not because it was contrary to religion but because it was contrary to reason. And to the evangelical protest that blood sports were morally degrading was added the 'enlightened' argument that they were primitive and obstructed the general progress of civilisation. Joseph Strutt noted of bear baiting in 1801 that:

'...it is not encouraged by persons of rank and opulence in the present day; and when practised, which happens rarely, it is attended only by the lowest and most despicable parts of the people; which plainly indicated a general refinement of manners and prevalency of humanity among the moderns.'

Such an assertion, however, not only overestimated the decline of bear baiting, but smacked of hypocrisy in that there was little attempt at this time to eradicate the upper-class sports of fox and stag hunting.

The attitude of the landed classes to the pastimes of the poor was increasingly ambivalent. Anti-puritan tolerance had marked the beginning of the eighteenth century, but was modified towards its end by the emergence of two new circumstances. There was a greater insistence on the need for social control. Magistrates became very conscious that the rights of property were being safeguarded only by a small, poorly trained and unprofessional militia in most counties. Secondly and more importantly, the growth of agrarian capitalism itself threatened popular recreation. Enclosure curtailed many activities in those villages where land was owned by an improving landowner. Thus in 1824, Robert Slaney wrote that in rural areas, 'owing to the inclosure of open fields and commons, the poor have no place in which they may amuse themselves in summer evenings,

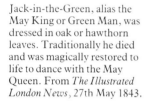

Jack-in-the-Green, alias the May King or Green Man, was dressed in oak or hawthorn leaves. Traditionally he died and was magically restored to life to dance with the May Queen. From *The Illustrated London News*, 27th May 1843.

when the labour of the day is over, or when a holiday occurs.' By 1844, William Howitt claimed that football 'seems to have almost gone out of use with the enclosure of wastes and commons, requiring (as it does) a wide space for its exercise.' Both statements were considerably exaggerated, but they were indicative of a trend.

The most insidious attack on popular custom and entertainment, however, came from the growth of an industrial economy. The accusation that traditional pastimes were a waste of valuable time stemmed in part from the puritan fear that 'Satan finds mischief for idle hands' and in part from the notion that recreation was subversive as far as productive labour and the advance of national wealth were concerned. Thus by 1758 William Temple could argue that 'the only way to make them [the labouring masses] temperate and industrious is to lay them under a necessity of labouring all the time they can spare from meals and sleep, in order to procure the common necessities of life.' The celebration of ancient customs was condemned as slothful, a diversion from the main business of life. Dorning Ramsbotham noted with disdain in July 1873:

'One evening I met a very large procession of young men and women, with fiddles, garlands, and every ostentation of rural finery, dancing Morris dances in the highway, merely to celebrate an idle anniversary, or what they had been pleased to call for a year or two a fair, at a paltry thatched alehouse upon the neighbouring common.'

During the first half of the nineteenth century, the farm labourer was subjected to a tightening up of his work routine, although the seasonal rhythm of many of his occupations still provided opportunities for leisure. But in the rapidly growing industrial towns during this period, the situation was different. Here, the need was for regular full-time employment, making the most intensive use of both labour and capital. Idle men or idle machines meant loss of production and loss of profit, perhaps even bankruptcy; by the mid century, public holidays were severely reduced and working hours extended to the limit of endurance. The urban working week acquired a uniform dullness throughout the year. In some areas, where labour was short or where small handicraft industries survived, the working man might still assert his right to 'Saint Monday', but more often recreation was confined to the brief pleasures of tavern and street. And in towns, even more than in the countryside, space was at a premium; the large areas needed for the old rural sports, particularly football, were no longer available as green land disappeared under ghettoes of working class housing. If such activities were to survive at all, they would have to be drastically modified.

Corn dolly making.

There were many traditional activities which could not in any form migrate to the cities. These included Plough Monday celebrations, where the plough boys or 'bullocks' drove their decorated ploughs through the streets; 'crying the neck', when harvesters ran with a bundle of straw taken from the last sheaf; beating the bounds of a parish; clipping and harvest suppers; church doles and audit dinners. As Malcolmson has commented, 'much of the rural past had to be set aside, and most of the migrants discovered that the expanding urban centres had, as yet, only an extremely raw and restricted recreational culture to put in its place.'

The new urban working class culture as it came into being had its own effect on traditional pastimes in the countryside. The old game of football, played by an unspecified number of players on a local field or even between two villages, in traditional Shrove Tuesday matches, gradually disappeared and was replaced by a highly disciplined sport, born in the public schools. A leading part of its propagation among the working classes was played by social reformers, churchmen prominent among them. There was an awakening of conscience in the mid century concerning excessive working hours, which led by degrees to the acceptance of the Saturday half-holiday; many reformers considered it essential that such time should be devoted to useful and improving pastimes. Football seemed to them to offer an appealing blend of healthy exercise, teamwork and sportsmanship. The working classes, who brought the habit of kicking a ball around to the factory yard, took to the new game with enthusiasm. It gave individuals an opportunity to shine and provided an exciting spectator sport which allowed a developing urban 'tribalism' to express itself. Thus, to the southern public school tradition was added the contribution of many thriving working class teams from the Midlands and North. The success of football nationally after the institution of the FA cup in 1872 meant that it attracted attention even in the rural areas, winning allegiance among the younger men, to whom the older sports, with the exception of cricket, seemed dull in comparison.

New forces, too, were threatening other traditional forms of recreation among rural workers from the 1860s. The greater use of labour-saving machines removed much of the uncertainty concerning such vital operations as harvesting, and the whole complex of ritual and superstition which had surrounded the long, difficult harvest by the old, laborious methods was devalued. No longer did reapers stand in a half-circle around the last strand of corn and throw their hooks at it—sharing the responsibility for the death of the corn spirit. And the traditional harvest supper, an almost pagan thanksgiving with the provision of an abundant feast of roast-beef, plum-puddings, apple-pies and unlimited quantities of ale or cider, was fast disappearing. Farmers felt less inclined to reward their men for the more limited effort of mechanical reaping, accomplished in a matter of days rather than weeks; although contemporary writers also

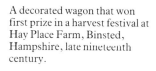
A decorated wagon that won first prize in a harvest festival at Hay Place Farm, Binsted, Hampshire, late nineteenth century.

blamed the decline on the social aspirations of farmers, who were more reluctant to sit down in open fellowship with their men and share a meal with them.

The harvest supper was to some extent replaced by the harvest festival. The ancient religious service of Lammas was revived in 1843 by Stephen Hawker, the vicar of Morwenstow, near Bude in Cornwall, and quickly spread to other areas. The Church stepped in to offer a wide variety of substitutes for traditional customs and pastimes as the century wore on. Sunday Schools for instance, grew in number from the 1780s. Many teachers opposed the playing of children's games which contained some trace of superstition as well as the playing of any games on Sundays. They offered instead, among other things, literacy. A literate child, as he or she

Sunday school outings. *Left:* using a wagon from Mapleton Farm, Horsington, Lincolnshire, about 1908. *Above:* Wiveliscombe, Somerset, about 1895.

There was a tendency for May Day customs to be revived in schools, usually after they had been discontinued as adult celebrations. *Left:* May Day celebrations, Iffley, Oxfordshire, about 1900. *Bottom:* Maypole dancing, also about 1900.

grew older, became less attached to the oral culture of early years and developed new and wider horizons. Something of this process is recalled by M.K. Ashby who, speaking of the establishment of a Methodist Sunday School at Bledington in Oxfordshire in the 1850s, observed:

'Their worship was as orderly as it was enthusiastic and the Sunday School prospered. Reading must have been taught to the children there, at home or by Mrs Benfield. It was almost impossible to be illiterate among them: Wesley's hymn book and the Bible were the basis of their religious life. Thus, they not only had letters but also literature and language and ideas. Cheap Bibles were obtainable: no home, no packed box of young man or woman going away was complete without it.'

Sunday Schools supplemented the education that children received during the week. Before the Education Act of 1870, schooling for many was scant and often meant no more than a brief spell at a dame's school, where even the rudiments of the three Rs were imperfectly instilled, thus the contribution of the Sunday Schools was an important one. They were, moreover, in the vanguard of the movement to give poor children a break from home. By organising at first excursions and then holidays, they gave the children a glimpse of a wider world and in doing so broke down the pockets of isolation that kept alive the old traditions in rural areas. As the *Norwich News* commented in 1846, following a visit of 5,000 working class children and 3,000 spectators to the seaside:

'Sunday school outings are better adapted to regenerate society, than the revival of the Maypole and the antiquated rubbish of the Book of Sports.'

Not all the clergy were opposed to folk customs, however, and some, especially Anglican clergy, sought to preserve them; the dissenting churches took their paganism altogether more seriously. When the Revd Hill took over the cure of Bledington in 1843, he took a simple delight in the performance of mumming plays and other ritual dramas. Ashby recounts:

'The brief memoir of Mr Hill by his son tells of the remnants of old songs, of the children's maypoles, and the rhymes with which they begged on St Thomas's and St Valentine's Days and of the Mumming Play acted in the Vicarage kitchen at Christmas time. Percy, the small son, saw it but could not later recollect the play, only the unwonted appearance of the men, with their false beards and strange garments and the quaintness of their antics. Once the Morris dancers with their Tom Fool came to the Vicarage lawn.'

Other Anglican clergy indulged their antiquarian tastes more actively; they felt that they had little time to lose if they were to record a fast-disappearing culture. The Revd John Broadwood took down some sixteen traditional Sussex songs in the 1840s. Later in the century, the formidable Sabine Baring-Gould, squarson and rector of Lew Trenchard in North

Copy stick, late nineteenth century. Under the inscription is another reading 'Deal not with the unjust'. On the other side is the legend 'Rememberances'.

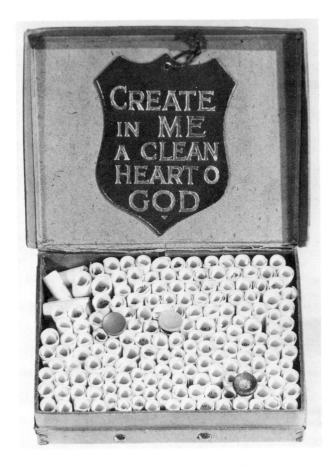

Devon, set out to record traditional Devon songs, as far as possible from the 'old singing men' who, by the 1880s, were a dying breed. Roger Luxton of Halwill, himself once a famous song-man, offered an explanation for this:

' "Ah, your honour," he said "in old times us used to be welcome in every farmhouse at all shearing and haysel and harvest feasts... All them things be given up... The farmers be too grand to talk to us old chaps, and for certain, they don't care to hear us zing. Why for nigh on forty years us old zinging fellows have been drove to the public houses to zing." '

Between 1888 and 1890, Baring-Gould, with the help of F.W. Bussell of Brasenose College, Oxford, and the Revd H. Fleetwood Sheppard, rescued an impressive number of songs, published in *Songs of the West* (1889), and also compiled a list of fifty-five surviving singers. By 1904, Baring-Gould noted, in a letter to Cecil Sharp, 'It is full late now to collect. All my old men are dead but one.' Baring-Gould's valuable service in collecting these songs, however, was diminished by his habit of changing any of the original words which he considered unsuitable for Victorian taste. The *Songs of the West* bore many signs of a too fastidious mind, although some contemporaries still considered his substitutions too down-to-earth: *Three Drunken Maidens*, even in its modified form, and with its last verse rewritten, could still cause a local sensation.

The Church brought about other changes, too, in the musical life of the countryside. The 1840s saw an Anglican revival—the Tractarian

The Cold Ash team of bell ringers at Newbury in Berkshire.

Movement—which attached great importance to beauty and ceremonial in church services; it sought to re-establish the altar rather than the pulpit as the focal point of the service. One consequence was that the old rustic musicians, depicted in Hardy's *Under the Greenwood Tree*, were displaced by organ and choir. However, the practice of communal hymn-singing gradually became popular. The Victorian period was a great age of hymn-writing, reaching its pinnacle with *Hymns Ancient and Modern*, published in 1868. As Miss Ashby has commented, this collection 'provided a choice of hundreds of hymns, many with fine rhythms, sometimes rousing tunes, suitable for children, for boys, for simple souls and cultivated minds, gathered from all ages and from churches, far and wide.' None of the words were improper, and the abundance of good hymn tunes, Wesley's included, provided stiff competition for the old folk songs. In fact a considerable number of them were borrowed from the old folk-songs; clergymen were not above plagiarism for their own purposes. When Baring-Gould organised a tour of folk dancers and singers in the South-West in 1890, he was disconcerted by the uproarious laughter which greeted the 'Dilly Song', an air which had been taken over as a hymn tune in local Methodist chapels.

The growth of musical literacy itself diverted attention from the traditional songs. John Hullat's tonic sol-fa system was taught widely in schools from the 1870s, and although it had its defects, Walvin notes that it was 'nonetheless responsible for the musical training of tens of thousands of pupils from the mid-century onwards.' Pianos became more widely available and within reach of the better-off working class household by the end of the century. Religious music was popular, and so increasingly were

Below: performance of the masque, *The Well in the Wood*, by Mrs C.M.A. Peake, written for the people of Boxford, near Newbury, 1913. *Right:* the Camel play actors at Queen Camel, Somerset, April 1912. Dialect plays, like this one by John Read, were quite widely performed in Somerset and neighbouring counties.

169

the new tunes from the music-hall and seaside, minstrel songs and the repertoire of symphony orchestras. Moreover, brass bands and choral societies were establishing their hold in working class areas, even among quite small communities. Thus at Bledington:

'The brass band arrived to provide for some a genuine and most superior hobby and diversion. It had become possible through the publication of cheap musical scores and the invention of valves that made wind instruments easier to play—not that they were put within easy reach of farmworkers, but passion solves difficulties. By 1872 the Chipping Norton Temperance Club had a brass band and the Wyck Rissington Band that played at the Bledington festivals at Lammas time had a similar origin.'

In the last decades of the century, the habit of reading for pleasure spread among the rural working class. An interest in serious literature—the Bible and works of philosophy and economics—had marked the reading of a small working class elite earlier in the century; now the cheap popular literature of the 1880s and 1890s found its way from towns to the countryside. Lloyd's 'gothic shockers' and penny dreadfuls struck a familiar note to a society nourished on folk tales about suicides, the supernatural and the works of the Devil; even such a well-intentioned journal as the *Rural World* was careful to include a plentiful reporting of violence and death, and serialised tales of 'mystery and the imagination'. The difference was that even the most avid consumer of horror literature knew it to be invention. In consequence, people learned to regard folklore also as fiction. Those who believed it in any other sense were held to be naive, simple-minded, primitive. The old oral culture, therefore, suffered not only from neglect, but also from the positive aversion of a newly sophisticated generation among the labouring classes.

The Churches too had to come to terms with the fact that they were now competing with the new secular entertainments. In the bid to recruit and hold members, Cunningham points out that both Anglicans and Non-Conformists began to tolerate what they had previously condemned.

'The young in particular, it was recognised, expected secular amusement and "if the Church will not provide it, the Devil will." At varying points in the second half of the century, most Methodists came to accept outdoor games, the religious novel was being serialised in the journals by the late 1870s and even dancing began to be admitted by the 1890s.'

The outcome was that Church life was more inviting: Joseph Lawson reflected in the 1880s that chapels not only had better music, but 'they have

Ballad pedlar, about 1890.

Birling village band, Kent, 1887. The band of fourteen to fifteen men was founded in the late eighteenth century.

New Inn, Stratton, Cornwall, about 1880.

New Inn, Stratton, Cornwall, about 1880.

sewing classes, bazaars, concerts and drama; cricket and football clubs, and harriers; societies for mutual improvement, and excursions to the seaside.'

Not all rural labourers, however, wished to take up some new entertainment or improving activity. The attraction of religion, the temperance movement, or even brass bands was far from universal. For some, an acute sense of dislocation accompanied the dying of their craft, the replacement of the careful skills of the hand by the crude efficiency of the machine, and the abandonment of a familiar way of life. The village pub, at least, was not much altered; the inn was the last refuge for the old singing men and authentic folk dancers. Most villages still had two or three. At Bledington, Ashby describes The King's Head '...two small low-ceiled rooms with fixed benches round the walls and a table on which mugs could be set, with little space for anything but drink and talk, and darts when there were few drinkers. There were similar rooms at The Five Tuns, one of them almost a cellar.'

The pubs provided the opportunity for playing a number of the old, popular indoor games: dice, cards, draughts, quoits and darts. Shove halfpenny, known in its present form from the end of the eighteenth century, gained a firm hold in the nineteenth; skittles was already well established and seems to have developed from the fourteenth century game of kayles, in which a truncheon rather than a bowl was hurled at a number

Cribbage-domino set.

171

of pins or skittles (usually nine). A board version of skittles, 'Devil among the tailors', in which a ball tethered to a mast was swung at the pins, was also to be found in some areas; it became rarer towards the end of the century. Spanish dominoes, introduced in the late 1870s, replaced an earlier version imported from France and enjoyed an enormous vogue, particularly in the North of England.

The trend, though, was for the great variety of regional games to be reduced. Some, like bat and trap, played in Kent, and knur and spell, mostly found in the North-East, virtually disappeared in the two or three decades before 1914. Such games waned, as cricket, a more skilful and competitive event, grew in popularity. The basic rules of cricket had been established in the eighteenth century; the game obtained a mass following from the mid nineteenth century with the development of county and then of international tournaments. Cricket became the leading summer game and football the leading winter game. The rural labourer, however, was still largely excluded from the growing practice of playing sport on a Saturday afternoon, as he continued to work long hours throughout this period, and despite the general improvement in the labourer's position after 1850, he did not obtain any extra holidays. Indeed, as the number of special holidays dwindled in the early nineteenth century, he was actually worse off in this respect. In the second half of the century, however much slack time off the

Left: skittle set. *Above:* knur and spell being played in Yorkshire in the early nineteenth century. The knur was a small, hard ball and the spell was a spring-loaded device that released the ball to a predetermined height in the air; the knur was struck with the mallet to land as far away as possible.

Cricket. *Left:* Horspath cricket team, Oxfordshire, about 1900. *Below:* Mr Turrill, the first man to spin the ball at Garsington, Oxfordshire.

labourer might get, he increasingly resented having to work on Saturday afternoons when other workers were free. To reformers the need was clear:

'Another thing that ought to be done is that the labourer should have a half-holiday every week and leave at 1 p.m. on Saturday. As it is, he has to work every day God Almighty sends. All the year round; no pleasure, no holiday; and the farmer keeps him at it, nay, he is so afraid of the poor labourer getting off earlier on Saturdays that he, the farmer, votes on the District Council to keep the poor roadman at work until 4 p.m. on Saturday, although the Urban roadman leaves at 1 p.m. on Saturdays; and he will tell you that it will never do to allow the roadman to leave at 1 p.m. on Saturday, or else the farm labourer will want to leave also early. The condition of the poor labourer is bad, nay rotten: no holidays, no recreation, miserable wages (14s. a week), and in winter he works on Sundays.' (from *The Land—A Report of the Land Enquiry Committee Vol 1 Rural 1913*)

In fact, as we have seen, labourers' wages varied greatly, but the time available for leisure was universally restricted.

Small wonder that after the toil of the fields many opted for the simple pleasures of the inn. The hardness of the labourer's life was also reflected in an enduring passion for violent or cruel sports, such as prize fighting, Cornish wrestling and dog fighting. Many of these sports did not die out naturally, but were suppressed in the second half of the century. Bull baiting was declared illegal in 1835 and cock fighting in 1849, although they lingered on in the remoter areas. However, the prohibitions on coursing and the taking of game and fish remained largely a dead letter—poaching provided welcome additions to a monotonous diet, a good sport and the excitement of outwitting the gamekeeper. The great residual sport, which united all sections of rural society in the nineteenth century, was hunting. It was the pastime, first and foremost, of the aristocracy and gentry as it required considerable wealth. Even in the 1830s, before costs soared, Carr notes that to maintain a top Midland pack in style might cost between £4,000 and £6,000 a year, while a good provincial pack needed around £2,000, unless the master was willing to work himself to death with the chores of the kennels.

Disciplined sport, such as athletics, became popular in the late nineteenth century, often under the patronage of the local squire or parson.

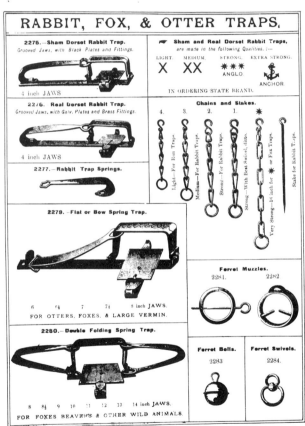

RABBIT, FOX, & OTTER TRAPS.

2275.—Sham Dorset Rabbit Trap.
Grooved Jaws, with Black Plates and Fittings.

4 inch JAWS

Sham and Real Dorset Rabbit Traps,
are made in the following Qualities:—

| LIGHT. | MEDIUM. | STRONG. | EXTRA STRONG. |
| X | XX | ✱✱✱ ANGLO | ⚓ ANCHOR |

IN ORDERING STATE BRAND.

22/6. Real Dorset Rabbit Trap.
Grooved Jaws, with Galv. Plates and Brass Fittings.

4 inch JAWS

Chains and Stakes.

2277.—Rabbit Trap Springs.

2278.—Flat or Bow Spring Trap.

6   6½   7   7½   8 inch JAWS.
FOR OTTERS, FOXES, & LARGE VERMIN.

Ferret Muzzles.
2281.   2282.

2280.—Double Folding Spring Trap.

Ferret Bells.   Ferret Swivels.
2283.   2284.

8   8½   9   10   11   12   13   14 inch JAWS.
FOR FOXES BEAVERS & OTHER WILD ANIMALS.

The numbers of those who could ride to hounds increased with the growth of subscription packs from the mid century, and gave scope to the hunting ambitions of small farmers as well as those of rural tradesmen and the commercial interest in the market towns. Participation was still far beyond the means of the agricultural labourer, other than as a foot follower. Nonetheless, as other blood sports were denied him, he became an enthusiastic devotee of the hunt. In the 1840s Jem Hastings daily followed Lord Fitzhardinge's hounds on foot 'over incredible distances, equipped with a red coat', while Ben Foulds, a framework knitter, similarly 'tramped after the Quorn'—one of the most exclusive of packs. Typically, however,

Top: hunting scenes, about 1900. *Left:* rabbit warrener in Herefordshire, about 1900. *Above:* animal traps from an early twentieth century manufacturer's catalogue.

the rural worker's involvement was only that of an interested spectator, although as Jefferies observes, he could still take great pleasure in the proceedings.

'The labourers on the rick, which stands on the side of a hill, are fully as excited as the riders, and they can see what the hunter himself rarely views, i.e. the fox slipping ahead before the hounds. Then they turn to alternatively laugh at, and shout directions to a disconsolate gentleman, who, ignorant of the district, is pounded in a small meadow. He is riding frantically round and round, afraid to risk the broad brook which encircles it, because of the treacherous bank, and maddened by the receding sound of the chase. A boy gets off the rick and runs to earn sixpence by showing a way out. So from the rick Hodge has his share of the sport, and at that elevation can see over a wide stretch of what he— changing the "d" into a "j"—calls the "juke's country".'

There were also other forms of incidental recreation. A break in the monotony of village life might be provided by one of many kinds of visitor: cheapjack, tinker, missionary, quack politician, ballad singer, ex-soldier or foreigner with a musical or animal act. Occasionally, a German band or circus—an invention of the late eighteenth century—might call. Often the circus was a modest affair, with perhaps no more than two or three horses: the first elephant appeared in a show in 1828. Later in the century circuses became grander and villagers might travel some distance to see one of the famous American companies on tour. Hugh Cunningham states that 'Barnum had established a familiarity with Europe with his 1840s tours with Tom Thumb and Jenny Lind' and by the 1870s, the circus was rivalling the popularity of Sanger and the other British companies. The circus provided an occasional treat, but other events, fixed within the agricultural year, were also eagerly anticipated by the rural community. These included agricultural shows and ploughing matches, and above all, local fairs. The commercial importance of the old fairs was declining, although in some localities reached easily by rail they remained a popular diversion. Sally Alexander points out that in Oxford 'St Giles came of age

The pig roast at Bidford 'Mop' (fair), Warwickshire, early twentieth century.

with the introduction of the excursion ticket', the first excursion bringing in 900 people from Banbury in 1850. Much later, in the years before the first World War, Alfred Williams could speak of the numbers who thronged to Highworth Fair in Wiltshire and of the bewildering variety of entertainment on offer:

'Here were exhibitions of all kinds—of beast and birds, waxwork figures, model machinery, glass-making, cotton-spinning, picture-galleries, and all sorts of things beside. We could not afford to see everything, but my mother took us into the waxworks show, and also to see the cotton-spinning. A great Zulu and several negros performed the war-dance outside the former of these places, and a man blew loud blasts and fanfares with a trumpet, and invited the people to "walk up and see the great Napoleon Bonnypart, the 'Dook' of Wellington and other celebrities, very lifelike and natteral".'

The fair, which survived in this way, as a spectacular event, also placed a Victorian emphasis on the exhibition of useful arts and manufactures. Agricultural machinery firms, notably Savage's of King's Lynn, specialised in providing steam-driven equipment of all sorts. A magnificent showman's engine might power a fairground organ or roundabout, or other novelties such as 'yachts, gallopers, gondolas, arks and palladium shows'. Transporting machinery by road, however, was expensive, and it was often not worth while to stop for one or two nights at the smaller fairs, many of which fell further into decline as they were no longer able to offer the latest attractions. In fact, those fairs which retained a strong traditional element were usually the earliest to be abolished. One such casualty was the Charlton Horn Fair, at which it was customary for fair-goers to wear horns and for men to dress up in women's clothing, giving rise to the expression 'All is fair at Horn-fair'. The origin of the fair is now lost; it may have developed from a medieval wake with the horns representing St Luke, the patron of the parish, but the ritual lost its meaning and became merely an occasion for rowdiness, and the fair was suppressed in 1872.

One event in the village calendar popular throughout the nineteenth century was club day, considered by some to be more of a 'red letter' day than either Christmas or Easter. Friendly societies were working class benefit clubs, sometimes dating from the eighteenth century, which insured against sudden disaster—usually illness or want of employment.

Left: village entertainers at Taplow, Buckinghamshire—fiddler and a one-man-band with a monkey to collect contributions. *Below:* gypsies with a Dancing Bear.

The club walk of the Meare Benefit Society in Somerset, headed by the village band, about 1910.

Contributors paid in a small regular contribution and could draw on the fund in time of need. Provision was also made for an annual celebration, in which the whole village joined. Alfred Williams recalled club day in South Marston in Wiltshire early in the twentieth century; in the morning of the second Tuesday in May, the club members and followers walked in procession through the village, wearing brightly coloured sashes and carrying banners, led by a brass band. They went first to the church, then to the manor, the farms and finally to the homes of the cottagers, and at one o'clock promptly,

'...all sat down to a substantial hot dinner of roast beef, and other cooked meats and vegetables, provided in the club-room; the band played selections; the foaming ale was brought in in large two-gallon cans; the greatest good nature prevailed. Farmers and all belonged to the gathering; it was no one-sided affair, and a great number of folk attended from neighbouring villages; all the old people made it their business to come to "Maason Club".'

There were set up 'stalls and booths, shooting galleries, swings and cocoa-nuts... There was generally a Punch and Judy show, with the "original dog Toby", and once a man brought a small menagerie with a "Rooshan" bear and a gorilla. The "show" consisted of a drama, a very crude affair, illustrated by means of shadows thrown on a sheet from behind, a sort of cinematograph entertainment, the charge to see which was one penny.'

In a sense, club-day represented a median point between two worlds; it encompassed the ritual procession, feasting and amusements which had characterised the older festivals, but it was an almost entirely secular occasion, fostered by the Victorian virtues of thrift and self-help, and patronised by the local gentry and leading tenantry.

Indeed, the rural establishment showed a renewed interest in organising the labourer's leisure towards the end of the century. To some extent, this reflected the unshaken belief of the landed interest in their own natural

177

authority and perhaps a desire to perpetuate their social standing at a time when their political and economic position was under attack. It also reflected the sincere wish of the upper and middle classes generally to encourage Christian and patriotic virtues, a robust manliness and a sense of British fair play among the labouring classes, and to promote a better understanding between all sections of society. The outcome was that many of the older spontaneous forms of recreation were discouraged, and were replaced by such organised events as fêtes, flower shows, village sports, concerts and local drama productions. 'Small events,' Cunningham notes, 'became pregnant with larger consequences.' The annual flower show evoked this comment from the *Banbury Guardian* in 1866:

'Floriculture and horticulture while being a health giving is also a pure and harmless recreation, which may be engaged in by individuals of either sex and of all stations of life, the peasant as well as the peer, the overtoiled man of business and the industrious artisan, on every imaginable scale from a single flower pot to the princely conservatory.'

Another innovation which flourished under the patronage of squire and rector was the Village Institute 'with its library of improving books, and its itinerant lecturers, propagating the values of the more refined levels of society.' To the village institute must be added reading rooms and working men's clubs. The Volunteer Force, founded in 1859 as a middle-class military organisation to face the threat of a French invasion also rapidly

Left: picnic at the Old Cottage, Northcutt Mouth, Cornwall, around 1900. People brought their own food and were provided with tables, chairs and hot water. *Above:* refreshment stall at Holmley House, Sibford Ferris, Banbury, Oxfordshire, about 1916.

August Bank Holiday on White Horse Hill, Uffington, Berkshire, about 1899.

acquired a working-class membership and sought to retain it by offering leisure activities. Cunningham records that in East Surrey, by 1872 the officers were keeping the men together 'by social gatherings, cricket clubs and quadrille parties.' Country people characteristically responded to these new attractions by taking what was offered and adapting them to their own purposes. The village institute helped those who wished to gain a better education and a better job outside the local community; the working men's club provided an alternative meeting place to the pub, and soon evolved its own forms of entertainment; village sports were enjoyed simply for their own sake.

Paternalism, however, lost its hold over the rural community as the labourer began to travel. Rare holidays might be used to visit relations in a place which had once seemed to have only a mythical existence, Bath, Birmingham or London. In a city, there was sight-seeing to be done: visits to be made to botanical gardens, zoos and museums, to the musical hall, to

Wrestling match at an annual club picnic, 1897.

Red Lion Hotel, Handcross,
West Sussex.

a pub, where the latest songs could be heard more cheaply, or to the park, to listen to the band. Those single men who had Saturday afternoon off regularly and lived close to a town, could afford trips to watch football, boxing or wrestling matches, well advertised in advance in the local press, or even part of a three-day county cricket marathon. Occasionally, a family outing might be accomplished to a local race meeting; horse racing in particular benefited enormously from the growth of cheap rail excursions in the third quarter of the century. By this time, it was not uncommon for the better-off labourer and his family to manage a day's outing to the seaside or some other popular resort—although usually out of season, since the harvest always took precedence.

By the turn of the century, the labourer was gaining first hand knowledge of the towns, and the town dweller was increasingly discovering rural England. The sporadic visits of the traditional itinerants were replaced by a flood of people, both tradesmen and tourists. After 1900, teashops and hotels appeared to meet the needs of charabanc parties, walkers, and the cyclists who spilled out of the cities in ever greater numbers from the 1880s. As early as 1883, the Cyclists' Touring Club, which had started life in 1878 as the Bicycle Touring Club, had 10,627 members, all enjoying the benefits of a *Monthly Circular*, a handbook of useful information, maps, guides and road routes. The invasion was well planned. Gradually, the better acquaintance of the agricultural labourer with his urban cousin served to make him restless, and to a degree envious. His earnings might be inferior, but his social expectations were no longer bounded by the old rhythms of the countryside and its limited horizons. The countryside was enclosed in itself no longer; it was part of a wider world, more mobile, moneyed, leisured and instructed, with different and desirable rhythms of its own.

As the century wore on, traditional customs survived in areas ever more remote from the centres of population and among the older, and usually less educated, inhabitants. Sometimes the vestiges of primitive superstition lingered for a considerable time. There was a persistent half-belief in the

180

The beach at Ilfracombe, North Devon.

'old knowledge'—in the protective virtues of holed stones, iron, especially in the shape of a cross, and other charms against misfortune; in the effectiveness of the remedies of 'wise-women'; in the advisability of carrying out certain actions at propitious times. More blatant evidence of paganism, however, was rare. In 1853, a Devon farmer at Meavy burned a sacrificial sheep on Catsham Tor to save the rest of his stock. In 1865, Robert Hunt recalled that when he was working on his book, *Drolls, Traditions and Superstitions of Old Cornwall*, he heard of a calf being burned on St John's Eve (the feast which, in its original form, celebrated the summer solstice) to protect the herd against the murrain. Margaret Baker records a fertility rite practised early in the twentieth century:

'On New Year's morning until at least 1913 in the West Midlands, farm-women plaited a new hawthorn globe as a fire and fertility charm to be baked in the oven and hung in the kitchen until the following year. While they worked, the men "burning the bush" fired the old globe in the field and carried it flaring over the first-sown wheat, smouldering twigs falling into every furrow.'

By this time, such rituals were uncommon enough to be worthy of notice, and survived as curiosities within a more intimate religious view of the workings of nature.

Some less overtly superstitious customs hung on a while longer, chiefly because of an innate love of the rituals involved. Margaret Ashby found this to be the case with the more precise of the morris dances, which had an 'intrinsic beauty' in 'figure, step and movement'. Similarly, an attachment to folk song persisted amongst those who found the airs, and the sentiments expressed, touched them deeply. Thus, Cecil Sharp was taking down a song from a woman, who had interrupted her work picking potatoes, when she suddenly stopped singing, seized the lapels of his coat in enthusiasm, and exclaimed, 'Isn't it lovely?' But in spite of this enthusiasm there were very few to pass on these customs, and they gradually dwindled away. As Ashby commented of the morris dancers at Bledington:

'Once it had been part of the inheritance of the whole village: in the early twentieth century it belonged almost exclusively to a small group of farm-workers—those whose minds and whose leisure were not absorbed by religion or the sociabilities of the inn and who had the necessary gift. The share of women and children in the old arts had come to an end as property and social division dominated life (though the school revived some May Day celebrations). Even among the men they were rapidly vanishing: yet, strangely, it had retained its fine quality to the last.

'By 1890 it had not always been possible to form a complete side in Bledington. Benfield and Hathaway had bestirred themselves to recruit and instruct a "young side" who should maintain the traditions of visits and competitions. But this plan, successful for a time, broke down. The swiftness of step and the elaborate figures are best learned by small boys, with their wonderful absorptive and imitative power, and by this time men, including members of the side, left the village too often for the old traditions to be steadily carried forward.'

Instead, in Bledington in the 1890s, the children learned especially written songs and did Swedish exercises, and 'no-one knew that they could have had already from their fathers that "grandest" most exacting of dances, the "Gallant Hussar".'

At the time when the folklorists like Sabine Baring-Gould and Cecil Sharp were recording the old culture, it had to all intents and purposes disappeared. Attempts at revival undertaken by middle class enthusiasts enjoyed only a limited success for the simple but sufficient reason that folk song and dance no longer corresponded to the real needs or beliefs of the community.

It would, however, be false to view rural culture purely in terms of the survival of primitive superstition and archaic customs, just as it would be a mistake to regard urban culture as entirely the product of industrialisation. Travelling showmen, circuses, itinerants and casual labourers of all kinds migrated from town to country and back again, while railway navvies, colliers, seamen and many others helped to create and sustain a popular tradition made up of many and diverse influences. Yet, the growing concentration of people in the towns, the routine of factory life, and the greater degree of labour discipline in the countryside produced new recreational forms, shaped by industrialisation, and led to the withering away of older agrarian pastimes. Indeed, as entrepreneurs and governments invested more and more heavily in urban-based public entertainment in the second half of the nineteenth century, the rural classes were drawn inevitably and with little resistance to the mass culture of the industrial age.

Bibliography

Introduction

The extract from Lord Rosebery's speech is taken from Thompson. Material on urban growth is from Mathias. The idea of a 'secret people', the last witnesses to the customs and beliefs of a much older rural England was developed by Martin, while the example of surviving belief in 'folk knowledge' is taken from Baker.

Baker, M. *Folk-lore and Customs of Rural England*. David & Charles, 1974.
Martin, E.W. *The Secret People: English Village Life after 1750*. Phoenix House.
Mathias, P. *Retailing Revolution*. Longmans, 1967.
Thompson, P. *Socialists, Liberals and Labour: the Struggle for London 1885-1914* Routledge & Kegan Paul, 1967.

The Landed Interest

A major source for this chapter has been Thompson, whose perceptive and detailed study is required reading for all students of the landed interest. Mingay, Spring and Holderness contributed information on the ways in which the aristocracy supplemented their incomes other than through agriculture. Olney deals with the effects of the third Reform Act on rural politics. Girouard and Wingfield-Stratford were consulted on country house living. The anecdotes about Barfield Lloyd Baker and Squire Biddulph are taken from Ditchfield.

Camplin, J. *The Rise of the Plutocrats: Wealth and Power in Edwardian England*. Constable, 1978.
Ditchfield, P.H. *Country Folk: A Pleasant Company*. Methuen, 1923.
Girouard, M. *Life in the English Country House: A Social and Architectural History*. Yale University Press, 1978.
Holderness, B.A. 'Agriculture and Industrialisation in the Victorian Economy' in Mingay (ed.) 1981.
Jefferies, R. *Hodge and his Masters*. Smith, Elder & Co., 1880; recent edition, Quartet, 1980.
Mingay, G.E. *The Gentry: the Rise and Fall of a Ruling Class*. Longman Group, 1978.
Mingay, G.E. (ed.) *The Victorian Countryside*. Routledge & Kegan Paul, 1981.
Olney, R.J. 'The Politics of Land' in Mingay (ed.) 1981.
Robinson, G. *Hedingham Harvest: Victorian Family Life in Rural England*. Constable, 1977.
Spring, D. 'English Landowners and Nineteenth Century Industrialism' in J.T. Ward and R.G. Wilson (ed.) *Land and Industry: the Landed Estate and the Industrial Revolution*. David & Charles, 1971.
Thompson, F.M.L. *English Landed Society in the Nineteenth Century*. Routledge & Kegan Paul, 1963.
Wingfield-Stratford, E. *The Squire and his Relations*. Cassell & Co., 1956.

Tenant Farms, Tied Cottages

Much of this chapter is based on original sources, but the two main general works of value are Mingay and Horn. Insights into village life are provided by the contemporary or autobiographical books of Jefferies, Thompson and Grey. The basic work on farmhouse and cottage architecture is Barley. The Yorkshire census details are quoted from Harris. Various aspects of domestic life and equipment are dealt with by Ayres and Lindsay.

Ayres, J. *The Shell Book of the Home in Britain*. Faber, 1981.
Barley, M.W. *The English Farmhouse and Cottage*. Routledge & Kegan Paul, 1962.
Grey, E. *Cottage Life in a Hertfordshire Village*. Fisher Knight, 1934.
Horn, P. *Labouring life in the Victorian Countryside*. Gill & Macmillan, Dublin, 1976.
Harris, A. *The Rural Landscape of the East Riding of Yorkshire 1700-1850*. University of Hull Press, 1961.
Jefferies, R. *Hodge and his Masters*. 1880; recent edition, Quartet, 1980.
Lindsay, S. *Iron and Brass Implements of the English Home*. Alec Tiranti, 1964.

Mingay, G.E. *Rural Life in Victorian England*. Hamish Hamilton, 1977.
Thompson, F. *Lark Rise to Candleford*. Oxford University Press, 1945, and numerous later editions.

Seed Time to Harvest

The brief survey of British agriculture before 1870 is largely taken from Jones, whose monograph is perhaps the best introduction to the subject. Holderness contributed information on the differences between the American and British grain milling industries, wool imports, dairy substitutes and the canning, preserving, fertilizer and seed compounding industries.

The concept of the Second Agricultural Revolution is from Thompson, as is much of the comment on technical changes associated with fertilizers and feeding stuffs.

A considerable debt is owed to Collins, the main author consulted on farm mechanisation. Further information on the development of the agricultural engineering industry was provided by Grace and Phillips.

In the last part of the chapter, the single most important reference work used was Fussell's pioneering study of the tools and implements of husbandry. Additional information came from Passmore, from Tyler and Haining, from Culpin and from Cheke. In general, however, the very abbreviated description of farm equipment given here is meant only to direct interested readers to Fussell.

Bagwell, P.S. 'The Decline of Rural Isolation' in G.E. Mingay (ed.) *The Victorian Countryside*. Routledge & Kegan Paul, 1981.
Cawood, C. 'The History and Development of Farm Tractors: Part I' in *Industrial Archaeology* August 1970.
Cheke, V. *The Story of Cheese-making in Britain*. Routledge & Kegan Paul, 1959.
Collins, E.J.T. 'The Age of Machinery' in Mingay (ed.) 1981
Collins, E.J.T. 'Migrant Labour in British Agriculture in the Nineteenth Century' in *Economic History Review* February 1976.
Collins, E.J.T. *Sickle to Combine*. University of Reading, 1969.
Culpin, C. *Farm Machinery*. Crosby, Lockwood and Son, 1938.
Fussell, G.E. *The Farmer's Tools 1500-1900*. Andrew Melrose, 1952.
Goddard, N. 'Agricultural Societies' in Mingay (ed.) 1981.
Grace, D.R. & Phillips, D.C. *Ransomes of Ipswich*. University of Reading, 1975.
Holderness, B.A. 'Agriculture and Industrialisation in the Victorian Economy' in Mingay (ed.) 1981.
Passmore, J.B. *The English Plough*. Oxford University Press, 1930.
Stephens, H. *The Book of the Farm*. William Blackwood and Sons, 4th edition 1891.
Thompson, F.M.L. 'Free Trade and the Land' in Mingay (ed.) 1981.
Thompson, F.M.L. 'The Second Agricultural Revolution 1815-1880' in *The Economic History Review*. 2nd series, vol. 21, no. 1, April 1968.
Tyler, C. & Haining, J. *Ploughing by Steam*. Model and Allied Publications, Hemel Hempstead, 1970.
Williams, M. *Farm Tractors*. Blandford Press, 1974.

Industries of the Countryside

Much of the information for this chapter has been derived from specialist articles and monographs, which are listed below. Darby (ed.), Mathias (1969) and Pawson set the general background for the role of rural industries in the pre-industrial period and the Industrial Revolution. The accounts of W.A. Henman, Alec Walker, Victor Shafer, W.F. Moore and A.J. Pool have been taken from material in the Document Collection of the Institute of Agricultural History, University of Reading.

Booker, F. *The Industrial Archaeology of the Tamar Valley*. David & Charles, 1967.
Booker, J. *Essex and the Industrial Revolution*. Essex County Council, 1974.
Brears, P.C.D. *The English Country Pottery*. David & Charles, 1971.
Burnett, R.G. *Through the Mill*. Epworth Press, 1945.
Census of Great Britain, 1851. Population tables, II, Ages, etc. vol. 1. 1854.
Census of England and Wales, 1891. Ages, etc. vol. III. 1893.
Census of England and Wales, 1911. General Report, 1917, Occupations and Industries parts I-II, 1914.
Cobbett, W. *Cottage Economy*. Oxford University Press, 1822.
Darby, H.C. (ed.) *A New Historical Geography of England*. Cambridge University Press, 1973.
Donald, J. 'The Crendon Needleworkers' in *Records of Buckinghamshire*, vol.19, 1971.
Edlin, H.L. *Woodland Crafts in Britain*. Batsford, 1949.
Forestry Commission *Report on Census of Woodlands, 1924, 1928; Census of Woodlands, 1947-49, (1952); Census of Woodlands, 1965-67, 1970.*

Gandy, I. *The Heart of a Village: an Intimate History of Aldbourne*. Moonraker Press, 1975.

Green, J.L. *The Rural Industries of England*. E. Marlborough, 1895.

Green, J.L. *Village Industries*. The Rural World Publishing Company, 1915.

Hammersley, G. 'The Charcoal Iron Industry and its Fuel, 1540-1750' in *Economic History Review*, 2nd series, vol.26, 1973.

Hartley, M. & Ingilby, J. *The Hand-knitters of the Dales*. Dalesman Publishing Company, 1969.

Hey, D. *The Rural Metalworkers of the Sheffield Region*. Leicester University Press, 1972.

Jones, E.L. 'Agricultural Origins of Industry' in *Past and Present*, no. 40, 1968.

Kelly's Directories: Berkshire, 1869, 1877, 1895; *Hampshire*, 1890; *Norfolk*, 1888, 1912; *Oxfordshire*, 1877, 1887; *Somerset*, 1906; *Suffolk*, 1879.

Major, J.K. 'A Berkshire Foundry' in *Berkshire Archaeological Journal*, vol.65, 1970.

Marshall, J.D. & Davies-Shiel, M. *The Industrial Archaeology of the Lake Counties*. 2nd edition, Michael Moon, 1977.

Mathias, P. *The Brewing Industry in England, 1700-1830*. Cambridge University Press, 1959.

Mathias, P. *The First Industrial Nation*. Methuen, 1969.

Morton, H.V. *In Search of England*. Methuen, 1927.

Palmer, F.A. *The Blacksmith's Ledgers of the Hedges Family of Bucklebury, Berkshire, 1736-1773*. Institute of Agricultural History, Reading, 1970.

Pawson, E. *The Early Industrial Revolution*. Batsford, 1979.

Rackham, O. *Trees and Woodland in the British Landscape*. Dent, 1976.

Reeves, M. *Sheep Bell and Ploughshare: the Story of Two Village Families*. Moonraker Press, 1978.

Robinson, D.J. & Cooke, R.U. 'Lime-kilns in Surrey' in *Surrey Archaeological Collections*, vol.59, 1962.

Rose, W. *The Village Carpenter*. Cambridge University Press, 1937.

Rowlands, M.D. *Masters and Men in the West Midland Metalware Trades before the Industrial Revolution*. Manchester University Press, 1975.

Shorter, A.H. *Papermaking in the British Isles*. David & Charles, 1971.

Strong, W.H. *Industries of North Devon*. B.D. Hughes (ed.) David & Charles, 1971.

Sturt, G. *The Wheelwright's Shop*. Cambridge University Press, 1923.

Sturt, G. (under pseudonym Bourne, G.) *William Smith: Potter and Farmer, 1790-1858*. Caliban Books, 1920.

Saville, J. *Rural Depopulation in England and Wales, 1851-1951*. Routledge & Kegan Paul, 1957.

Tann, J. *Gloucestershire Woollen Mills*. David & Charles, 1967.

Thirsk, J. 'Industries in the Countryside' in Fisher, F.J. (ed.) *Essays in the Economic and Social History of Tudor and Stuart England*. Cambridge University Press, 1961.

Williams, W.M. *The Country Craftsman*. Routledge & Kegan Paul, 1958.

Wilson, G.B. *Alcohol and the Nation*. Nicholson & Watson, 1940.

Woods, K.S. *The Rural Industries Round Oxford*. Oxford University Press, 1921.

Water, Road and Rail

Very little of the vast literature on transport is directly concerned with rural transport. Much information has therefore been derived directly from contemporary sources, although some statistics quoted have come from the unpublished theses of Doble and Caroe. Two general books of value are those of Bagwell and of Dyos and Aldcroft. On waterways, the main books are those of Hadfield. Recent work on stage coaches has largely been confined to periodicals, and two articles by Kennett have been particularly useful. Droving is covered by Bonser and Colyer.

For railways, the most valuable general books are those of Perkin and Thomas. County carriers are covered in articles by Everitt, while the quotation about the Magdalen carrier is from Randell. Bird provides a useful guide to changes in road transport. The influence of the motor car is poorly represented in the literature, although information is to be found in Richardson. Early bus services of the railways companies are covered by Lee, and bicycles are dealt with by Caunter and Alderson.

Alderson, F. *Bicycling, a History*. David & Charles, 1972.

Bagwell, P.S. *The Transport Revolution*. Batsford, 1974.

Bird, A. *Roads and Vehicles*. Longman, 1969.

Bonser, K.J. *The Drovers*. Macmillan, 1970.

Caroe, L. *Urban Change in East Anglia in the Nineteenth Century*. Unpublished thesis, Cambridge University, 1966.

Caunter, C.F. *The History and Development of Cycles*. H.M.S.O., 1955.

Colyer, R. *The Welsh Cattle Drovers*. University of Wales Press, 1976.

Doble, E. *History of the Eastern Counties Railway in Relation to Economic Development*. Unpublished thesis, University of London, 1939.

Dyos, H.J. and Aldcroft, D.H. *British Transport: an Economic Survey from the Seventeenth Century to the Twentieth Century*. Leicester University Press, 1969.

Everitt, A. 'Town and Country in Victorian Leicestershire: the Role of the Village Carrier' in Everitt, A. (ed.) *Perspectives in English Urban History*. Macmillan, 1973.

Fletcher, W. *The History and Development of Steam Locomotives on Common Roads*. 1891; reprinted as *Steam on Common Roads*. David & Charles, 1972.

Hadfield, C. *British Canals*. David & Charles, 4th edition, 1969.

Kennett, D.H. 'The Pattern of Coaching in Early Nineteenth Century Norfolk' in *Norfolk Archaeology*, xxxvi, 1977.

Kennett, D.H. 'The Geography of Coaching in Early Nineteenth Century Northamptonshire' in *Northampton Past and Present*. 1974.

Lee, C.E. 'One Hundred Years of Railway Associated Omnibus Services' in John Hibbs (ed.) *The Omnibus: Readings in the History of Road Passenger Transport*. David & Charles, 1971.

Perkin, H. *The Age of the Railway*. David & Charles, 1972.

Randell, A. *Sixty Years a Fenman*. Routledge & Kegan Paul, 1966.

Richardson, K. *The British Motor Industry 1896-1939*. Macmillan, 1977.

Thomas, D. St John *The Country Railway*. Penguin, 1976.

Thomas, D. St John *Regional History of the Railways of Great Britain*. several volumes, David & Charles, 1961

In the Market Place

Much of the information on itinerant trading is from Alexander, while details of the decline in livestock fairs and droving are from Perren. One of the co-authors of this book, Jonathan Brown, was responsible for the description of market towns and of the changes in corn and livestock markets in this period. Davis was consulted on some aspects of traditional retailing, but the principal reference work on the 'retailing revolution' is still that of Jefferys. Chartres provides information on country tradesmen, and Fraser offers a useful summary of the appearance of the mass market in the late Victorian era.

Alexander, D. *Retailing in England during the Industrial Revolution*. Athlone Press, University of London, 1970.

Burnett, J. *A History of the Cost of Living*. Penguin, 1969.

Chartres, J.A. 'Country Tradesmen' in G.E. Mingay (ed.) *The Victorian Countryside*. Routledge & Kegan Paul, 1981.

Davis, D. *A History of Shopping*. Routledge & Kegan Paul, 1966.

Fraser, W.H. *The Mass Market 1850-1914*. Macmillan, 1981.

Hindley, C. (ed.) *The Life and Adventures of a Cheap Jack*. 1876.

Jefferies, R. *Hodge and his Masters*. Smith, Elder & Co., 1880; recent edition, Quartet, 1980.

Jefferys, J.B. *Retail Trading in Britain 1850-1950*. Cambridge University Press, 1954.

Johnson, C. *Among English Hedgerows*. Macmillan, 1899.

Kelly's Directories for the various English counties, published in four-yearly editions, from about 1850.

Mathias, P. *Retailing Revolution*. Longmans, 1967.

Perren, R. *The Meat Trade in Britain 1840-1914*. Routledge & Kegan Paul, 1978.

Pulbrook, E.C. *English Country Life and Work*. Batsford, 1923.

Rees, J.A. *History of the Grocery Trade*. Duckworth, 1932.

Thompson, F. *Lark Rise to Candleford*. Oxford University Press, 1945 and numerous later editions.

Williams, M. *Thomas Hardy and Rural England*. Macmillan, 1972.

For the Public Good

The main source for the treatment of poverty—including the working of the New Poor Law—was Rose, supplemented by Digby, particularly on rural charities, and by Midwinter. Material on the Benthamites and the reference to Sir John Simon are from Perkin. Much of the description of medical provision in the countryside is from Horn, from whom are also taken some apt quotations for the section on education. The principal authors on rural education, also extensively quoted, are Sturt and Sellman, but useful advice on the growth of the voluntary school movement was provided by Jonathan Brown. Information about the history of the police force was taken almost entirely from Critchley, while the account of the changing pattern of rural crime is largely from Jones, with additional comment from Dunbabin.

Ashby, M.K. *Joseph Ashby of Tysoe 1859-1919: a Study of English Village Life*. Cambridge University Press, 1961.

Ashby, M.K. *The Changing English Village: Kineton*. The Roundwood Press, 1961.

Critchley, T.A. *A History of the Police in England and Wales, 900-1966*. Constable, 1967.

Davey, B.J. *Ashwell 1830-1914: the Decline of a Village Community.* Leicester University Press, 1980.

Digby, A. 'The Rural Poor' in Mingay (ed.) 1981.

Dunbabin, J.P.D. *Rural Discontent in Nineteenth Century Britain.* Faber, 1974.

Horn, P. *Education in Rural England 1800-1914.* St Martin's Press, New York, 1978.

Horn, P. *Labouring Life in the Victorian Countryside.* Gill & Macmillan, Dublin, 1976.

Jefferies, R. *Hodge and his masters.* Smith, Elder & Co., 1880; recent edition, Quartet, 1980.

Jones, D. 'Rural Crime and Protest' in Mingay (ed.) 1981

Midwinter, E.C. *Victorian Social Reform.* Longmans, 1968.

Mingay, G.E. (ed.) *The Victorian Countryside.* Routledge & Kegan Paul, 1981.

Moore, D.C. 'The Gentry' in Mingay (ed.) 1981.

Perkin, H. *The Origins of Modern English Society 1780-1880.* Routledge & Kegan Paul, 1969.

Rose, M.E. *The Relief 1834-1914.* Economic History Society & Macmillan Press, 1972.

Sellman, R. 'The Country School' in Mingay (ed.) 1981.

Sellman, R. *Devon Village Schools in the Nineteenth Century.* David & Charles, 1967.

Sturt, M. *The Education of the People: a History of Primary Education in England and Wales in the 19th Century.* Routledge & Kegan Paul, 1967.

The Labourer's Leisure

Description of recreation before 1850 is taken mainly from Malcolmson, though in a greatly abbreviated form. Walvin and Cunningham were the principal sources for the period after 1850. Information on pub games is from Brander and field sports from Watson, Beach-Thomas and Carr. The chief sources on folksong are Lloyd, Karpeles and Dickinson. Comments on village life are largely from Ashby.

Ashby, M.K. *The Changing Village: Kineton.* The Roundwood Press, 1974.

Baker, M. *Folklore and Customs of Rural England.* David & Charles, 1974.

Beach Thomas, W. *Hunting England.* Batsford, 1936.

Brander, M. *The Life and Sport of the Inn.* Gentry Books, 1973.

Carr, R. *English Fox Hunting: a History.* Weidenfeld & Nicolson, 1978.

Cunningham, H. *Leisure in the Industrial Revolution c1780-1880.* Croom Helm, 1980.

Dickinson, B.H.C. *Sabine Baring-Gould: Squarson, Writer and Folklorist 1834-1924.* David & Charles, 1970.

Ditchfield, P.H. *Country Folk: a Pleasant Company.* Methuen & Co., 1923.

Dorson, R.M. *The British Folklorists: a History.* Routledge & Kegan Paul, 1968.

Hole, C. *English Custom and Usage.* Batsford, 1941-47.

Hole, C. *English Folklore.* Batsford, 1940.

Hole, C. *English Sports and Pastimes.* Batsford, 1949.

Jefferies, R. *Hodge and his Masters.* Smith, Elder and Co., 1880; recent edition, Quartet, 1980.

Karpeles, M. *Cecil Sharp: his Life and Work.* Routledge & Kegan Paul, 1967.

Lloyd, A.C. *Folk Song in England.* International Publishers, New York, 1967.

Malcolmson, R.W. *Popular Recreations in English Society 1700-1850.* Cambridge University Press, 1973.

Strutt, J. *Glig-Gamena Angel-Dead; or the Sports and Pastimes of the People of England.* London, 1801.

Walvin, J. *Leisure and Society 1830-1950.* Longman, 1978.

Watson, J.N.P. *Victorian and Edwardian Field Sports from Old Photographs.* Batsford, 1978.

Williams, A. *A Wiltshire Village.* Duckworth & Co., 1912.

Index

Abbeydale forging mill 76
Abbots Bromley (Staffs) *160*
Aberavon 21
Abergavenny, 1st Marquis of 20
activities, social 170-171
administration, rural, reorganised 159
administrators, trained 18, 159
advertising 126, 128, 134, 138
agriculture, changes in 42-65
agricultural engineering industry 44-65
agricultural implements and machinery 44, 48, 51-66, 88, 89
agricultural productivity 44
agricultural products/produce: bulk transport of 99-101, 103-104; processing 76-81; trading in 114, 118, 122
Agricultural Revolutions, The 42, 44
agricultural shows 48, *119*, 175
agricultural tools 182
Akeld Farm (Northumberland) *51*
Aldridge, H. (fruiterer) *43*
alum production *43*, 67
ammonia 44
Andover (Hants) 47, *110*, 143
animal traps *174*
arable farming 38, 39, 42
Agricultural Holdings Act (1883) 15
Albone, Dan 64, 65
Aldbourne (Wilts) 98
Alexander, David (quoted) 116-117
Alexander, Sally (quoted) 175-176
Alexandra Mill 79
Aldermaston Wharf 84
Allan, William 88
Allen, the Revd John (quoted) 149
Alton (Hants) *50*, 84, 108
Arch, Joseph 24, *24*
Argentina (cereals) 39, 42
arsenic production 71
Arts & Crafts Movement 97
Ashby, Joseph 148
Ashby, Miss K. (quoted) 152-153, 154-155, 167, 169, 170, 171, 182
Ashtead (Surrey) 94
Ashwell (Derbys) 155
Askrigg (Yorks) 76
auctioneering 123
Australasia 40, 60
Austria-Hungary (milling technology) 78
Aveling & Porter 53
Avon, River (Glos) 86
Axholme, Isle of 42
Axminster (Devon) *149*
Aysgarth (Yorks) 76

Badcock's 133
baker's shops *140*
Baker, Margaret (quoted) 181
Bakewell (Derbys) 150
baking, domestic 25, *26*
ballad pedlar 170
Bampton Horse Fair *118*
Banbury (Oxon) 61, 121, 176, *183*
bands, brass 170, *170*, 171
Bank Holiday Act (1870) 12
Barford & Perkins 60
Barnet (Herts) 119
'bargain' system (in mining) 70
Baring Gould, the Revd Sabine 167-168, 169, 182
bark industry *85*
barley 39, 59, *59*
barn machinery *61*
Barnstaple (Devon) *100*, 131, *131*
Barnstaple pottery 73
Barnum 175
Barrow-in-Furness (Lancs) 16
basic slag 44
basket making *80*, *87*
basket willow 86-87
Bath (Somerset) 133, 179
Beadnall (Northumberland) *51*
beaker, horn *35*
Bearwood estate (Berks) *28*
Beaufort, Duke of 18
Bedale Market (Yorks) *124*
Bedford 45, 53
Bedford, Duke of 16, 27, *28*

Bedfordshire 81, 97, 104, *137*
Beesley family (basket makers) *87*
beggars *146*
Belbroughton (Worcs) 75, *75*, 76
Bell, the Revd Patrick 58
bell founding 98
bell ringers *169*
Bell's Weekly Messenger 48
Bellairs (quoted) 154
benefit and friendly societies 31, 144, 148, 176, *177*
Bentham, Jeremy 141
Benthamites 141, 150, 157
Berkshire 82, 100, 103, 154
Berkshire, Directory of (Kelly's) 69
Berry & Son (millers) *100*
Bibby's 44
bicycles 12, *110*, 112, 113, *137*
Bicycle Touring Club 180
Biddulph, Mr 21
Bidford 'Mop' (Warwickshire) *175*
Biggleswade (Beds) 64
binders 59
Bingham (Notts) 124
Binsted (Hants) *165*
Birling (Kent) *170*
Birmingham 100, 154, 179
biscuits 12, *129*
Black Country 16, 68, 74
blacksmithing 46, 66, 74, 93-94
Blackstone's 47, 57
Bledington (Glos) 152, 153, 167, 170, 171, 182
Blenkinsop, Dora and Hannah *26*
Bletchington (Oxon) 88
Blofield (Norfolk) *14*
BOCM 44
Boards of Guardians 143, 145
bone (fertilizers) 43
Boot, Jesse 131
Booth, Charles 144
Boston (Lincs) 46, 100
Bourne, George *see* Sturt, George
bowl turning 96, 98
Boxford (Berks) *169*
Boyce, James 58
Bradfield Woods (Suffolk) 88
Bradford (Yorks) 78
Bradiford (Devon) 86
Bramlett's 56
Brandon (Suffolk) 71, *71*
brass bands 170, *170*, 171
Bratton (Wilts) 56, 95
Bratton Ironworks 95
Breakspear, Richard, Jesse and Henry 88
brewing: commercial 39, 42, 80-81; domestic 25
brick manufacture 66, 72, *72*
Bridstow (Herefordshire) *110*
Brinkworth, John *142*
Bristol 62, 63, 100, 102
Bristol Wagon and Carriage Works 91, *104*
British and Foreign Schools Society 149, 150
Brixton Deverill (Wilts) 137
broadcloth industry 77
Broadwood, the Revd John 167
Brown & May 47
Buccleuch, Duke of 13
Buckinghamshire 33, 75, 78, 81, 97, 154
Bucklebury (Berks) 93, 94, 96, 98
Bucknell (Shropshire) *85*
Bude Canal 100
building and contracting 16, 89-91
Burnford & Evershed (agricultural engineers) 45
Burford (Oxon) *118*, 119, *119*
Burge, Robert 97
Burnham Beeches (Bucks) 82
Burrell's 45, 53
Burton-on-Trent (Staffs) 80
Bury & Norwich Post (quoted) 104
buses *see* omnibuses
Bussell, F.W. 168
butter making 62, *62*

Caird, James (quoted) 37, 39
California 39, 60, 106
Cambridgeshire 71, 104, 162
Canada (wheat imports) 42
canals 67, 84, 100-101, *100*, *101*, 114, 119
Capitalism 160, 163
Cardiff 63
Cardington (Beds) *28*
Carlisle (Cumberland) *103*
Carlton Curlieu (Leics) 158
Carmylie (Scotland) 58
Carnegie, Andrew 23
carpentry 90-91
Carr (quoted) 173
carriages 109, *109*

carriers, village 106-109
Carson & Toone 63
carts *104*, *105*, 107, *107*, *110*
Catsham Tor (Devon) 181
cattle markets *120*
Central Chambers of Agriculture 15
Chadwick, Edwin 144
chaff cutters 60-61, *60*
chair making *85*, 98
Challow (Berks) 59
Chamberlain, Mrs Harriet 88
Chamberlain, Joseph 38
Chandler's Patent liquid manure drill 56
Chaplin family 13-14
charcoal 66, 67, 73, 84-84, 87
charcoal iron industry 66, 73, 74, 82, 84
Chard (Somerset) 29
charity, private 143-144
Charity Organisation in Society 144
Charlton Horn Fair 176
Charter Gas Engine Co. 64
Charton-on-Otmoor (Oxon) 88
cheapjack *see* retailers, itinerant
cheese making 62-63
cheese presses 62-63, *63*
Cheltenham (Glos) 133
cherry picking *43*
Cheshire 30, 71
Chesterfield (Derbys) 100
Chicago 64
Chichester (Sussex) 100, *130*
Childwick Green (Herts) *142*
Chile (nitrates) 44
Chippenham (Wilts) 91, *91*
Chipstable (Somerset) 95
Chithurst (W. Sussex) *161*
choral societies 170
Christchurch (Hants) 64
Christian Socialists 146
church music 169
Church of England: and education 148, 149-50, 154, 156; and entertainment 165, 170-171; and musical literacy 169; and traditional customs 166-168
churns 62, *62*
circuses 175
Civil War (American) 38
Clarence Mills 79
Clarion Club 12
Clarke, J.A. (quoted) 57-61
Clausen, Sir George 142
clay digging 66, 70, 72
Clayton & Shuttleworth 45, 56, 59, 60-61
clothing: home made 114, 135; ready made 129, 134, 135
clothing industry 66, 76
club days 176-177
Clyst St Lawrence (Devon) 12
coaches 109
coal 33, 34, 67; (transport) 100, 101, 105-106
coal fields 68, 69, 70, 97
coal mining 16, 67, 70, 97
Coalbrookdale 74
Cobbett, William (quoted) 81
Cocks, John and Charles *129*
Codford St Mary (Wilts) 137
coke smelting 73, 84-85
Collins (quoted) 46, 47, 49
combine harvesters 60
confectionery industry 39
Congregational School 150
Conservative Party 38, 147, 150, 151
consumer products 114, 138; growth in demand 115; mass produced 129
Cooke, the Revd James 55
cooking 30, 32, 33-36
coolers 62, 63
Co-operative Movement 128
copper mining 68, 71, *71*, 97
coppice woods 73
coppicing 82-88, *82*
coprolite 43, 71
copy stick *167*
Corbett, Thomas 63
corn dolly making *164*
corn drill 56
corn exchanges 122
Corn Laws, Repeal of (1846) 37
Cornwall 67, 71, 104
Corringham (Essex) *122*, *140*
Cort (ironmaster) 74
cottages 26-28, *28*, *29*, 33-36
cottage hospitals 145
cotton 76; mills 67, 86
Councils, County, Parish and District 18, 156-157, 159
Country Life *146*, *147*
County Agricultural Protection Society (Durham) 37
country houses 21-22

Cowthorpe (Yorks) *135*
craftsmen, rural 20, 97-98
Crewe (Cheshire) 123
cricket 165, 172, *172*
crime 157, 158-159
Crimean War 38
Critchley (quoted) 159
Croford (Somerset) 96
Crookham Common (Berks) 86
cultivators 53, 54
Cunningham, Hugh (quoted) 170, 175, 178
curd breakers 62
cutlery 74
Cyclists' Touring Club 180
cylindrical roller mill 78

Daily Express 139
Daily Mail 139
Daily Mirror 139
dairy farming 104-105
Dairy Supply Co. *62*
dairy utensils and equipment 47, 49, 61-64, *129*, *131*
dairying 25, 47, 49, 61-64
Darent Valley 78
Dartmoor, traditional cultivation 51
Davey, B.J. (quoted) 155, 157
David, Dorothy (quoted) 126
Dean, Forest of 82, 84
Dedrick's Hay Press 60
Denmark (dairying) 38, 62
department stores 127, 132-133
depression 15, 37-42, 46, 154
Derbyshire 68, 99
'Derbyshire Farmer', 'Plain (quoted) 48
Devizes (Wilts) 47
Devon & Somerset Show *132*
Devon & Somerset Stores 133
Devon Great Consols Mine 68, 71
Devonport 16
Devonshire 30, 42, 71, 76, 79, 168
Devonshire, Duke of 16
Dewsbury (Yorks) 78
Dickens, Charles (quoted) 151
Digby (quoted) *142*
Digger, Darby's *54*
Dinsdale (Durham) *26*
dispensaries 144
distilling 42
distribution of goods 118-119, 124, 139, 140
doles 144
dolly, laundry *26*
Domesday Book (quoted) 78
Domesday Survey, New 9, 13
domestic self-sufficiency 114
domestic service 21, 26, 98
Don, River 74
Doncaster (Yorks) 125, *125*
Dorchester (Dorset) *131*
Dorset 71, 82, 88, 99, 120
Dorsetshire Labourer, The 120
drama *161*,167, *169* 177, 178
draper's shops *130*, 133-134
Dray, William, & Co. 46
drills 55-56
Drolls, Traditions and Superstitions of Old Cornwall 181
droving 102-103, *103*, 104, 114
Dudley, Lord 16
Dunbabin (quoted) 159
Durham 16
Dursley (Glos) 47, 2063
dye works 97
Dyos, H.J. (quoted) 16

'Eagle' mower 56
East Anglia 42, 66, 67, 80, 87, 100, 101, 103
East Clandon (Surrey) *139*
Eastern Counties Agricultural Labourers and Smallholders Union 24
East Kent Hop Gardens *156*
Eastman's (butchers) 131
Ecclesfield (Yorks) 74
Eden Bridge *103*
education 148-157, *157*, 159; cost of 149; government grants for 150, 152, 153, 156; influence of 157; non-sectarianism in 149, 154; Revised Code (1862) 153; rural 154, 156; and seasonal work 153, 155; spread of 12, 30, 167, 179; state system 150
Education Acts (1870) 150, *152*, 154-55, 156, 159, 167; (1876) 155; (1880) 155; (1902) 156
Education, Committee of the Privy Council on 151, 152
Education, Diocesan Boards of 151
Edwards, George 24, 142, 142-143
enclosure 163
enfranchisement, widened 154

Engineer 48
engineering, agricultural 45-49, *45*
engineers, village 92, 93, 95-96
English Land Restoration League 23, 142
entrepreneurs 67, 68, 74
epidemics 144-145
Epping Forest 82
Ernle, Lord (quoted) 37
Essay on Liberty 150
Essex 81, 102
Eustace, William 89
Evangelical Movement 162, 163
Evesham (Worcs) *137*
Evesham, Vale of 12, 42, 104
excursions 167, 176
Exeter (Devon) 133
Exmoor, traditional cultivation 51

Fabians 146
factories, urban 68
factory-made goods 66, 114, 115, 140
Fairford (Glos) *110*
fairground equipment 176
fairs 115, 118-121, *118*, 175-176
Fairs Act (1871) 121
Fairs, Owen's Book of (quoted) 124
Far from the Madding Crowd 120
Faringdon (Berks) *104*, 105, 108
Farm and Machinery Review (quoted) 64-65
farm houses 25-26, *25*, *26*, 28-32, *31*, 33-36
farm improvements 14
Farmer's Magazine 48
Farmer's Journal 48
farmers: education 149, 150, 154, *157*; leisure 19; living conditions 25-26, 31-33; numbers 25
Farmers' Alliance, The 15
Farnborough (Hants) 73
Farnham (Surrey) 73, *73*, 91, 107, *107*, 122
feeding stuffs, animal (purchased) 44
Fens, The 87
fertilizers 43-44, 56
fertility rites 181
fiddle broadcaster 55
fiddler *176*
Finch Foundry 69, 76
fish, transport of: by rail 105; by road 102
Fison, Joseph & Co. 43-44
Fitzhardinge, Lord (hounds) 174
Fletton bricks 72
flint knappers *71*
Flitton, Mr (quoted) 155
flour, white 38, 79
flower shows 178
Fobbing Church School (Essex) 152
fodder 44
folk dances 169
food processing 115, 129
foods 38, 44, 123, 124, 125, 128, 138
football 164, 164-165, 181
footwear, ready made 129, 135
Forster's Education Act (1870) 152
Foulds, Ben 174
Fourdrinier paper making machine 78
Fowler's 45, *54*
Fowler, John 53
frail making *80*
free trade 37, 38
freight 'wars' 101
friendly societies *see* benefit and friendly societies
Frimley Common (Surrey) 73
Frisby's shoe shops *130*
Froyle (Hants) 95
fruit farming 41, 104
fuller's earth 71
fulling mills 66, 69, 77, *77*
Funtley (Hants) 74
Furness, coppicing in 82, 85
furniture manufacture 85
Fussell, James, Isaac and John 75, *75*
fustian trade 98

Gainsborough (Lincs) 53, *110*
'Gallant Hussar' 182
galvanised metal 36
game preservation 14
games 171-172, *171*, *172*
Gandy, Ida (quoted) 98
Gardner's 61
Garrett's 45, 56, 59
Garsington (Oxon) *172*
Germany (dairy industry) 41, 62
Gibbon, J.V. 57
Gilbert, W.H. 43
Gilbey, W. and A. 137
Gill, T.H. 16
Girouard, M. (quoted) 21

Gislingham (Suffolk) *50*
Glasgow 63
gleaning *51*
Glendale (Northumberland) *51*
Gloucester 55
Gloucestershire 29, 77, 82, 100
Godalming (Surrey) *140*
Goddard (quoted) 48
Goddard, Philip 88, 89
grain, transport of 38, 100, 101, 102
Grand Junction Canal *101*
Grantham (Lincs) 45
grassland farming 41
Great Eastern Railway 104, 112
Great Exhibition (1851) 45, 58, 60
Great Western Railway *104*, 105, 110, 112
Green, J.L. (quoted) 97
Green, T.H. 146
Gresham (Norfolk) *29*
grinding mills 61
grocery 127, *133*, *135*
Ground Game Act (1880) 15
Grounsell 55
Guildford (Surrey) 58, 108, *120*
guising 161
gun flint industry 71, *71*
gypsies *176*
gypsum mining *71*

Haddenham (Bucks) 89
Haggard, Rider 120
Halesworth (Suffolk) 102
Halifax (Yorks) 78
Halwill (Devon) 168
Hambleton, drove road 103
Hammond, J.L. 147
Hampshire 70, 82, 88
Handbook of House Property 16
Handcross (W. Sussex) *180*
harbour development 16
Hardwicke Court (Glos) 18
Hardy, Thomas (quoted) 83-84, *120*, 169
harness making 66, 92
Harris, Joshua 88
Harrison, D. (blacksmith) *93*
harrows 54, *54*
harvesting (grain) 47, 49-51, 57-58, 60, 76, 84
harvest festival *165*, 166
harvest gangs 12, 49-50
harvest supper 165
harvest stripper 60
Hastings, Jem 174
Hawker, the Revd Stephen 166
hawkers *see* retailers, itinerant
hay forks 57
hay kickers 57
hay making 56-57, *57*, *58*
Hay Place Farm *165*
Hayley Wood (Suffolk) 88
Hayward, Miss C. 97
'Hazeley' swathe turner 57
health, public 144
Health, Poor Law Board on 146
heating, cheap 33, 106
Hedges (Hants) 93, 94
Hedges, John 93
hedging and ditching *142*
Hedingham Harvest 20
Helston (Cornwall) 110
Hemmingford Grey Mill 79
Henley-on-Thames (Oxon) 102, 159
Henman, William 88, 89, 93
Hepworth's 131
Hereford *110*, 119
Herefordshire, coppicing in 82
Herriard estate (Hants) *83*
Hertfordshire 80, 81, 97, 101, 102
Heydon (Norfolk) *91*
Heytesbury (Wilts) 137
Highway Act 158
High Wycombe (Bucks) *43*, *85*
Highways and Byways 113
Highworth (Wilts) Fair 176
Hill, the Revd 167
Hill, Thomas 88
Hindley, Charles (quoted) 116, 117
Hinton Lake 13
hiring fairs *119*, 120-121
History of Shopping, A 126
Hitchin (Herts) 105
hobby horse, Padstow *161*
hoe, horse-drawn 56
Hoffmann (brick) kiln 72
Holbeton (Devon) 152
Holderness, B.A. (quoted) 39, 41, 42, 44
Holderness Road Mill 79
Holtzendorff, Professor von (quoted) 17
holidays 160, 161, 164, 167, 172
Holsworthy (Devon) *128*, *132*
Home & Colonial Stores 131

Hop Day *43*
hop growing *107*
hop poles 82, 87
Horn, Pamela (quoted) 145, 149, 152, 156, 158, 159
Horn Dance *160*
Horn Fair, Charlton 176
Horncastle (Lincs) 119
Horndean Farm (Sussex) *50*
Hornsby & Son 45, 47, 59, *59*, 64
Hornsby-Ackroyd Patent Safety Oil Traction Engine 64
horse-hoes 56
horse racing 180
horse sales *118*, *119*
Horsington (Lincs) *166*
Horspath (Oxon) *172*
Hoskyns, C. Wren (quoted) 53
House of Commons, composition of 17
household goods: production 28-30, *32*, 36, 114, 129; supply 132, 133, 134, 135-136
Howard, J. & F. 45, 53, 57
Howitt, William (quoted) 121, 160, 164
Hull 79
Hullat, John 169
Humphries & Sons' Wagon Works 47, 59, 91, *91*
Hungerford (Berks) 102
Hunt, Robert (quoted) 181
Hunter, H.J. (quoted) 26
hunting 163, 173-175, *174*
hurdle making *83*
Hussey & McCormick 58
Hymns Ancient and Modern 169

ice cream sellers *146* (*see also* retailers, itinerant)
Iffley (Oxon) *166*
Ilfracombe (Devon) *181*
Illustrated London News 163
Implement and Machinery Review 48, *54*, 65
imports: and farming 37-39, 40, 41, 42-44, 106; and food supply 115, 123
In Search of England 98
India 46
industrial development (by landowners) 16
industrial economy, growth in 30, 164
industrial goods, transport of 100
industrial plant 67
Industrial Revolution 21, 66, 68, 74, 77, 81
industrial villages 74
industrial work (as alternative employment) 67
industry, growth of 42, 68, 69
industry and the rural economy 16, 30, 42, 67, 68, 69, 74, 100, 164
internal combustion engine 47, 54, 64-65
International Tea Co. *130*, 131, *131*
Ipswich (Suffolk) 44, 45, 53
Irish itinerant labour 50
iron working 46, *93*, 94-95
iron industry 66, 73, 74, 84
ironmongery 67, 129
Islip (Oxon) 88
Ivel Agricultural Motor 64-65, *65*

Jack-in-the-Green *163*
Jarmain, T.M. 57
Jefferies, Richard (quoted) 13, 19, 20, 21, 31-32, 38-39, 41, 132, 133, 135, 139, 143, 175
John, Hugh 149
Johnson, Clifton (quoted) 125
Joice (coachbuilders) *109*
joinery 28-29
Jones (quoted) 37, 158

Kay (later Kay-Shuttleworth), Dr Joseph (quoted) 151
Kell Brothers 55
Kennet and Avon Canal 100
Kennet Valley 70, 86, 87
Kent 12, 42, 51, 82, 88
Kidlington (Oxon) 88
King's Lynn (Norfolk) 53, 102, 108, 121, 176
Kings Stanley (Glos) *142*
Kingsley (Hants) 102
Kingston Deverill (Wilts) 137
Kirton (Lincs) 104
Kirton Lindsay (Lincs) 124
kitchen hearth *30*
kitchen ranges 34-35, *35*
Knibworth (Leics) 158
knife grinder *107*, *108*
Knight, J.H. *107*
knitting: hand 67, 68, 76, 148; framework 76
Knottingley (Yorks) 102
knur and spell *172*

Labour Party 147
labour shortages 49-51
labourers *14*, 18, 20-21; earnings 30-32, 114; education 152-153, 155, 156; employment 25, 45, 50, 106, 120-121, 164, 172; and friendly societies 31; housing 25-28, 31, 135-136; numbers 43, 97; recreations 160-182; and trade unionism 24; travel 106, 113, 179-180; welfare and Poor Law 141, 142, 144, 145
lace making 77, 97, 154
Lailey, George William 96, 98
Lake District 67, 84, 86
Lambarde, William *13*
Lambourn (Berks) 97, 110
Lammas 166
Lancashire 30, 77, 82, 84, 87
land: clearing 53; ownership 14, 24, 37; taxes 23; uses 15-16, 23; value 15, 16
Land, Return on Owners of 9, 13
Land, The 173
landed classes 13-24; attitudes to 18-21; concern for workers 24, 27, 163-164, 177-178; decline *22-24*; and government 17-18, 22, 159; income and investment 39, 173-174
landlord-tenant system 14, 24, 37
Larke, River 100
lathes 86, 96
laundering, domestic 26, *26*
Laval separator 62
Lavergne, Leonce de (quoted) 37
Lawes, J.B. 43
Lawrence & Kennedy 63
Lawson, Joseph (quoted) 170-171
Lea, River 101, 102
Lea Valley 80
lead mining 67, 68, 71, 76, 97
Leeds (Yorks) 45, 53, 154
Leeds Castle (Kent) *109*
Leicestershire, basket willow in 86
Leiston (Suffolk) 45
Lewes (Sussex) *50*
Lew Trenchard (Devon) 167
Liberal Party 147, 150, 154
Lichfield (Staffs) *93*
Liebig, Justus 43
Life and Labour of the People of London 144
lighting *32*, 33, *33*
lime burning 71, *71*, *97*
Lincoln 45, 100, 121
Lincolnshire 25, 30, 43, 80, 99, 100, 103, 104
Lind, Jenny 175
linotype 139
Lipton's 131
Lister's 47, 63, *63*
literacy, growth of 139, 166-167; need for 154
literature 170
Liverpool 100, 154
livestock: production increased 38, 39, 41; sale 40, 119, 123, 140; transport of 102-104
Lizard, The (Cornwall) 110
Lloyd Baker, Barwick 18
Lloyd George, David 19
Local Government board 145, 146
locksmithing 74
Locomotives Act (1865) 109
London 41, *43*, 46, 57, 58, 62, 67, 72, 74, 80, 84, 100, 101, 102, 103, 105, 114, 123, 144, 179
London Labour and the London Poor 144
London Lead Co. 67
Londonderry, Marquess of 16
Long Crendon (Bucks) 75
Long Handborough (Oxon) *110*
Lowe, Robert (quoted) 154
Lowestoft (Suffolk) 102
Luxton, Roger 168

Macadam, John 102
Magdalen 73
magic, practice of 12, 181
Maidenhead (Berks) 105, *146*
Maidstone (Kent) 78
Malcolmson (quoted) 162, 164
Malmesbury, the Revd T.R. 144
malting 39, 42, 67, 76, 78, 80-81, 101
Manchester 58, 64, 100, 154
Mapleton Farm *166*
Mark Lane Express 48
market equipment 125, *127*
market gardening 41-42
market towns: and carriers 108; and education 148; and rural industry 105; and trading 40, 88, 121-123, 124-125, 126, 131, *131*, 133, 135; and workhouses 142

markets 115, *118, 119, 120*, 121-125, *131;* (types listed) 122
Marshall, Edward *150*
Marshall, Miss J.E. *150*
Marshall tractor 65, *65*
Marshall's 53, *110*
Martin, E.W. (quoted) 12
Massingham, H.W. 147
Masterman, C.F.G. 147
Mawdsley (Lancs) 87
May Day 161, *166*
Mayor of Casterbridge, The 120
Maypole Dairy *40*, 131, *131*
maypole dancing 16
McConnell, Primrose 49
McKenzie, T. 56
McLaren's 53
Meare (Somerset) *177*
Mears (bellfounders) of Whitechapel 98
meat 106, 123
Meavy (Devon) 181
mechanisation 44-65; factors governing 46, 48-49, 51; and school attendance 155
Medical Department, Privy Council 145
medical officers, county 146
Medical Relief, Select Committee on 145
medical treatment 144-146
Meikle, Andrew 59
Mells (Somerset) 75, *75*
Menzies, J. (quoted) 119
metal workers 67, 73
metal working 74-76
metals: forging 66, 73, 74; importation 71; mining 66, 67, 70; non-ferrous 71
Metcalf 102
Methodist Magazine, The Primitive (quoted) 162
Methodism 167
Methodists, Primitive 162
Metropolitan Poor Act (1867) 144
Midlands 25, 41, 67, 74, *83*, 84, 100, 102, 104; East 67, 68, 71, 76, 82; South 77, *81*, 97; West 16, 67, 74, 82, 181
Milbourne (Dorset) *24*
milk production and supply *40*, 41, 61-62, *63*
milking *50*
milking machines 46, 63-64
Mill, John Stuart (quoted) 150
mill machinery 78-79
milling 42, 66, 68, 69, *72, 73*, 76, 78-79, *79, 100*, 101, 123
millstone industry 92
millwrighting 90, 92
Milne, Miss *152*
miners, mining 67, 68, 70, 97
Mingay, G.E. (quoted) 39
mining 67, 68, 70, 97
mixed farming system 38, 40, 42
Model T Ford 112
mole catcher *168*
monitorial system 149, 150
Monmouthshire, coppicing in 82
Moore, F.W. (quoted) 95, 159
Moore, James *116*
Moore, William 95
Moore, Hannah 162
morris dances 182
Morris Oxford 112
Morton, H.V. *96*, 98
Morwenstow (Cornwall) 166
Mosdell, Joseph 70
motor cars 12, *107*, *110*,112-113
mowers 56-57, *57*
multiple retail chains 130-131
mumming plays 161, 167
music, popularity of 169-170

nail making 74
Nalder's 59
Nash, Isaac 75-76
Nash, Isaac, & Co. 75
National Agricultural Labourers' Union 24, *24*
National Union of Agricultural Workers 24, 142
National Society for the Promotion of the Education of the Poor in the Doctrine and Discipline of the Established Church 150
needle making 75
Netherlands (development of butter substitutes) 41
New Domesday Survey (*Return on Owners of Land*) 9, 13
New Forest *90, 119*
New Zealand (lamb) 106
New Zealand Mutton Co. 131
Newbury (Berks) 52, 100, 110, *169*
Newcastle-upon-Tyne 100, 101

newsagents *140*
newspapers 12, 30, 139
newspaper vendors *see* retailers, itinerant
Newton Abbot (Devon) 133
nitrogen 44
non-conformity 18, 149, 150, 162
Norfolk 77, 97, 102, 103, 137, 158
Norfolk Directory (Kelly's) *134*
Norfolk Directory (White's) 137
North, the 67
North Eastern Railway 112
North Stoke (Oxon) 159
Northampton 121
Northamptonshire (lace factories) 97
Northcutt Mouth (Cornwall) *178*
Northumberland 71, 99
Norton (Yorks) 74
Norwich 101, 121
Norwich Mercury (quoted) 101, 121
Norwich News (quoted) 167
Nottingham 77, 124
Nottinghamshire 80, 86, 97, 99, 100
Nunney (Somerset) *75*

Oak House School, Axminster *149*
Oakridge (Glos) *93*
oats 39
oilcake 44, 61, *61*
oil engines 47, 64, 65
Okehampton (Devon) *15*, 76, 131
Oliver Twist 151
Oliver's, George *130*, 131
Olney, R.J. (quoted) 14, 17
omnibuses 109, *109*, 110, *110*
outwork 68
overseas competition 166
Overton (Hants) *112*
oxen, plough 51
Oxford 87, 88, 159, 175
Oxford Canal 100
Oxford School (of philosophy) 146
Oxfordshire 154

pack horses 67
packs, subscription 174
Padstow hobby horse *162*
paganism, survivals of 161, 180-181
Pangbourne (Berks) 93
paper making 66, 69, 76, 78
paraffin lamps 33
Park Iron Works 95
partnerships (in mining) 70
Paul, R. & W. 44
paupers, pauperism 142, 143, 144
Peak District 67, 70, 71, 92
Peake, Mrs C.M.A. *169*
Peasenhall 55
peat, as industrial fuel 67
pedlars *see* retailers, itinerant
Peel, Sir Robert 37, 157
Pennines 71, 76, 92
pensions *142*, 144, 147, 148, 158, 159
Pershore (Worcs) 47, 59
petrol engines 47
Petter's 47, 65
phosphate rock 44
piece work 31
Perkin (quoted) 145
pianos 169
Player, John (clockmaker) *30*
Plenty's 52-53
Plough Monday 164
ploughs 51, 52-54, *52, 54, 64*
ploughing 49, 53
ploughwrighting 46, 91-92
Plymouth (Devon) 131
poaching 162, 173
Poaching Protection Act (1862) 158
police 106, 157-159
Police Act, County (1839) 157
Police, Royal Commission on the Rural 157
pollarding 82
Pontefract (Yorks) 102
Pool, A.J. 95-96, 97
Pool, W.H. 95
Poor Law Amendment Act (1834) 141-142, 148; inadequacy of 144, 146, 150, 153-154
Poor Law Boards (originally Poor Law Commission) 142, 144, 145, 146
Poor Laws and the Relief of Distress, Royal Commission on the 147
population, changes in 97, 114, 141, 158
Portland (Dorset) 71
Portland, Duke of 16, 112
post office 106, 137, *139*
potash 44
potatoes 49, 56, 104

Potteries, The 73, 84
pottery 36, 66, 67, *73*
poverty, attitudes to 141, 144, 146-147
Poverty: A Study of Town Life 144
Preference, Imperial 38
preserving and canning industry 42
prices 31, 37, 42
production, domestic system of 67
Protestantism 162
public houses, village 171, *171*, 173, *186*
public schools, influence on sport 165
Pulbrook (quoted) 136, 138, 139
pupil-teachers 151-152, 153
Purbeck (Dorset) 71
Puritanism 162, 164

quarrying 66, 70-71
Quedgeley 97
Queen Camel (Somerset) *169*
Quorn Hunt 174

rabbit warrener *174*
Rackham (quoted) 88
railways 12, 30, 34, 41, 45, 69, 70, 84, 97, 99, *100*, 101-112, *105*, 115, 117, 119, 123, 124, 132, 176, 180
Ramsbotham, Dorning (quoted) 164
Randell, Arthur (quoted) 108
Rank, Joseph 79
Ransome, J.R. & A. *61*
Ransome, Robert 93
Ransome's 45, 46, 53, *54*, 59, 65
Ransome's & Sims 52
Ransome's, Sims & Jefferies 45, 47, 57, 59, 64
rape dust 44
rating system 143, 159
Read, John *169*
reading for pleasure 170
Reading (Berks) 84, *92*, 102, 105, 107, 108, 133
Reading Iron Works 46
reaper-binders 58
reaping equipment 50, 58, *58*
Redditch (Worcs) 75
Reed, John *149*
Reeves 56
Reeves, Marjorie (quoted) 95
Reeves Robert 95
refining, iron 74
Reform Acts (1832, 1867, 1885) 17
refrigeration 40
relief 141, 143, 144-146
rents 15, 27
repair and maintenance of machinery 89, 93
retailers: itinerant 114, 115, *115*, 116-118, *116, 117*, 139, *140;* traditional 123, 126-128, 133-135; village 115-116, 127, 137-138
retailing 126-129
Retford (Notts) 100
Richmond (Yorks) 121
Richmond's chaff cutter 60
Ridgeway (drove road) 103
rivers, navigable *see* waterways, inland
road transport 67, 70, 99, 119; local *105*, 106, *107;* long-distance 101-102
Robinson, Geoffrey (quoted) 20
Rochdale Pioneers 128
Rochester (Kent) 53
rock salt 71
rollers 54-55
Rolling Stock of the Farm, The 56
root slicer 61
rope making 76
Rose, Walter (quoted) 89-91, 146
Rothamsted (Herts) 43
roundsmen system 139
Rover bicycle *112*
Rowntree, Seebohm 31, 144
Royal Agricultural society of England 43, 48
Royal Barum ware 73
Royal Shows:(1895) 63; (Cambridge, 1848) 63; (Cardiff, 1872) 63; (Bristol, 1879) 63; (London, 1879) 62; (Manchester, 1879) 58; (Norwich, 1911) *48*
rural craftsmen 20, 116, 137; listed 70
Rural Economy of England, Scotland and Wales 37
rural industries 66-98; children employed in 154; decline 70, 95-96, 97-98; listed 70; location 66-67
Rural Industries, The 70
Rural Life of England, The 121
rural trade, changes in the pattern of 105

Rural World 170
rush plaiting *80*
Russia 38, 46
Rutland 97

saddle and harness making 92-93
St Giles's Fair 175-176
Salford Priors (Worcs) *45*
Salisbury, 3rd Marquess of 17
Samuelson *61*
Sandford St Martin (Oxon) *150*
Sandwich (Kent) 100
Sanger, Lord George 175
Sanitary Act (1866) 146
Sanitary Boards, Local, Rural and Urban 146
Sanitary Conditions of the Labouring Population of Great Britain, Report on the 144
Saunderson tractor 65
Savage's 53, *176*
Saville, J.D. (quoted) 97
sawyers 90, *90*
Saxmundham (Suffolk) 102
Scandinavia, dairy mechanisation in 47
Schleswig-Holstein 38
School Boards 154
schools 148-157, *149, 150, 152*
scythe making *75*
Seaham Harbour (Northumberland) 16
Seahouses (Northumberland) 71
Sedbergh (Yorks) 76
seed compounding industry 44
Selby Cross (Yorks) *135*
self-binders 58, 60
Sellman (quoted) 152, 156, 157
Senior, George (chemist) *132*
separators 62
Sevenoaks (Kent) *13*
Severn, River 100
Severn Valley 86
sewage 43
Seymour, Edward, & Sons 92
Shafer, Victor (quoted) 94
Shalbourne (Wilts) 92
Sharp, Cecil 168, 182
Sharp tractor 65
sheaf-binders 58
sheep farming *50*
sheep shearing *113*
Sheffield (Yorks) 68, 74, 76, 92, 133
Sheppard, the Revd H. Fleetwood 168
Shepton Mallet *130*
Shields, Andrew 63
shipping 38, 99, 100, *100*, 101, 102
shoemaker *136*
shops 126, *126*, 127, *128, 129, 130, 131, 132, 133, 134, 135*, 136-139, *136, 137, 138, 139, 140*
Shopkeeper's Guide, The 126
Shropshire 66, 82
Sibford Ferris (Oxon) *183*
Silcock's 44
silver mining 71
Simon, Sir John 145-146
Singer Manufacturing Co. 131
Singer Sewing Machine C0. 130
Sixty Years a Fenman 108
skittles *172*
Slaney, Robert (quoted) 163-164
slaughterhouses 123
smelting 67, 71, 73, 74
Smith, W.H., & Sons 130
Smith, William (blacksmith) 88
Smith, William (potter) 73
smock, working *31*
Smyth, James 55; 56
Somerset 42, 75, 77, *80*, 87, 100
Somerset & Dorset Railway *103*
Songs of the West 168
South Marston (Wilts) 176
South Molton (Devon) 131
Southport (Lancs) 133
sowing 55-56
Spalding (Lincs) 102
Spoenhamland System 141
Spencer, Earl 48
sport *20*, 21, 23, *172, 173*
sporting rights 15, 27
sports: blood 16, 19, 163, *174;* cruel, suppressed 173; spectator 165
Spring, David (quoted) 15-16
Spring Farm (Suffolk) *50*
squatters 27
Staffordshire 68, 73, 74, 80
stage coaches 101-102
Stanneries 70
Stannington (Yorks) 74
Stanneries 70
Starley, J.K. *112*
Stead & Simpson's 131
steam contractors 49
steam power 68, 69, 77, 78; in agriculture 45, 49-54, 59, 60, 61

188

steam engines 46, 49, 53, 64
steam vehicles 109-110, *110*, 113
Steele, Edward 88, 89
Stevens, Henry 88
Sticklepath(Devon) 69, 76
Stockton & Darlington Railway 99
Stoke Gifford (Glos) 18
stone picking *142*
Stort Valley 80
Stour, River (Suffolk) 72, 100
Stratfield Mortimer (Berks) 69, 70
Stratford St Mary (Suffolk) 72
Stratton (Cornwall) *138*, *171*
straw 66; hat making 76; plaiting 81, *81*, 97, 98, 154
straw elevator 60
Strong, W.H. (quoted) 79
Strutt, Joseph (quoted) 163
Stuart & Binney 64
Studley Royal (Yorks) *16*
Sturbridge (Cambs) 118
Sturt, George 91, 106, *107*; (quoted) 33, 73, 90, 106
Sturt, Mary (quoted) 149, 153, 154
Sudbury (Suffolk) *131*
Suffolk 71, 81, 88, 102
Sunday Schools 148, 166-167, *166*
superphosphates 43
Surrey 71, 82, 88
Surtees, R.S. (quoted) 37-38
Sussex 82, 84, 167
Sutton's Seeds 20
Swanton Morley (Norfolk) 137
Swanwick (Hants) *105*
swathe-turners 57, *57*
Sweden (dairy equipment) 62
Swedish exercises 182

Tadcaster (Yorks) 79
Tadley (Hants) 84
tallyman *see* retailers, itinerant
Talpa 53
Tamar Valley 68, 71
tanners 67
tanning industry 76, 84, 85
Tangye, Richard (quoted) 109
Taplow (Bucks) *176*
Tarbuck's *Handbook of House Property* 16
tariffs 38
Tasker, W. 47, *110*
Taunton (Somerset) 96, *132*, *133*
Tavistock (Devon) 131
Taylor, Tom 145
teachers 148-153
Teesside 74
Telford, Thomas 102
Temple, William (quoted) 164
tenant farmers 14, 18, 143
tenant-rights 14-15
Tenbury (Worcs) 19
tennis 21, *22*
textiles 40, 66, 67, 68, 69, 74, 76-78
Thames, River 100
Thames Valley 87, 100
Thatcham (Berks) 84, 86
Thetford (Norfolk) 45, 53
Thirsk (Yorks) 56
Thistle Mechanical Milker 63
Thompson, Flora (quoted) 116, 117, 118
Thompson, S.M.L. (quoted) 13, 17, 18, 22, 40, 42, 43
Thorley, Joseph 44
'Thorley's Food for Cattle' 44
'Three Drunken Maidens' 168
thresher 60
threshing and barn work 45, 49, 59, *59*
Thumb, Tom 175
Tideswell (Derbys) 124
tile manufacture *73*
tiles, drainage 72, 73
timber 82, 87
tin 67, 68, 71, 97
tinker *see* retailers, itinerant
tinsmithing 94
Tipteerer's Play *73*
Tittleshall-cum-Godwick (Norfolk) 137
tobacco salesman *see* retailers, itinerant
Toll board *120*
tonic sol-fa system 169
tools 66, 69, 74, 75
Torridge, River 79
Totnes (Devon) 131
Tractarian Movement 168-169
traction engines 45, *110*
trade unions 18, 24, 39, 158
tradesmen (rural) and poor relief 143
tractors 46, 64-65, *64*, 65
traditions, oral 167-168, 170, 182
tramways 109
transport, mechanised 109-113
transport, motor 12, 112-113, 123, 124
transport networks 87
Trent, River 100

Trent Valley 71, 86
'tribute' system (in mining) 70
Tring (Herts) *81*
truck system 128
Tull, Jethro 55
turnery 84-86, *86*, 96,
turnpike trusts 102
Turrill, Mr *172*
Tuxford's 46
Tyneside 16
Tysoe (Warks) 148

Uffington (Berks) *178*
Under the Greenwood Tree 169
undertaking 90
underwood *see* coppicing
unemployment 39, 143, 147
Unemployment Insurance 147-148
Union Chargeability Act (1865) 143
Unions (workhouses) 142
United States of America 38, 41, 42, 46-47, 58, 60
Universal Cow Milker 63
Upton (Berks) 28
urban influences: on reading habits 170; on recreation 160; on retailing 127-128; social 12, 32-36; on taste 132
urbanisation, rapid growth of 96-97

Vaccar 64
vans *108*
Vaughan, Mr 83
vegetable farming 41, 104
Vernon Cross (Somerset) 96
Verulam, 2nd Earl of 22
Village Carpenter, The 89-90
Village Institutes 178, 179
village sports 179
villages: charity in 144; primary schools 148-149; service trades 88
Volunteer Force 178-179

Waddingham's Mill 79
Wadebridge (Cornwall) *116*
wages, agricultural 18, 30-31, 38, 155
wagons *104*, *105*, *107*, *108*
waifs and strays 154
wakes, church 161, 176
Wales 71, 74, 84, 104
Wales, Prince of 21
Walter, Alec 91-92
Walters family 28
Walton-on-Trent (Derbys) 148
Walvin (quoted) 169
Wantage (Berks) 124
Ward, John, and family *15*
Ward, Sadie and John Kingdon *157*
Ware (Herts) 101, 102
Warland, John 88, 89
Warminster (Wilts) 62
Warner, Thomas 88, 89
Warwickshire, rural metal working in 74
water power 67, 68-70, 69, 74, 77, 86
water wheels 68-69, 69
Waters family (tenant farmers) 14
waterways, inland 67, 69, 99-102
Watkins, the Revd Frederick 151
Weald, The 82, 84
Wear Gifford (Devon) 79
weavers 67, 68
Webb, James 88, 89, 93
Wedgwood pottery 114
Wedlake, Mary 49, 57
weeding 56
Well in the Wood, The 169
Wellington (Shropshire) 86
Wem (Shropshire) *120*
Wesley, John 169
West, Mr (miller) 79
West Country 66, 70, 77
West Riding (Yorks) 77
Westbrook, Cuthbert *83*
Westminster, Duke of 16
Westmorland, knitting in 76
Weyhill (Hants) 119, 121
Weymouth (Dorset) 100
wheat 37, 38, 39, 78
Wheelwright's Shop, The 90
wheelwrighting 66, 91-92, *91*, 94
whisky distilling 39
White *110*
Whitechapel 73
Whitehead, John *73*
Whitstable (Kent) 100
Wilkins of Tiptree 42
Wilkinson, T.W. 113
Williams, Alfred (quoted) 176, 177
willow bonnet making 98
Wiltshire 30, 41, 51, 77, 82, 88, 100, 103, 137-138
Wiltshire Directory (Kelly's) 137
Windsor chair *29*
wine and spirit trades 80

Wingfield Stratford, Esme (quoted) 19-20, 22, 23
winnowing machine 59
Wisbech (Cambs) 42, *122*
Witham, River 100
Wiveliscombe (Somerset) 96, *166*
Woburn (Beds) 27, *28*, 102
Women, employment of 50-51, *51*, 72, 81, 138
Women and Children in Agriculture, Reports ... on the Employment of 83, 154
Wood, Walter A. 58
wood: as fuel 33, *82*, 84, 86; as raw material 35, 66, *83*
wood working 66, 68, 69
Woodbridge (Suffolk) 102
woodland 67, 81-84
Woodlanders, The 83-84
Woodley (Berks) 26, *33*
Woods, K.S. (quoted) 70, 86
wool 40, 76
wool manufacture 77
Worcester *130*
Worcestershire 74, 75
Worker's Union (Agriculture Section) 24
workhouses 141-143, 145, *146*, *147*, 150, 151
working hours 164, 172-173
Workshops Act (1867) 154
worsted wool 77
Wortley Forge 74
Wrecclesham Pottery 73, *73*
Wyatt, James and John 94
Wye Valley (Bucks) 78
Wyre Forest 82

Yare, River 100
Yarmouth (Suffolk) 100, 101, 102
yeomanry, new class of 24
Yeovil (Somerset) 47, 65
York 144
Yorkshire 26, 67, 74, 76, 99, 100, 103
Young, Arthur 32

zinc baths 36, *17*
zinc mining 71